Strange Fits of Passion

Epistemologies of Emotion,
Hume to Austen

Strange Fits of Passion
Epistemologies of Emotion, Hume to Austen

෴

Adela Pinch

Stanford University Press, Stanford, California

Stanford University Press
Stanford, California
© 1996 by the Board of Trustees of the
Leland Stanford Junior University

Printed in the United States of America

CIP data are at the end of the book

For Harry and Judith Pinch

Acknowledgments

One of the subjects of this book is how people come to know their own feelings and the feelings of others; one of my anxieties is that the people who have helped to shape this project will not truly know my own vast sentiments of gratitude, affection, and indebtedness.

I have relied heavily on the conversation, the insights, and the readings of Amanda Anderson, Ann Cvetkovich, Lynn Enterline, Marilyn Ivy, Maryjo Marks, Kate Mehuron, Dick Moran, and Jeff Nunokawa. My debts to Webb Keane, for his intellectual companionship, his rigorous questions, his patience, and his labors, know no end. Mary Jacobus, Laura Brown, Harry Shaw, Cynthia Chase, and Dorothy Mermin have my abiding gratitude for their comments on earlier versions of several of these chapters. I sincerely thank my friends at the University of Michigan who helped me immeasurably by listening, and by reading and commenting on portions of the manuscript: Julie Ellison, Chris Flint, Andrea Henderson, Anne Herrmann, June Howard, John Kucich, Marlon Ross, and especially Athena Vrettos. Special thanks go as well to Austin Booth, not only for her assistance with the research for the Coda but also for her shrewd, supportive presence during the last stages of this project.

Paul Fry and Susan Wolfson reviewed the manuscript with extraordinary generosity and insight. I am grateful to them, and to Claudia Johnson and Esther Schor for their kindness in sharing with me their forthcoming books. Pamela Moody patiently checked facts and quotations; Lynn Enterline generously looked up passages; and Peggy Berg scrupulously edited the manuscript. I remain responsible for all of the book's shortcomings.

The research for Chapter 2 was made possible by a Research Grant in Women's Studies from the Woodrow Wilson National Fellowship Foundation, and a Beatrice Brown Award in Women's Studies, Cornell University. The research for the Coda was funded by a Faculty Assistance Fund Grant, University of Michigan. My thanks to these institutions for their assistance.

A section of Chapter 3 appeared as "Female Chatter: Meter, Masochism, and the *Lyrical Ballads*," *ELH* 55 (Winter 1988): 835-52, and another section appeared as "The True Colors of 'Poor Susan'," *The Wordsworth Circle* 25.1 (1994): 14-17. A version of Chapter 5 appeared as "Lost in a Book: Jane Austen's *Persuasion*," *Studies in Romanticism* 32.1 (Spring 1993): 97-117. I am grateful to the Johns Hopkins University Press and to the Trustees of Boston University for permission to use material here.

Contents

Introduction: Emotional Extravagance and
the Epistemology of Feeling   1

1   The Philosopher as Man of Feeling:
    Hume's Book of the Passions   17

2   Sentimentality and Experience in
    Charlotte Smith's Sonnets   51

3   Female Chatter: Gender and Feeling in
    Wordsworth's Early Poetry   72

4   Phantom Feelings: Emotional Occupation in
    The Mysteries of Udolpho   111

5   Lost in a Book: Jane Austen's *Persuasion*   137

    Coda: Quotation and the Circulation of Feeling
    in Early Nineteenth-Century England   164

Notes   195
Works Cited   219
Index   237

Strange Fits of Passion

Epistemologies of Emotion,
Hume to Austen

Introduction

Emotional Extravagance and the Epistemology of Feeling

Feelings often seem to have lives of their own in eighteenth-century writing. Not always lodged within the private, inner lives of individual persons, they rather circulate among persons as somewhat autonomous substances. They frequently seem as impersonal, and contagious, as viruses, visiting the breasts of men and women the way diseases visit the body. Hume, among many others, declares that "the passions are so contagious, that they pass with the greatest facility from one person to another, and produce correspondent movements in all human breasts." In Hume's understanding, feelings spread about freely and fluidly; they do not know the boundaries of individuals. He stresses that the claims of individuals are subordinate to the feelings that visit them from without: "Hatred, resentment, esteem, love, courage, mirth and melancholy; all these passions I feel more from communication than from my own natural temper and disposition."[1] In poetry and in prose, moreover, emotions indeed live as autonomous forms, stalking about as personifications, often in vexed and detached relations to the persons presumed to be feeling them.

There were persistent murmurings, in the second half of the eighteenth century, that feelings were getting out of hand. A satire on the "*Sentimental* stile" of poetry complained that feelings had become so feverish and wayward that they were crowding true passion out, swirling about " 'till damp'd, and chill'd, by sentimental sighs, / Each stifled passion in a vapour dies." The author of the satire found that fashionable feeling had attached itself to all objects and occasions, large and small. He instances "a Noble Author," who "has lately published his works, which consist of *three* compositions. *One*, an Ode upon the death of Mr. Gray; the *two* others, upon the death of his Lordship's *Spaniel*."² Even the average late eighteenth-century individual at her religious devotions had to be careful that her feelings for the deity did not exceed the mark. Hester Chapone counseled that the worshiper guard against "those factitious feelings which we have the art of raising in ourselves," that "heated fancy, that, in a kind of frenzy, adds an unnatural force to our sentiments," turning the "ardours of devotion" into a dangerous religious "enthusiasm."³ Extravagant feelings could cause the greatest acts of benevolence; they could also lead women to their ruin. Hannah More, like many others, warned that a sensibility that opened one up to strong feeling was highly dangerous to a woman's virtue; Mary Wollstonecraft argued that women had been made "slaves" of their senses and their passions, to be "blown about by every momentary gust of feeling" and plunged into a wide "variety of meannesses, cares, and sorrows."⁴

As these remarks suggest—and many critics have confirmed—the attack on emotional extravagance, sensibility, and the sentimental came from a variety of positions, including conservatism (More), feminism and radicalism (Wollstonecraft), and fear of religious enthusiasm (anti-Methodism).⁵ My point will not be to weigh the different claims about the passions' wondrous virtues or their dangerous "tendency to excess";⁶ indeed, I hope this book will show that many opposing views may share some common assumptions about passions, their expression, and their objects. The subject of this book is rather the meaning of the very gesture of calling feelings extravagant, and the relationship of that gesture to this period's fascination with trying to account for where feelings come from and what they are. A passage from Joanna Baillie's "Introductory Discourse" to her *Series of Plays on the Passions* can suggest the kind of epistemological drive to know feelings that I wish to trace. According to Baillie, the merest hint of the presence of extravagant feelings compels us to find them out:

Let us understand, from observation or report, that any person harbours in his breast, concealed from the world's eye, some powerful rankling passion of what kind soever it may be, we will observe every word, every motion, every look, even the distant gait of such a man, with a constancy and attention bestowed upon no other. Nay, should we meet him unexpectedly on our way, a feeling will pass over our minds as though we found ourselves in the neighbourhood of some secret and fearful thing.

Baillie begins with the premise that strong passion can be concealed within a man, concealed from the "world's eye." But our insatiable desire to find out feelings converts the whole man into a walking embodiment of what he harbors: even his distant gait becomes evidence, and his mere presence becomes like that of a "fearful thing." The very secretness of his passion not only incites people to discover it; it also makes him a strangely affecting being whose presence sends feelings to haunt us. A feeling "passes" over our minds like a shadow, a ghost, or an angel. Baillie continues:

If invisible, would we not follow him to his lonely haunts, into his closet, into the midnight silence of his chamber? There is, perhaps, no employment which the human mind will with so much avidity pursue, as the discovery of concealed passion.[7]

The gothic language suggests that the drive to know passions converts its object into a compelling mystery.

This book explores how writers of the late eighteenth and early nineteenth centuries account for the relationships between persons and passions. It sees a range of kinds of writing—the philosophical treatise, the lyric poem, the novel—as being motivated, though sometimes less explicitly, by the kind of inquiry into feelings that Baillie describes. Eighteenth- and early nineteenth-century writers seek after the origins and locations of feelings; as they try to pin feelings down, I shall argue, they often discover that one's feelings may not really be one's own. The romantic period and the era that precedes it often appear to us as eras in which people increasingly learned to claim their emotions as the guarantors of their individuality, buried in their breasts as in Baillie's impassioned man's. The books I study here also reveal the period's concomitant tendency to characterize feelings as transpersonal, as autonomous entities that do not always belong to individuals but rather wander extravagantly from one person to another. I explore the origins and the tensions between these ways of representing feelings in late eighteenth- and early nineteenth-century social thinking, epistemology, gender ideology, aesthetic theory, and literary form.

Thus, I use the phrase "emotional extravagance" to indicate two crucial aspects of writing about feeling in this period. The first connotation that "extravagance" has in the context of this study is derived from its obsolete, etymological roots: that which strays beyond boundaries. Thus Hume, among many others, declares that "all the affections readily pass from one person to another, and beget correspondent movements in every human creature."⁸ The second connotation is the more familiar sense "emotional extravagance" might have: excessive, lavish, unrestrained emotionality, or sentimentality. The chapters that follow demonstrate that these two meanings are intimately connected: feelings in late eighteenth- and early nineteenth-century writing appear most excessive when that writing raises questions about whom those feelings belong to, about whether those feelings come from without or from within a person.

The period's tendency to link extravagance in feeling with epistemological questions can be briefly exemplified by a few passages from Kames's discussions of false sentiments in his *Elements of Criticism* (1762). An influential text in late eighteenth-century aesthetic theory, the *Elements of Criticism* typically considers literature in terms of both its emotional effects on its readers, and its representations of its characters' emotions. Under the latter heading, Kames concerns himself with judging whether literary, especially dramatic, characters' expressions of their passions—what Kames calls their "sentiments"—are appropriate to the passions they are presumed to be feeling. As Kames details the ways in which the expression of passion can be faulty—"sentiments that accord not with the passion," sentiments that are "unnatural," sentiments that are "pure rant and extravagance"—it is often unclear where exactly the fault lies. Is Kames judging the language that a writer attributes to his or her character? Is the problem that a writer may not know the true feelings of a character well enough? Or is Kames scrutinizing the emotions themselves of a literary character? The issue of whether someone's language is suited to their passion quickly slides into the problem of whether that person's feelings are suited to their situation—whether their feelings are authentic or false. Kames appears to find most offensive literary characters who in accounting for their own emotions seem merely to be "describing the passion another feels."⁹

One of Kames's examples of a sentiment that accurately suits the passions of the speaker—that illustrates specifically the tendency of the impassioned to sway back and forth between different passions "like a pendulum"—is an enraged Othello ordering Desdemona about before Lodovico:

> Oth: Ay; you did wish that I would make her turn:
> Sir, she can turn and turn, and yet go on;

> And turn again. And she can weep, Sir, weep:
> And she's obedient: as you say, obedient;
> Very obedient—proceed you in your tears—
> Concerning this, Sir—oh well painted passion!
> (1:466–67; IV.i.252–57)

Though he does not say so, Kames may be admiring in this passage the correspondence between what he sees as Othello's pendulum-like swings of passion—between love, jealousy, and anger—and Desdemona's obedient swings back and forth across the stage, as Othello orders her to "turn and turn . . . and turn again." The turning Desdemona thus provides a visual demonstration of Kames's point about the passions. But if Desdemona illustrates Kames's—and Othello's—point, she also suggests a paradox at the heart of Kames's inquiry into sentiment. For Kames, Othello's passions seem true just when Shakespeare's hero is denouncing Desdemona's expressions of emotion—her tears—as false, insincere, not her true feelings. He also quotes approvingly Othello's adjacent cry: "Oh devil, devil! / If that the earth could teem with woman's tears, / Each drop she falls would prove a crocodile" (1:467; IV.i.244–46). Othello is making the kind of judgment, in other words, that Kames makes throughout his discussion of false sentiments; and Othello is of course wrong in his judgment. Desdemona's "well-painted passion" may suggest that Kames's discussions about whether literary passions are well painted are inevitably drawn into questions about how one knows whether the feelings someone expresses are truly theirs. Kames's example of a grand passion "vibrating like a pendulum" turns on a question about someone else's feelings; and such questions, we shall see, often turn on a woman's feelings.[10]

Kames's concern with the evidence by which one could know, and hence make a judgment about, the extravagance or appropriateness of people's words to their sentiments, people's sentiments to their passion, or their passion to their character or situation extends to the question of what would count as evidence of one's *own* feelings. This question is given philosophical form in one of his last examples of unnatural sentiment, an impassioned speech by Osmyn after the departure of Almeria in Congreve's pathetic tragedy, *The Mourning Bride*:

> Yet I behold her—yet—and now no more.
> Turn your lights inward, Eyes, and view my thought.
> So shall you still behold her—'twill not be.

> O impotence of sight! *mechanic sense*
> Which to exterior objects ow'st thy faculty,
> Not seeing of election, but necessity.
> Thus do our eyes, as do all common mirrors,
> Successively reflect succeeding images.
> Not what they would, but must; a star or toad;
> Just as the hand of chance administers! (1:489; my emphasis)

This outburst on the nature of vision and mental imagery does seem rather grandiose in the situation at hand: the speaker's beloved has simply temporarily left the stage. Kames's comment focuses on the first four lines: "No man, *in his senses*, ever thought of applying his eyes to discover what passes in his mind; far less of blaming his eyes for not seeing a thought or idea" (1:489; my emphasis). It may indeed be ludicrous to ask the eyes to turn into the mind to see what is going on in there. However, in censuring this passage, Kames is putting his finger on a problem, one that symptomatically links a theory of knowledge with the approach to emotion he is pursuing. How *is* one ever supposed to find out accurately the passions and sentiments that lurk within? The crux of the matter lies precisely in Kames's inadvertent pun on "sense": he transforms the "mechanic sense" that Osmyn deplores into a metaphor for mental self-presence itself. The pun that leads from "sense" to "senses" notes the trajectory described by an empiricist approach to the mind: empiricism regards our mechanic senses as the foundations of our capacity to have sense, or reason. In spite of their disagreement, both the dramatic hero Osmyn and the aesthetic philosopher Kames are exploring the limits of an empiricist approach to mind. While empiricist philosophy does not exactly advise that we turn our eyes inward to see the mind, it does generally imagine that we learn what passes there through a process *modeled* on visual perception: we observe and "reflect" (Osmyn's word) on the contents of our minds. Moreover, while Kames scorns Osmyn's desire to see his desire, his own *Elements of Criticism*—like many of the books in this study—maintains that the way to understand feelings is to find their empirical, observable causes. That Kames is drawn into a disagreement about the grounds for self-knowledge with a literary character whose sentiments he finds unnatural suggests that there may be a connection between an empiricist theory of knowledge and the waywardness of feelings in late eighteenth-century writing.

One of this book's central claims, then, is that the eighteenth century's revolution in epistemology, which both gave feelings empirical origins and declared their social benefits, had strange effects on how writers represented people's relations to their feelings. The writers I discuss tend to tell—often within a single work—conflicting stories about the status of feeling. On the one hand, they assert that feelings are personal, that they have origins in an individual's experience and are authenticated by their individuality. On the other hand they reveal that feelings may be impersonal; that one's feelings may really be someone else's; that feelings may be purely conventional, or have no discernible origins. The chapters that follow show how and why these two stories occasion each other by focusing on extravagantly affective passages or scenes: Hume's extraordinary confession of his own melancholy; a woman poet's insistence that she really feels the gloomy feelings her poems portray; Wordsworth's witnessing of a woman poet reading and weeping; tearful exchanges between fathers and daughters in the gothic novel; the climactic debate about the comparative strengths of men's and women's feelings in *Persuasion*; and finally the public mourning for a dead princess. The book treats the romantic and preromantic attachment to sentiment and gloominess not by diagnosing the age, but by showing that emotion emerges in each text when epistemological concerns confront specific questions about society, gender, or aesthetics. Thus, after a first chapter on how Hume's epistemology and social philosophy combine to make it difficult for the philosopher to account for his own feelings, the second chapter shows how a formal version of this problem affects the gender politics of women's sentimental poetry. The third chapter then shows how the conjunctions of gender and feeling in the material of Chapter 2 influence Wordsworth's early aesthetics. In Chapter 4, the gothic novel reveals how the conflicting accounts of feelings first seen in Hume took sensational narrative form in the 1790's. Chapter 5 defines the situation of the woman as knower of feelings in the epistemological dramas of Austen's novel, while the book's Coda explores the early nineteenth century's culture of emotion.

 The first chapter addresses the ways eighteenth-century philosophers and aestheticians conceive of emotions, linking rhetorical practices to broader social and epistemological aspects of the period's conception of personhood. Focusing mainly on Hume's *Treatise of Human Nature* allows me to show the extent to which empiricism rendered feelings authoritative grounds for aesthetic and social experience, but only by suggesting that people's feelings are not always authentically their own. Hume's notion of the social force of feelings underlies his theory of knowledge itself: his understanding of the movement of feelings between people depends upon the rhetorical status of a crucial concept in his epistemology, the relation of force between impressions and ideas. This chapter proceeds through readings of some of the strangely sympathetic characters in Hume's examples in the *Treatise*, ultimately considering Hume's story about his "own" feelings in the famous conclusion to book 1. The chapter's focus on representations of emotions and their epistemological consequences concludes in an exploration of late eighteenth-century defenses of the practice of personifying emotions. I ask what it means to represent feelings as persons and reveal the assumptions this practice implies about the knowability both of feelings and of the concept of "person."

The book begins with Hume not to provide a philosophical explanation of the literary works that follow, but rather to show how similar questions about our knowledge of feelings and the forms they take structure both literary and philosophical texts. Focusing on the work of sentimental women poets, for example, the second chapter seeks to show how both the poetry and the politics of emotion in the late eighteenth century are shaped by the epistemological issues described above. The chapter is devoted to the gloomy *Elegiac Sonnets* (first edition, 1784) of Charlotte Smith, the popular poet of sensibility whose revival of the sonnet enabled the romantic poets' use of the form. Seen in the context of both intertextual, formal concerns and Smith's letters and reviews, the sonnets explain why the sentimental woman poet may be in the odd position of sympathizing with her own feelings. If sentimental verse was inevitably a woman's genre in the late eighteenth century, it was so only by making the feelings expressed not her own. Smith's poems claim simultaneously that the feelings in them are derived from the transmission of literary tropes and that their authority comes from their personal idiosyncrasy. Feeling itself is thus revealed as that which constructs and mediates between the categories of literary "convention" and personal "experience." I suggest that the concept of sentimentality itself may be defined precisely as a confrontation between the personal and the conventional, and I conclude the chapter by discussing both the productiveness and the limitations of this confrontation for eighteenth- and nineteenth-century feminism.

The third chapter places Wordsworth's early writing within late eighteenth-century understandings of feeling by exploring the poet's relations both to sentimental women poets and to the sentimental figures of female suffering he frequently borrows in his early work. I take seriously the charges of extravagance—excesses of attention or emotional response—that Wordsworth received from his contemporaries, noting that the poet's writing thus marks part of this period's disruptions in its understanding of emotional authenticity, of the relationship between emotions and their objects. A discussion of Wordsworth's first published poem, "Sonnet on Seeing Miss Helen Maria Williams Weep at a Tale of Distress," demonstrates how Wordsworth links the transmission of feeling to the transmission of literary form in his response to a woman responding to someone else's suffering. The chapter pursues Wordsworth's experiments in the movement of feeling through his representations of suffering in the *Lyrical Ballads*. His interest in the transpersonal nature of feelings centers on the problem of pain. Wordsworth was the most radical romantic theorist of the relationship between affect and language, and his notion of words produces a nondialectical understanding of the relationship between pleasure and pain, posing a counteraesthetic in which other people's pain is the theoretical origin of representation. Through readings of the Preface to *Lyrical Ballads*, "Goody Blake and Harry Gill," and "Poor Susan," the chapter argues that these feminine figures of woe mediate Wordsworth's relations to literary form, in particular to popular literary forms, as sources of poetic power.

The next two chapters of the book turn from lyric poetry to novels of the romantic period, focusing on narrative accounts of the origins of feeling. The fourth chapter explores how and why Radcliffe's gothic novel provides complex and often conflicting narrative solutions to the question of where feelings come from. It contends that approaches to the gothic that seek to determine the genre's attitudes toward individual feeling, or "sensibility," must do so by seeing how the novels understand the relationship between "feeling" and "individual." *The Mysteries of Udolpho* reveals emotional life to be a kind of occupied territory: it represents its characters' minds as filled in by feelings that are not always their own. Focusing on the melancholy nostalgia that seeps through the novel, the chapter argues that *Udolpho*'s narratives of the origins of feelings are shaped by the gothic novel's reflections on its own conventions and modes of representation. Concomitantly, by reading scenes from Radcliffe's 1794 novel along with her work most clearly marked by the French Revolution, the *Journey Made in the Summer of 1794 Through Holland and Germany*, I suggest that its aesthetics of feeling respond as well to problems of representing historical change. Radcliffe marks these issues by exploring the transgenerational journeys feelings make: What would it mean to locate a daughter's feelings in her father's? In the very process of telling a story about the origins of the daughter's feelings in the father, her book also tells a counternarrative in which the daughter's feelings have no determinate human origins.

Some readers may be surprised to find Jane Austen—seen by many as, at best, a somewhat ambivalent enemy to sensibility and extravagances of all kinds—in a book about emotional extravagance. Though less conventionally "sensational" than *Udolpho*, Austen's last and most "romantic" novel, *Persuasion*, is similarly concerned with telling stories about the origins of sensation, devoted to exploring memory, nostalgia, and the extent to which women in particular may be occupied by others. *Persuasion's* narrative accounts of the conditions of sensation also return us to some of the questions of empiricism that have been, since Hume, shaping the representations of feelings. Like the writings discussed throughout this book, Austen's 1818 novel often suggests that the origins of feelings are "unnatural." I read this novel as a phenomenological exploration of what it feels like to derive one's "sentiments and ideas" from reading, as women in particular were imagined to do. Affiliated both with late eighteenth-century women's writings about feeling and with romantic modes of representing the origins of consciousness, *Persuasion* explores the effects of literature upon women's emotional lives by comparing them to the conditioning effects upon consciousness of the presence of other people. Finally, my Coda traces feelings beyond the novel of manners and into the drawing rooms and public dramas of Regency England. I consolidate this book's testimony to the legacy of eighteenth-century epistemologies of emotion in the culture of the romantic period by exploring two popular manifestations of the circulation of feeling: the practice of sentimental quotation, and the national outpouring of extravagant feeling on the death of the Princess Charlotte in 1817.

꙲

As this description might suggest, this book seeks to show that a concern with the vagrancy of emotions persists from the eighteenth century through the romantic period: the chronological spread of the writers I discuss reflects a polemic about the existence of important continuities between eighteenth-century and romantic aesthetics. Thus, while the three central chapters are clustered around two decades—the 1780's and 1790's—in which the nature of emotion was being hotly debated, in treating Hume's early *Treatise* and Austen's last novel this study looks at works that fall significantly on either side of the "age of sensibility" as it is usually defined. This book should confirm that it is possible to talk about a long "era of sensibility" stretching from the end of the seventeenth century into the beginning of the nineteenth. Politically, this long age of feelings is framed by the emergence of feeling as the center of civic identity in postabsolutist English political thought, the reformulation of questions about rights during the late eighteenth-century revolutionary period, and the development of theories of relations to others and to objects necessitated by colonialist and commercial expansion. Socially, the long era of sensibility defines relations not only between middle-class British men and women but also between middle-class men and women and their social others: Indians, slaves, the poor, and the mad.[11] Central to both aesthetic and social experience, feeling was thus a compelling subject for the searches for origins typical of both eighteenth-century and romantic thought: attempts "to trace the passions to their sources," in Samuel Johnson's phrase, constituted "the fashionable study."[12] In this view, the romantic period appears primarily as the last phase of this longer era of sensibility, continuing its investment in finding feelings out.

 It is important to situate romanticism in this context in part because contemporary criticism still seems afraid of seeing romanticism as being in any way about emotion—as if to do so would involve believing that poetry really *was* the spontaneous overflow of powerful feeling. Romanticism has been treated in the past thirty years as being about everything but emotion. Though the most affect-laden of romantic aesthetics, the sublime, has perennially fascinated critics, the sublime's best readers have often subordinated its affective dramas to linguistic and semiotic predicaments.[13] It should be possible to counter some of the critical nervousness about romantic emotion by rescuing romantic texts from some of the postromantic assumptions about feeling for which romanticism is held to be embarrassingly responsible: the assumption, for example, that feelings are fundamentally private and prelinguistic but knowable only in their representations. In this respect I am particularly indebted to recent studies of romanticism that consider the role of gender in both men's and women's writing.[14] It is precisely by attending to the role of gender in the affective aesthetics that inform both eighteenth-century and romantic writing that one can place romanticism within a longer and more complex history of concern for where feelings come from.

The social currency of feeling in the eighteenth century and the romantic period is inseparable from its complex interactions with ideas about gender. Feminist debates on gender and emotion often start by accepting that there is a cultural association between women and emotion, and beginning the debate there: Has the association between women and emotion led to a devaluation of emotion? Do women's interests suffer or gain from their association with emotion? To begin the debate with these questions suggests that contemporary critics have already resolved some of the issues that troubled the late eighteenth century, for as I am arguing, debates about feelings' social effects were always paired with epistemological questions.[15] In the introduction to Chapter 2 I will discuss further why it has been necessary for feminism to focus on feeling. My study will insist on seeing how crucial questions—is feeling men's or women's domain? what or whose interests are served by the gendering of certain kinds of feeling?—are inseparable from broader epistemological questions: How do feelings come to be anybody's? Where do they come from and how do they travel? Thus, some readers may be disappointed that I do not definitively designate the late eighteenth-century problem of feeling as a property belonging either to men or to women, and evaluate it as such. However, I do hope to show that the writings I study affirm, in feminist philosopher Lorraine Code's words, "that moral and political questions have an epistemological dimension that must be addressed, just as epistemological questions are at once moral and political."[16]

Readers will also find that in these chapters questions about gender and the origins of feelings are often motivated by an author's formal dilemmas. For example, I focus on Radcliffe's concern about the gothic novel's status as a purveyor of highly conventionalized terrors, and on Wordsworth's relationship to popular poetic genres. It is in formal issues—and not in their own personal relationships to feeling—that the differences between the male and female authors I discuss emerge. As such my book's special plea for the need to take into account the period's epistemological point of view also includes a plea for a contextualized, gender-sensitive formalism. Formalism—by which I mean simply a commitment to reflection on a text's modes of representation—can prevent us from taking a text's expressions of emotion at face value. It opens up a space that allows us to theorize our own epistemologies of emotion and gender in relationship to those of an earlier historical period. In other words, it is my desire *not* to take for granted what the relations among gender, language, and emotion might have looked like in the eighteenth century and romantic period that has made the readings in this book more rhetorical and formal than overtly historical in orientation.[17] A commitment to both gender and form has contributed, therefore, to my choice of texts: the book brings together writers—the moral philosopher Hume, the romantic poet Wordsworth, the gothic novelist Radcliffe, the popular sentimental poet Smith, and Austen, the novelist of manners—who are sometimes strictly segregated in literary studies by genre and gender. This study links its chapters not genealogically as intellectual history, but conceptually across these generic differences: it is by traveling across genres and genders that the epistemological preoccupations of these strange fits of passion can emerge.

Hunting down the relationships between persons and passions, this study borders on central issues in eighteenth- and nineteenth-century studies: the rise of individualism and the construction of the subject. This study does not question the notion that "individualism" is a crucial term for eighteenth-century and early nineteenth-century culture; perhaps we should say "individualisms" to allow for the number of accounts of the autonomous political person that developed throughout the period.[18] It does, however, pursue the following propositions. First, some of the very articulations of "individualism" may have contributed to the notion of feelings as transindividual. Second, and more important, this book holds that the history of feeling and the history of the individual are not the same thing.[19] I am less interested in determining whether the persons who feel the feelings that circulate through the period's texts were individuals than in exploring the history of what was thought to authorize and authenticate those feelings. Thus these chapters ask questions such as these: Do feelings have meaning insofar as they belong to someone? When does it become possible to say that feelings are personal? The discussion of Charlotte Smith's poetry in Chapter 2, for example, suggests that the relationship between feeling and the personal was a subject of contestation and struggle in late eighteenth-century women's writing. Throughout this study, I seek to determine whether it is possible to question the notion that, in Paul Ricoeur's phrase, an emotion must always be my own.[20]

My interest in separating the study of emotion from the study of the individual—or at least in arguing that the relationship between the two is not self-evident—stems from a skepticism about the claims that have been made in "histories of the subject" by scholars of the Renaissance through the nineteenth century. While American, Marxist, and Foucauldian sociologists of culture have always seen the late eighteenth and early nineteenth centuries as crucial to the emergence of the unified, bourgeois, private, psychologically and affectively oriented modern subject, recent studies have been able to date this figure's birth in both the most narrowly defined and the most various ways.[21] That the subject is historically, socially constructed is an increasingly uninteresting truism: the difficulty concerns what we take for granted as depending, philosophically and politically, on the demonstration that she is. Renaissance scholar Katherine Eisaman Maus has discussed how accounts of the construction of the subject often start from both historicist and philosophical motives. The historicist impulse is to demonstrate the distance of earlier cultures from our own, or to see ourselves as belonging to a particular historical moment; but this historicist impulse is often in the service of a theoretical or philosophical commitment to seeing any notion of subjectivity autonomous from social determination as illusory. Maus's point is that the two projects—historicist and philosophical—need not depend on each other, that the claims of the one can and perhaps ought to be made independently of the claims of the other.[22]

Maus is correct that it is not always clear what exactly is gained, either historically or philosophically, by a demonstration that private or unified subjectivity is illusory, not least because such delusions can be quite powerful. Poststructuralist-historicist literary criticism (I aim to indicate the extent to which historicism and poststructuralism have worked together, rather than seeing them, as is often the case, as opposed) has tended to argue that the production of a gendered, unified, affective subject supports the development of a conservative bourgeois politics; conversely, textual or social effects that expose the constructedness of that subject have sometimes been linked to social subversion. That Hume's skepticism about personal identity and his account of how the person is constructed in his book on the passions, discussed in

Chapter 1, was inseparable from his conservative vision of a society based on sympathy should suggest that philosophical, political, and historical arguments about the subject require some disentangling.[23] Focusing on the epistemological and transpersonal status of emotion in eighteenth- and nineteenth-century writing, rather than seeing affectivity as subordinate to the question of subjectivity, might be one way to begin such a disentangling. My allegiances to poststructuralist, rhetorical readings and my own debts—particularly in the Coda—to historicism will be evident in these pages. However, my emphasis on how eighteenth- and nineteenth-century writers may have either understood or revealed feelings not as the property of the self-possessing individual but rather as alien influences is not designed to prove, once again, that the subject is always already inhabited, is nothing but the sum of its affective identifications: my goal is to understand the conditions under which it becomes attractive, or troubling, to see feelings as doing their work in such extravagant ways. I do not assume in this study that emotions are inherently difficult to know; my goal is to explore how and when it became productive to know feelings as difficult and wayward.

In order to pursue these goals, this project reflects, implicitly and somewhat intermittently, on the afterlife of the eighteenth and early nineteenth centuries' fascination with the movement of feelings. This manifests itself in some brief discussions, in the last three chapters, of the following topics in contemporary psychoanalytic theory: the status of affect in psychoanalytic theory; the relationship between affect and language; the process of transference; the relationship between pleasure and pain. Psychoanalysis, like the writings this book explores, traces the circulation of feelings between and within persons, the ways in which feelings get from one place to another.[24] These chapters do not perform psychoanalytic readings of their romantic texts; rather psychoanalysis makes its presence felt as a heuristic analogy, as the body of writing that inherited some of these problems from the earlier period. It may seem strange to go about an exploration of the conditions that produce emotional extravagance in eighteenth- and nineteenth-century writing by comparing these texts to psychoanalytic ones. My argument, however, is that the conditions that cause psychoanalysis to be drawn to strange theories about—for example—how one person's feeling can secretly pass to another (as I discuss in Chapter 4) are precisely psychoanalysis's own conflicted relationships to empiricism. Thus a comparison to psychoanalysis can make the epistemological dramas in eighteenth-century and romantic writings more visible.

This book seeks to explore how philosophers, poets, and novelists account for their feelings and the feelings of others. It therefore considers the ways in which feelings get their names. Of the writers discussed here, Wordsworth—as we shall see in Chapter 3—most explicitly considers the relationship between feelings and the words that represent them. He conceived of "words, not only as symbols of the passion, but as *things*, active and efficient, which are themselves part of the passion."[25] Chapters 1 and 4 also describe Hume's search to find words for the mind's motions, and the role that the naming and unnaming of feelings plays in *The Mysteries of Udolpho*. This project should also involve some reflection on the words I use to name emotions in the texts I discuss. Readers may find that in these pages I tend to use "passion," "emotion," and "feeling" almost interchangeably. I try to stay close to the shades of meaning that generally distinguish these words in eighteenth- and nineteenth-century writing—passion tending, on the one hand, to evoke the powerful force of an autonomous entity, and feeling, on the other hand, sometimes approaching physical sensation. However, my practice reflects the fluidity these terms had in the period I discuss. Some writers attempted a carefully delineated taxonomy of emotion: Kames, for example, distinguishes between a passion, which is a feeling accompanied by a desire for action, and emotion, which is an "internal motion or agitation of the mind" that "passeth away without desire" (1:41).[26] But for most writers, the many names for emotion travel as freely as emotions themselves.

Chapter 1

The Philosopher as Man of Feeling
Hume's Book of the Passions

> A gloomy, hair-brained enthusiast, after his death, may have a place in the calendar; but will scarcely ever be admitted, when alive, into intimacy and society, except by those who are as delirious and dismal as himself.
>
> Hume, *An Enquiry Concerning the Principles of Morals*
>
> What beings surround me?
>
> Hume, *A Treatise of Human Nature*

The fate of "individual feeling" is an instructive issue on which to examine accounts of the relationship between eighteenth-century empiricism and romantic aesthetics. Historians of the movement from Locke to Wordsworth have traditionally characterized romanticism as a transcendence of empiricism's dualism, its pale versions of self, its allegiance to the object world and its vision of a mind passive before sensory experience; dissenting views have stressed romanticism's particular and sometimes unexpected debts to Lockean language theory, theories of imagination, and associationism.[1] On the issue of feeling, however, the line between empiricism and romanticism has always seemed fairly direct. Critics concerned with the neoclassicism of eighteenth-century aesthetics have of course contrasted the clarity, generality, and universality of the expression of feeling in eighteenth-century drama, verse, and painting to the messy particulars and rampant individualism of romantic feeling.[2] Nevertheless, searches for the origins of the latter always start with Locke and Hume. Hence the "preromantic" aesthetics of sensibility and the gothic are often treated as the missing link in the chain from Locke to Wordsworth: both the romantic egoist and the man and woman of feeling are seen to be indebted to the emphasis on feeling in eighteenth-century philosophy.

And the feeling in that philosophy is generally taken to be individual feeling. Writing of Hume's famous privileging of passion over reason ("reason is, and always ought to be, slave to the passions") in his study of sentimental literature, R. F. Brissenden notes that "the feelings, the passions, and the rational considerations which went into the making of moral judgments were, of course, one's own."[3]

There are, however, aspects of the *Treatise of Human Nature* that should make us uncertain whether the passions and feelings in Hume's discussions are or are not "of course, one's own." Speaking of *other* people's feelings, he declares, "Hatred, resentment, esteem, love, courage, mirth, and melancholy; all these passions I feel more from communication than from my own natural temper and disposition."[4] Hume appears to encounter this train of passions the way a figure in Spenserian romance might encounter a parade of allegorical feelings ("sterne *Strife* and *Anger* stout, / Unquiet *Care* and fond *Unthriftihead*, / Lewd *Losse of Time*, and *Sorrow* seeming dead"): the mere listing of the passions he receives by communication from without tends to make them seem like a gang of personified abstractions, heightening the externality of passion he refers to. Passions—as we shall see at the end of this chapter—have a close relation to personifications. This representation of passions as a train of exterior entities may seem strange, because we tend to see eighteenth-century understanding of passions as quite removed from such wayward, archaic forms. Late seventeenth- and eighteenth-century empiricism inaugurated a fundamental shift in the way modern European culture conceptualized emotion. In early modern thought, all emotional experience falls under the heading of "the passions," which are treated not only as innate, natural forces tied closely to the body but also as the essence of volition. Thus Descartes places emotion within the category of volition, in opposition to understanding, and seventeenth-century political theorists see the passions as fundamentally destructive and in need of restraint. The revolution in social and philosophical notions of emotion in the eighteenth century consists of two related trends. First, anti-Hobbesian "moral sense" philosophers rehabilitated the moral and political dimensions of feeling, arguing for the benevolence of innate emotions. Certain emotions could be "harnessed" for the social good.[5] Second, the writings of the empiricists shifted feeling from the realm of volition to the realm of understanding. For Locke, who complains of Descartes's confusion of feelings with the will, both emotions and ideas are derived from sensation.[6] Desire, feeling, and emotion are variants of pleasure and pain, which are states of understanding. This movement brings feeling closer to epistemological matters: empiricism allows emotion to be a way of knowing. Almost all eighteenth-century thinking about feeling, including Hume's, concerns the relationship between its epistemological and ontological status, and its social character.

This chapter will discuss Hume's *Treatise* in order to show that this revolution in epistemology, which both gave feelings empirical origins and declared their social benefits, had strange effects on how philosophy represented people's relationships to their own feelings. Hume's *Treatise* tells two different stories about the status of feelings. On the one hand, it asserts that feelings are individual, and that philosophy itself as well as social and aesthetic experience depends on individuals who can rely on the individual authenticity of their own emotional responsiveness. On the other hand, it also contends that feelings are transsubjective entities that pass between persons; that our feelings are always really someone else's; that it is passion that allows us to be persons, rather than the other way around. These two stories are inseparable in the *Treatise*, as are Hume's notion of the social "force" of feelings and his theory of knowledge. That is, the movement of feelings between persons—what is called "sympathy"—is crucial to Hume's moral philosophy, but I hope to show that it is also surprisingly crucial to his empiricism itself.

This chapter will also explore the movement of feeling in Hume's own prose. In the opening of the *Enquiry Concerning Human Understanding* (Hume's later revision of the notoriously difficult and famously unsuccessful first book of the *Treatise*), he defines the most socially responsible kind of philosophy, "easy philosophy," as using the colors of eloquence to move the passions. The easy philosophers paint virtue "in the most amiable colours; borrowing all helps from poetry and eloquence . . . they make us *feel* the difference between vice and virtue."[7] The conclusions of hard or abstract philosophy, by contrast, are "dissipate[d]" by "the feelings of our heart, the agitation of our passions, the vehemence of our affections" (*E*, 2). Hume saw himself as attempting to reconcile the two kinds of philosophy, raising hard questions about what we know about our understanding and our beliefs in a new kind of philosophic writing that would find favor with the reading public. Thus as a writer he is concerned with how his readers' feelings determine his ability to affect their beliefs about belief.

Hume's concern about how the account he has to tell of our understanding and beliefs can affect his readers' emotions, and hence their beliefs, might find an analogy in his discussion of miracles. Like the tenets of "easy philosophy," stories of miraculous events gain people's credibility because the stories raise "agreeable" emotions. Stories of miracles are thus highly seductive and likely to spread:

The passion of *surprise* and *wonder*, arising from miracles, being an agreeable emotion, gives a sensible tendency towards the belief of those events, from which it is derived. And this goes so far, that even those who cannot enjoy this pleasure immediately, nor can believe those miraculous events, of which they are informed, yet love to partake of the satisfaction at secondhand or by rebound, and place a pride and delight in exciting the admiration of others. (*E*, 78)

In fact, the last sentence suggests, the pleasures of exciting an audience can dangerously seduce even unbelievers into becoming tellers of amazing accounts: stories of miracles are so pleasurable that they circulate among believers and nonbelievers alike. There is a narcissistic "pride" or pleasure in retailing these stories even second- or thirdhand. Is there a danger as well that the philosopher—especially the skeptical philosopher who has amazing things to tell about the baselessness of many of our beliefs, the limits of our reason, and the fictiveness of our identities—may be seduced by the pleasures of raising emotions in his readers? Might the vertigo of skeptical demystification be as narcissistically gratifying as incredible stories? Hume himself asserts that the presence of skepticism itself can be detected by the feelings it creates. In a footnote, Hume insists that Berkeley's philosophy is to be counted as skeptical in spite of that writer's protestations, because of the way Berkeley's arguments make one feel: "Their only effect is to cause that momentary amazement and irresolution and confusion, which is the result of scepticism" (*E*, 107).

Hume himself, as we shall see, has had to contend with the charge that his skepticism was sensational, designed merely to cause amazement. This charge attaches itself above all to his most notable use of extravagant affective language, the amazing tale Hume tells in the famous conclusion to book 1 of the *Treatise*, where he speaks, presumably, of his own feelings. There, having undone our understanding of the relations between cause and effect, and having proven the fictiveness of the identity both of ourselves and of all external objects, Hume pauses to reflect on his philosophical "voyage" and plunges into an abyss of doubt: "My memory of past errors and perplexities, makes me diffident for the future. The wretched condition, weakness, and disorder of the faculties, I must employ in my enquiries, encrease my apprehensions. And the impossibility of amending or correcting these faculties, reduces me almost to despair" (*T*, 264). What is the place of the philosopher's own feelings in the *Treatise*? What is at stake in his representation of himself? One of the earliest reviews of the *Treatise* accused Hume not only of sensationalism but also of vanity, opining that the text obtruded too much notice of the author's self on his readers. Speaking of Hume's use of the first person singular throughout the book, the reviewer in the *History of the Works of the Learned* remarked, "This Work abounds throughout with *Egotisms*. The Author would scarcely use that Form of Speech more frequently, if he had written his own Memoirs."[8] Hume's use of personal pronouns will be one of the topics of this chapter. It will conclude by considering the "emotional extravaganza"[9] of Hume's conclusion to book 1, but it will arrive there by first visiting some other strangely moving figures in the *Treatise*—a plagiarist, an exile, a person in a painting.

The chapter's coda will extend some of these arguments into eighteenth-century aesthetic theory, focusing on the moving figures of late eighteenth-century poetry, personifications. Personifications of emotions—figures of intense feeling that may belong to no real person—reveal the extent to which the knowability of emotions themselves may depend on rhetorical forms. Thus my goal in the coda is to link the epistemological concerns of this chapter to the questions of feeling and form of the chapters that follow.

Passions and Persons: The Case of Pride

Book 2 of the *Treatise*, Hume's "natural history" of the passions, immediately follows the outburst of affective language in the conclusion to book 1. For some readers of the *Treatise*, books 2 and 3 have seemed unrelated to the skepticism about personal identity of book 1, where the sense of an individual, unified self is called a fiction: "But setting aside some metaphysicians of this kind, I may venture to affirm of the rest of mankind, that they are nothing but a bundle or collection of different perceptions, which succeed each other with an inconceivable rapidity, and are in a perpetual flux and movement" (*T*, 252). The persons of the later books seem to feel and act on their feelings with perfect self-possession and hence (such a reading assumes) with no question about the fictiveness of the self from whom these feelings confidently flow.[10] This would seem to be especially true in the case of the first passion discussed in book 2, pride: feelings of pride are feelings about oneself; thus surely the self can be confident of the propriety and authenticity of such a feeling that would seem to depend on nothing but itself. Hume's decision to begin the book entitled "Of The Passions" with the egotistical feeling of pride seems particularly interesting in light of the charge of egotism described above.

However, as Amelie Rorty has argued, Hume turns to the passions precisely to elaborate the consequences of the "problems that arose from his attempts to do justice to the precisions of skepticisms and the claims of common sense"; in particular, to demonstrate the sources and the strength of the fictions that constitute personal identity.[11] She argues that though pride is the passion that seems most to originate *from* a sense of personal identity, that seems unimaginable without one, in fact for Hume the reverse is true: the passion of pride produces a sense of self. The "object of pride and humility" (pride's obverse) is the "self" or "individual person" (T, 286); "here the view always fixes when we are actuated by either of these passions" (T, 277). The self as "object," however, is not the "cause" of the passion but rather its *effect*. The self cannot in and of itself produce pride (T, 288); the cause is rather the feelings aroused by other objects and the qualities of objects that are close to the self—the self's house, horse, or clothes, the temperature of the climate in which one was born, the fertility of one's native soil. Hume's emphasis on qualities and objects close to the self in the constitution of pride might be seen as providing a solid basis for the contingency of self by introducing a more properly proprietary category, such as property: the self may be a fiction, but its horses, carriages, and clothes are not. However, Hume's turn to the object world has a strange circularity to it. Objects close to us are fit sources of pride because we are attached to them; we are attached to them because they are close. We learn to take pride even in the disagreeable streets and buildings of a new city after we have lived there a while (T, 354–55).

In Hume's analysis, a complex mix of factors produces pride: the objects and qualities that provide the feelings that are pride's source must be worked on by some disposition in the mind: "'Tis evident we never shou'd be possest of that passion, were there not a disposition of mind proper for it; and 'tis as evident, that the passion always turns our view to ourselves, and makes us think of our own qualities and circumstances" (*T*, 287). While there may be some original disposition in the mind toward pride, it is the passion that "turns" us to a sense of self. That "turn" toward the self is quite powerful. In a crucial paradox, Hume implies that it is *because* the self is "in reality nothing" that, once "turned" in that direction, our passion and attention can only with difficulty turn elsewhere. In one of his "experiments" to see in what directions feeling can flow, Hume demonstrates that while the love inspired by the virtue of a son or brother can be a source of pride for ourselves (we are proud to have such a virtuous and lovable brother), a feeling of pride for ourselves cannot of itself spill over into a love for a relative. "The passage is smooth and open from the consideration of any person related to us to that of ourself," but the passage from self to other is difficult. Here is Hume's explanation:

Ourself, independent of the perception of every other object, is in reality nothing: For which reason we must turn our view to external objects; and 'tis natural for us to consider with most attention such as lie contiguous to us, or resemble us. But when self is the object of a passion, 'tis not natural to quit the consideration of it, till the passion be exhausted. (*T*, 340–41)

We get stuck on ourselves precisely because the self is "in reality nothing," held in place by being the "object" of a passion. Passion fixes the self.

The notion that a passion can *produce* an "individual person" (*T*, 286) as its object (the idea of self is one that pride "never fails to produce" [*T*, 287]), rather than coming from an individual person as its source, alerts us to other ways in which the notion of "person" comes into being in the *Treatise*. Passions often act *like* persons: the form of personhood is assumed by many mental entities. In the *Treatise*, relations between ideas and impressions are like relations between persons. In her discussion of Hume's account of associationism, Annette Baier argues that his notions about relations between ideas are modeled on human relations between kin and co-conspirators. In this respect she sees Hume practicing the kind of pseudo-personification of mental entities found in Locke's account of association, in which "whole Gang[s]" of unruly ideas rudely invite themselves into the mind's "presence room,"[12] and so on. For Hume these pseudo-personifications are pervasive, as perceptions "introduce" each other, "follow" and "attract" each other, as images "are always wandering in the mind" (*T*, 119), and "passions 'attend' one another, giv[ing] life to their resembling successors, or deal[ing] death to opposing rivals."[13] Baier finds the text full of foundational analogies to both biological and social human life (parenthood cited early in the *Treatise* as an instance of causation, for example), and sees even in Hume's privileging of "liveliness" or "vivacity" as the motor of mental "life" evidence of an integral connection between rhetoric and subject matter in the *Treatise*. For Baier, the *Treatise* is always already peopled, populated with hypothetical and rhetorical persons, even before it gets to the social concerns of books 2 and 3.

What passion does in Hume's *Treatise*, as exemplified by pride, is enact a kind of person-ification. It ties the "bundle of perceptions" into a recognizable human form we can claim as our own, just as Hume's prose turns impressions and ideas—the basic particles of empiricist philosophy—into recognizable, personified agents. Pride is a meta-passion that organizes relations between emotions and individuals. The last section of this chapter will elaborate the connection between person and passion that Hume's text reveals by looking at eighteenth-century analyses of personification; but now we must move on to Hume's discussions of real people. Having seen how relations between mental entities construct the image of "person" in the *Treatise*, we will next determine how relations between real persons might have consequences for Hume's understanding of mental entities.

Other People's Feelings: Sympathy

For Hume, sympathy is the mechanism by which people can catch the feelings of others. People's ability to feel other people's feelings is the sign of humankind's essentially social nature. People are fundamentally linked through their common feelings, and what allows those feelings to be shared is sympathy: "As in strings equally wound up, the motion of one communicates itself to the rest; so all the affections readily pass from one person to another, and beget correspondent movements in every human creature" (*T*, 576). A number of readers have illuminated the extent to which Hume's understanding of sympathy shaped his conception of social relations. They have stressed the utopian potential and historical distinctiveness of a sociability based on communicated feeling, as well as the limited and often conservative nature of such a vision. While some critics have focused on Hume's attempts to articulate, via sympathy, a society of moral and sentimental relations that replaces or stands apart from political institutions, some, like Carol Kay, have demonstrated the obedience of Humean sympathy to traditional forms of authority. Humean sympathy communicates feelings along well-worn paths: it causes us to admire the rich and powerful; and because "the imagination naturally turns to whatever is important and considerable" (*T*, 308), it strengthens our ties to our fathers and loosens our ties to our mothers (see also *T*, 355–57).[14] In Hume's *Treatise*, maternal feeling is a relatively weak bond, and women have no special place as either objects or subjects of feeling. Beginning an account of late eighteenth-century feeling with Hume thus can further help us (as Chapter 2 will show) denaturalize and recontextualize the link between women and emotion.

Moreover, sympathy, the faculty that makes passions "pass with the greatest facility from one person to another, and produce correspondent movements in all human breasts" (*T*, 605), first enters Hume's account of the passions not as a component of our moral relations with others but as an accessory to pride. In the case of pride, the opinions and feelings of others constitute a "secondary" cause, of "equal influence on the affections" (*T*, 316). Thus, when Hume declares, "hatred, resentment, esteem, love, courage, mirth and melancholy; all these passions I feel more from communication than from my own natural temper and disposition," this radical assertion of the transsubjectivity of feelings, of the superior force of feelings that visit from without, is paradoxically part of an attempt to account for the self-directed feeling of pride (*T*, 317). We feel pride, Hume argues, when we feel sympathetic versions of other people's feelings about us; "*a communication of sentiments*" (*T*, 324) can foster the pride that consolidates our sense of self. Not only is our sense of self constituted through having feelings of pride inspired by contingent objects, but the feelings we have about ourselves may be largely versions of other people's feelings about us. I will discuss Hume's account of the mechanics of sympathy in the following section; first I'd like to look at two of the strange characters who emerge in Hume's examples of the role of sympathy in the love of fame: the exile and the plagiarist. The former spells out some instructive lessons in the structure of sympathy; the latter suggests the special place of pride and its opposite—humility—in the fictions of the self.

The most extended example of the role of sympathy in pride and humility is, oddly, one in which the possibility of sympathetically catching the feelings of others is at all costs to be shunned. Hume tells a narrative about "men of good families, but narrow circumstances," who leave home and conceal their birth in order to flee the disdain of their friends and relations: "Nothing is more usual than for men of good families, but narrow circumstances, to leave their friends and country, and rather seek their livelihood by mean and mechanical employments among strangers, than among those, who are acquainted with their birth and education" (*T*, 322). These men find that their "poverty and meanness" "sit[s] more easy" upon them if they can avoid the threat of feeling the humility that would be the inevitable result of their relations' contagious contempt. Even the contempt and indifference of strangers who don't know their true station in life, according to Hume, is preferable to the contempt of their kindred and countrymen. In this section on how the sympathy of others can contribute to a sense of self, Hume's example is rather of men who salvage or construct some sense of self by fleeing sympathy: they give up the identity they have that is dependent on their relations, their birth, and define themselves in opposition to both strangers and friends, absorbed by miseries only they will know.

Both the story of the exiles and the example of the plagiarists that follows it might shed some light on the asymmetry of Hume's discussion of pride and humility. Theoretically, part 1 of book 2 is equally about pride and humility: both have the same object (the self); sympathy can play an equal role in both. But as many readers have pointed out, Hume's discussion is almost entirely about pride. Even though feeling bad about oneself has the same relation to the idea of self that pride does, humility—the sympathetic reinforcements of which the exiles must flee—is perhaps too close to Hume's assessment of the real state of the self: "ourself . . . is in reality nothing" (*T*, 340). Humility and skepticism about personal identity are not strange bedfellows, and pride has a special relation to the fictions of the self. This is evidenced, tellingly, in one of Hume's last examples of sympathy in this section, the case of plagiarists: "Plagiaries are delighted with praises, which they are conscious they do not deserve; but this is a kind of castle-building, where the imagination amuses itself with its own fictions, and strives to render them firm and stable by a sympathy with the sentiments of others" (*T*, 324). What is strange about Hume's plagiarists is that they seem genuinely pleased with the praise of others, rather than with their cleverness in having fooled people or with their access to recognition and fame. Hume, that is, rejects an instrumental explanation of the pleasures of plagiarism and insists instead on the practice's sheer gratification of the self. A plagiarist tries to pass off something appropriated as his or her own. Trying to render his or her fictions of self-worth and propriety "firm and stable" through sympathetic appropriation of the feelings of others, Hume's plagiarist in fact seems to resemble all Humean persons, consolidating the imaginative fiction of personal identity not only through objects which the laws of association allow them to call their own but also through perversely wandering feelings that originate in other people. The example of the plagiarist brings home the fictions of the self.

The story of the men who leave home is striking as well in its narrative form and fictional quality. The story of the poor relation, the youngest son perhaps, who leaves an indifferent and proud family to take up a new identity far away among rude strangers and support himself by his own labors finds, loosely, countless versions in eighteenth-century narratives, from *Tom Jones* to the pathetic tragedy, *Douglas*, by Hume's own cousin John Home. The exiles are cousins of Edgar in *King Lear*, and countless romances and novels tell the second half of their story, in which a character forced into obscurity makes a name for himself, regains his standing, and reclaims the esteem of his family. More melodramatically, this is an eighteenth-century woman's story, the narrative of the fallen daughter who must find a place to toil in obscurity. We could also see it as Hume's story, as Jerome Christensen has suggested. The youngest son of a distinguished Scottish family, Hume left his home and homeland first to work as a clerk (a "mean and mechanical employment"?) to a Bristol merchant, and then retreated to France where, making "a very rigid frugality supply [his] deficiency of fortune," he wrote the *Treatise*.[15] Hume did not conceal his family identity, but on leaving home he changed the spelling of his name from Home to Hume so that the English wouldn't mistakenly pronounce it "home." He changed his name, that is, to identify himself as "not-home."[16] This story may cast Hume as the hero of his own romance.

Both as narrative plot and philosophical example, this story encodes some pervasive eighteenth-century ideological contradictions: between the claims of sociability and those of individualism; between notions of identity based on family and status and claims of identity based on individual worth. We could thus see this story as a counternarrative to the *Treatise*'s championing of a pervasive, sympathetic sociability, and, perhaps, as a hint of *ressentiment* against the social arrangements that his own mechanics of sympathy underscore, in which our feelings of concern always flow toward those greater than us but not toward those lesser (see *T*, 342–43). The men who leave home and labor for themselves suggest that a sociability based on sympathy is claustrophobic to the individual. Are we justified in feeling, however, that there is something autobiographical, as well as something social and something literary, in this example? Is Hume here—as the reviewer annoyed at Hume's first-person pronouns joked—writing his memoirs? Tracing the progression of pronouns through the several paragraphs of the example reveals a shifting set of loyalties and identities between analyst and exemplum. It begins, somewhat strangely, in the third person plural: "Nothing is more usual than for men of good families. . . ." The plural underlines the typicality Hume wants to stress, but it is odd in that the narrative described is such an individual one. There is something unusual about a whole chorus of men in hiding speaking of their hiding: "We shall be unknown, say they, where we go. No body will suspect from what family we are sprung" (*T*, 322). The analytic "I" that is posed against the chorus of fleeing men ("In examining these sentiments, I find they afford many convincing arguments for my present purpose") turns into a "we" in the next paragraph. Yet as the paragraph continues, the analytical "we" quickly seems to have fallen into the story:

> We may infer from them [the fleeing men], that the uneasiness of being contemn'd depends on sympathy, and that sympathy depends on the relation of objects to ourselves; since we are most uneasy under the contempt of persons, who are both related to us by blood, and contiguous in place. Hence we seek to diminish this sympathy and uneasiness by separating these relations, and placing ourselves in a contiguity to strangers, and at a distance from relations. (*T*, 322)

The "we" of the commentary would seem to be no stranger to this predicament but rather a relation. And indeed shortly thereafter, the writing voice assumes the story: "Suppose *I* am plac'd in a poor condition. . . ." In the last paragraph of the example, the story is in fact that of the solitary individual, a "he." This seems most fitting because his experience is that of the self-enclosed individual whose miseries are known only to himself—and to an omniscient commentator: "Here he himself knows his misfortunes; but as those, with whom he lives, are ignorant of them, he has the disagreeable reflexion and comparison suggested only by his own thoughts, and never receives it by a sympathy with others; which must contribute very much to his ease and satisfaction" (*T*, 323–24). The structure of this example underscores the self-enclosedness of the figure. Self-reflection is defined as deprivation, in opposition to sympathy.

While vacillations of pronoun and pronoun reference are not uncommon in Hume, here the coming together and separation of the philosopher and fictional character (or characters), in conjunction with the claims of epistemological isolation made on behalf of this character ("we shall be unknown"; "he himself knows" "only his own thoughts"), produces an odd effect. Hume is, after all, a philosopher who believes that "nice and subtile questions concerning personal identity . . . are to be regarded rather as grammatical than as philosophical difficulties" (*T*, 262). Just what is Hume's relationship to this character whose essence is that no one knows his identity or his misfortunes? Why is Hume vacillating between omniscience and identification? And why would such an example from the realm of romance be attractive to Hume at this point? One name for this relationship between commentator and example might be "self-representation"; another might be "sympathy." Sympathy could also be the name of the relationship that might obtain between the reader of this interesting example and its protagonist(s). For Hume as for most middle and late eighteenth-century aesthetic theorists, sympathy described not only interpersonal relationships but also relations between persons and representations. In the *Treatise*'s discussion of compassion, for example, Hume easily moves from interpersonal examples to an aesthetic one: "A spectator of a tragedy passes thro' a long train of grief, terror, indignation, and other affections, which the poet represents in the persons he introduces. As many tragedies end happily, and no excellent one can be compos'd without some reverses of fortune, the spectator must sympathize with all these changes, and receive the fictitious joy as well as every other passion" (*T*, 369). While Hume elsewhere carefully distinguishes the way passions derived from literature feel from those derived from real life (a literary feeling "feels less firm and solid" ["Appendix," *T*, 631]), in this passage—and in many other places—

feelings from the world of representation and feelings from real people are equally illustrative.[17]

What train of sentiments do readers of the example of the fleeing man pass through? Might we sympathize with his need to escape his contemptuous relatives? His aloneness with his misfortunes and his gloomy reflections? There is a lesson about the structure of sympathy in this example. If we the readers sympathize with the fleeing man's misfortunes, his indignation at his relatives and his loneliness, rather than—like his relations—feeling contempt for his meanness, it is because of the privileged access we have: knowing, through an omniscient narrator, the misfortunes of a person who conceals them from the world. The man who flees sympathy turns out to be one of the most "sympathetic" figures in the text.

We could back this notion up by pointing out that one of Hume's paradigms of an ideal situation is one precisely like that set up between the reader—or the philosopher—and the private, self-enclosed man of the example: access to a person's private feelings. Life is made worth living, for Hume, by experiencing a series of lively external objects and the "brisk and lively emotions" they produce: "Man is altogether insufficient to support himself; . . . when you loosen all the holds, which he has of external objects, he immediately drops down into the deepest melancholy and despair" (*T*, 352). And the best, the "liveliest of all objects" that can wake us as if from a dream and give us vigor is "a rational and thinking Being like ourselves"

> who communicates to us all the actions of his mind; makes us privy to his inmost sentiments and affections; and lets us see, in the very instant of their production, all the emotions, which are caus'd by any object. Every lively idea is agreeable, but especially that of a passion, because such an idea becomes a kind of passion, and gives a more sensible agitation to the mind, than any other image or conception. (*T*, 353)

This ideal, the person to whose "inmost sentiments and affections" we are privy—total knowledge of another's emotions—is one that may be hard to attain in real life. In the *Treatise*, Hume seems relatively unconcerned with the question of how we really know what other people's feelings truly are, a problem Adam Smith makes central to his account of sympathy in *A Theory of Moral Sentiments*. There is nevertheless—as this description of the ideal encounter by contrast implies—an epistemological uncertainty in Hume's formulation of sympathy. If we derive our sympathetic reproductions of other people's feelings from our observation of external signs (gestures, expressions), "how do we know," as Christensen puts it, "that the passion which by virtue of our idea of it we conceive to belong to another person is in fact the passion that that person actually feels?"[18]

That ideal and its very difficulty are dramatized by the relation of the narrator to the fictive character who conceals his emotions from everyone else, both family and strangers. The lesson of the men who flee sympathy may be that the transsubjective, spontaneous flow of feelings—the privilege of having such a lively idea of another's passion that the "idea becomes a kind of passion"—may truly be most possible in the context of such fictive, narrative relations. Because he is a hypothetical, fictional character, this person is indifferent to our sympathy. But in this respect he explains another of Hume's points about sympathy—that we feel *more* sympathy with someone when she seems to be indifferent to or unconscious of her predicament. Speaking of the case of persons murdered in their sleep, or of little princes imprisoned, Hume argues: "As we ourselves are here acquainted with the wretched situation of the person, it gives us a lively idea and sensation of sorrow, which is the passion that *generally* attends it [the situation]; and this idea becomes still more lively, and the sensation more violent by a contrast with that security and indifference, which we observe in the person himself" (*T*, 371).[19] The fleeing men are, of course, conscious of their predicament, unlike the persons murdered in their sleep. But they have in common their indifference to sympathy; in both cases the onlooker, reader, or narrator imagines what the hypothetical feeling might be and then catches, sympathetically, that feeling. The example of the fleeing men may suggest to us that the notion of "private feeling," like personal identity, is fictional, something we project into the interior of another.

At this point we could return to the question of self-representation, the possibility of Hume secreting himself away in the figure of the fleeing men. We might begin by detecting a similarity—a relationship of kin—between the fleeing men and Hume's representation of himself as a *Frankenstein*-like monster fleeing society in the conclusion to book 1:

I am first affrighted and confounded with that forelorn solitude, in which I am plac'd in my philosophy, and fancy myself some strange uncouth monster, who not being able to mingle and unite in society, has been expell'd all human commerce, and left utterly abandon'd and disconsolate. Fain wou'd I run into the crowd for shelter and warmth; but cannot prevail with myself to mix with such deformity. (*T*, 264)

As in the case of the fleeing men, there is a slight ambiguity in this self-representation as to whether Hume has truly been cast out by his "exposure" (*T*, 264) to the enmity and contempt of others or is suffering a self-imposed, strategic exile. In the last sentence he seems poised between longing and contempt; it is unclear whether "such deformity" refers to himself or to others. But unlike the fleeing men, who turn out to become more sympathetic the more they flee, Hume has received very little sympathy for this outburst of feeling. The review in the *History of the Works of the Learned* drips with sarcasm at this point: "What Heart now would not almost bleed? what Breast can forbear to sympathize with this brave Adventurer? For my part, I cannot, without the utmost Emotion and Solicitude, take even a transient Prospect of the Dangers and terrible Catastrophe to which he is exposed."[20] We will defer until the end of this discussion a consideration of why, when Hume declares his feelings, expressions of irony emerge more readily than feelings of sympathy.

Sympathy and the Force of Impressions

We've seen how epistemological questions emerge in the workings of sympathy; I'd like to turn now to the place of sympathy in Hume's theory of knowledge. Writing of Hume's account of pride, Jerome Christensen ponders whether Hume's attempt to account for the passion in experimental, highly schematic or diagrammatic terms ultimately eviscerates the need to account for a *cause* of the passion: "The diagram makes pride intelligible while finessing or perhaps abolishing the supposed necessity of a causal explanation. What 'produces' pride ... in Hume's text is the systematic *representation* of the passion. System seems to imitate or reflect, but system also constitutes."[21] In Christensen's Bourdieuian reading of book 2, Hume becomes progressively less systematic in his approach to the passions, drawing attention to his own rhetorical position in the text, and ultimately defining passion as a form of practice that "goes without saying." The question of what would count as a "cause" of a passion is indeed ambiguous and strangely irrelevant (see, for example, *T*, 303). In Hume's account of the passions, questions of cause—for all that such questions are elaborately and inconsistently worked out—are subordinated to a concern with what we could call the performative or quantitative dimensions of affect. What authorizes feelings, what gives them their authenticity, their ontological status, their moral value, is not their causes but their force or liveliness. Hume's Newtonian framework allows his absolutism about feelings: they authorize themselves, refer only to themselves, and thus cannot be invalidated: "A passion is an original existence, or, if you will, modification of existence, and contains not any representative quality, which renders it a copy of any other existence or modification. When I am angry, I am actually possest with the passion, and in that emotion have no more a reference to any other object, than when I am thirsty, or sick, or more than five foot high" (*T*, 415). To many commentators, this passage is a mistake, an anomaly: feelings, as in the case of pride, clearly do refer to things. However, this striking passage allows Hume to stress how much he wants to *exclude* certain kinds of explanations for feelings: they are neither mimetic nor semiotic in any way nor subordinate to statements of fact. They are quantities of force.

The issue of force is at the heart of Hume's theory of where our ideas and feelings come from. All perceptions are divided into two categories, impressions and ideas; impressions are those perceptions that enter the mind with the "most force and violence," while all ideas are, without exception, the fainter copies of impressions. Hume's notion of "impression" is strikingly different from, say, Locke's. For Hume an impression is not a copy, a mark made on the surface of the mind by something from outside the mind; it is rather an original, the sensation itself.[22] An impression has no representational content. Unlike Locke, who is extremely concerned to explain how exactly perceptions of the outside world enter the mind, Hume leaves this as a matter of the sheer force or liveliness of whatever impresses itself upon us. The "*firmness, or solidity, or force, or vivacity*" (*T*, 106) of an impression would seem to operate like a physical property, and to be measurable as such: for example, Hume compares the consequences of the diminishing or increasing of the vivacity of an impression to the workings of "pipes" that "convey no more water than what arises at the fountain" (*T*, 386). The progression from a lively impression—say, pain—to the less lively *idea* of something—the idea of pain—would also seem to obey a law of physics. "Simple impressions always take the precedence of their correspondent ideas, but never appear in the contrary order," Hume writes: "To give a child an idea of scarlet or orange, of sweet or bitter, I present the objects, or in other words, convey to him these impressions; but proceed not so absurdly, as to endeavor to produce the impressions by exciting the ideas" (*T*, 5). The latter would be an absurd procedure because the relation between impression and idea is a unidirectional one: forceful impressions first, fainter ideas second. The difference between an impression and its corresponding idea is only "in the degrees of force and liveliness" (*T*, 1), and that difference marks out the fading of force into an idea. An idea becomes a "perfect idea" "when it intirely loses that vivacity" (*T*, 8). Since most passions are impressions of reflection for Hume, questions of force and liveliness are what define the emotions.[23]

As Hume describes the mechanism of sympathy, it seems that sympathy can reverse the seemingly unidirectional flow of force. Sympathy works precisely by converting ideas into their corresponding impressions. Here is what happens when we respond sympathetically to another person: "When any affection is infus'd by sympathy, it is at first known only by its effects, and by those external signs in the countenance and conversation, which convey an idea of it. *This idea is presently converted into an impression, and acquires such a degree of force and vivacity, as to become the very passion itself*" (*T*, 317, my emphasis). This may seem very mysterious to us: how can an idea take on the vivacity and force of an impression? How can sympathy reverse the law that forceful impressions precede their paler ideas? The problem of other people's feelings thus appears to have a crucial connection to the key terms and operations of Hume's theory of understanding. Sympathy seems to be the basis not only of ideal social relationships but of an ideal theory of mind, one that would overcome the passivity of mind of the empiricist account as it is usually understood. This mind would not merely suffer the fading of force but could reverse the process. Hume calls this power of sympathy a confirmation of his system and simultaneously an instance of the limits of philosophy:

What is principally remarkable in this whole affair is the strong confirmation these phaenomena give to the foregoing system concerning the understanding.... 'Tis indeed evident, that when we sympathize with the passions and sentiments of others, these movements appear at first in *our* mind as mere ideas, and are conceiv'd to belong to another person, as we conceive any other matter of fact. 'Tis also evident, that the ideas of the affections of others are converted into the very impressions they represent, and that the passions arise in conformity to the images we form of them. All this is an object of the plainest experience, and depends not on any hypothesis of philosophy. That science can only be admitted to explain the phaenomena; tho' at the same time it must be confest, that they are so clear of themselves, that there is but little occasion to employ it. (*T*, 319–20)

How might the reversals that sympathy can perform confirm Hume's system? How can an idea convert itself into the force of an impression? Where do the vivacity and force in this case come from? How might Hume's theory of sympathy cause us to rethink a crucial "hypothesis of philosophy," the meaning of "force"?

The possibility of sympathy depends upon the general resemblance between people. We saw earlier how the transsubjective and the individual are intertwined in Hume: here the force of sympathy begins with our "idea of our own person" (*T*, 318). Sympathy is predicated on our perception of a resemblance between another person and our idea of ourselves: the more resemblance we perceive, the more conversion of idea to impression takes place: "In that case resemblance converts the idea into an impression, not only by means of the relation, and by transfusing the original vivacity into the related idea; but also by presenting such materials as take fire from the least spark" (*T*, 354). The "force" or "vivacity" that causes the conversion of sympathy comes from some aspect of the mind perceiving resemblance. Furthermore, the question of what "force" or "vivacity" is, if it is not simply the property of impression, comes down in part to a semantic problem.

Hume is notable for his lack of interest in questions of language, of the relations between words and ideas that preoccupy Locke in the third book of the *Essay Concerning Human Understanding*. The words "strong" and "lively," however, occasion a reflection on the abuse of words and the process of naming. In the discussion of the causes of belief in book 1 of the *Treatise*, Hume concludes that it is hard to discuss the operations of the mind "with perfect propriety and exactness" because common language does not have enough names for the mind's different functions. As an example, he remarks: "Thus my general position, that an opinion or belief is *nothing but a strong and lively idea de-*

riv'd from a present impression related to it, may be liable to the following objection, by reason of a little ambiguity in the words *strong* and *lively*" (*T*, 105). In the course of his account of what he means by "strong" and "lively" he discusses the force of memory: "In thinking of our past thoughts we not only delineate out the objects, of which we were thinking, but also conceive the action of the mind in the meditation, that certain *je-ne-scai-quoi*, of which 'tis impossible to give any definition or description, but which every one sufficiently understands" (*T*, 106). It is the undefinable sense we have of our mind moving—its own actions, in addition to whatever the contents of our thoughts might be— that is called "force." Of a lively idea, Hume says, "it must be able to bestow on whatever is related to it the same quality, call it *firmness, or solidity, or force, or vivacity*, with which the mind reflects upon it" (*T*, 106). Here force is the quality of the mind's attention to its own ideas. "Force" and its cognates are the names of the "je-ne-scai-quoi," the actions we sense of our mind working.

A footnote in the *Enquiry Concerning Human Understanding* on the ambiguity of the words "force, power and energy" revises this point more clearly, suggesting that these motions of the mind become projected onto the objects the mind contemplates: "With regard to energies, which are exerted, without our annexing to them any idea of communicated motion, we consider only the constant experienced conjunction of the events; and as we *feel* a customary connexion between the ideas, we transfer that feeling to the objects; as nothing is more usual than to apply to external bodies every internal sensation, which they occasion" (*E*, 52). The last phrase suggests that empiricism, as a theory of ideas derived from experience, is set in motion when we take that "je-ne-scai-quoi" of the mind's own motions, give it the names of life—vivacity, liveliness, energy, force—and project it out into the world. If force is the mind's relation to itself, then empiricism is the relationship between the mind's relation to itself, and the relation between the mind and the world.[24]

By suggesting that the workings of the mind can turn ideas back into impressions, Hume's theory of sympathy causes us to rethink the meaning and the status of the notion of force. His understanding of the social character of feeling is intimately related to the status of a crucial concept in his epistemology, the relation of force between impressions and ideas.

Falling Figures

We have seen that sympathy appears to be a phenomenon that complicates the "mechanistic" or Newtonian aspects of Hume's understanding of force, impression, and idea and reverses the unidirectional fading of force. However, the one place where Hume worries about the fading of force is a passage in which sympathy seems to be responsible for the fading of feeling, rather than for its revivification. At the end of the discussion of how sympathy explains our esteem for the rich and powerful, Hume remarks that "the minds of men are mirrors to one another, not only because they reflect each others emotions, but also because those rays of passions, sentiments and opinions may be often reverberated, and may decay away by insensible degrees" (*T*, 365). The use of the mirror metaphor here is odd, the second half of the sentence implying that mirroring decays, rather than preserves or repeats. With the mirroring metaphor, sympathy seems in fact like an empty repetition. Interestingly, the narrative of feelings that is framed by this remark seems rather to tell the story of how sympathy fruitfully generates feeling, producing a new one to reinforce the old: A rich person takes an original pleasure in his objects of wealth; the beholder esteems him; this increases the pleasure of the rich man; and this in turn "become[s] a new foundation for pleasure and esteem in the beholder." The "secondary" pleasure of being esteemed for one's riches is said to be one of the "principal" motives for acquiring wealth. Sympathy thus appears to break down the distinction between an "original" feeling and its followers. In this passage, however, this multiplication is accompanied by a diminishing: "Here then is a third rebound of the original pleasure; after which 'tis difficult to distinguish the images and reflexions, by reason of their faintness and confusion" (*T*, 365).

While it is hard to say why Hume sees sympathy as decaying away as well as revivifying people's feelings here, this turn to decay might be connected to the paragraphs that precede this passage. The role of sympathy in our esteem for the rich and powerful leads Hume to hypothesize that our ideas of beauty are based on sympathy: when we find something beautiful, we are feeling sympathetically the pleasure that its proprietor takes in its usefulness. The extended example Hume uses to illustrate this rather utilitarian aesthetic theory concerns our sentiments when a man takes us on a tour of his beautiful house. This man "takes particular care among other things to point out the convenience of the apartments, the advantages of their situation, and the little room lost in the stairs, antichambers and passages; and indeed 'tis evident, the chief part of the beauty consists in these particulars" (*T*, 363–64). Our pleasure consists in "our sympathizing with the proprietor of the lodging" (*T*, 364), feeling, perhaps like Elizabeth Bennet visiting Pemberley, that the proprietor of such a house deserves more of our sympathy. The next several paragraphs are devoted to extending this argument, extending it, as Hume says, "to tables, chairs, scritoires, chimneys, coaches, sadles, ploughs, and indeed to every work of art"; to the fact that our pleasure in a beautiful field is essentially our sympathy with the proprietor of its fertile acres; to the fact that our conceptions of personal beauty are based on our sympathy with the health of the person. Though it is not explicit, the train of the example can lead one to assume that the proprietor of the tables, chairs, scritoires (etc.), of the fertile field, of personal health and beauty, is the same hypothetical happy man whose house we toured; after viewing the structure of the house we are led to admire its contents, then its grounds, and finally the personal advantages of the man himself. The train of our sympathies, that is, causes the figure of an individual to emerge in the text, person-ified through feeling. This happy figure is one who would be as much at home in the section on pride that began book 2 as he is in his own elegant house: he is a man whose sense of self is constituted by his qualities, his extensive objects and, in particular, the esteem of others.

Amidst this illustration, however—sandwiched between the view of the fields and the contemplation of physical health—is a paragraph which, while presumably also proving that our perceptions of beauty are based on sympathy with the possessor of the object, seems like a significant interruption: "There is no rule in painting more reasonable than that of ballancing the figures, and placing them with the greatest exactness on their proper centers of gravity. A figure, which is not justly ballanc'd, is disagreeable; and that because it conveys the ideas of its fall, of harm, and of pain: Which ideas are painful, when by sympathy they acquire any degree of force and vivacity" (*T*, 364–65). The train of the example might first lead us to expect that we are contemplating a painting in the fortunate man's collection, being asked to sympathize with his pleasure or unpleasure in his possession. But this is not the case: the object of our sympathy is a figure *in* the painting.

This move into a representation may momentarily surprise us. It is an another instance of how eighteenth-century discussions of feelings, and of sympathy in particular, move with unconcern between examples of "real" people and examples of representations of people. But how does this figure exemplify the notion that beauty lies with the proprietor? The only thing that is proper to this figure is unbalance; other than that it has nothing. This figure is in this respect like another falling figure of a man in the *Treatise*, cited earlier: "Man is altogether insufficient to support himself; . . . when you loosen all the holds, which he has of external objects, he immediately drops down into the deepest melancholy and despair" (*T*, 352).

According to Hume, we see the unbalanced figure in the painting and sympathetically receive the idea of its fall. The placement of this example in the sequence can't help but make us contemplate the contrast between the figure in the painting and the man with the house: the person in the painting without his or her proper center of gravity, the man with the house so balanced and centered in his world by his possessions, qualities, and the esteem we feel for him. (Indeed, in *my* idea, the figure is definitely falling down those elegant and economical stairs on which so "little room" is "lost" in the fortunate man's house.) We might, with a stretch of the imagination, also see this figure as kin of the exiles discussed earlier, who flee the contempt of their well-to-do relations: surrounded by the example of "our esteem for the rich and powerful," the figure in the painting is a poor relation in a rich man's house. As in the example of the fleeing men, this figure—like them, a "negative" example of a sympathy to be avoided—sets up a counternarrative. Viewed in the picture frame, this falling figure produces "disagreeable" or unbeautiful sympathetic pains in the viewer. But "framed," as this example is, within the example of the man who has everything, the picture of the falling figure may find a sympathy which identifies with the figure's nothingness. Drawing these analogies, I am certainly over-reading this figure who appears in view only briefly. There is, however, a structure of sympathy worth noting at work here. As with the fleeing figure, our access to knowledge of this figure's predicament seems a private privilege: since he or she is merely a figure in a painting, it is only we who can, through the associations of our minds, produce ideas about this person's future (it contains falling, pain, and harm) by feeling the force of those ideas sympathetically.

This painting is a representation that makes us uneasy: it is a representation that sympathy causes us to attribute a fall to. We might turn now from this sympathetic "fall" of ours into a representation to another off-balance figure in the *Treatise*, the confessional Hume in the conclusion to book 1. There, we also witness a figure on the brink of a fall: "When I look abroad, I foresee on every side, dispute, contradiction, anger, calumny and detraction. When I turn my eye inward, I find nothing but doubt and ignorance. All the world conspires to oppose and contradict me; tho' such is my weakness, *that I feel all my opinions loosen and fall of themselves, when unsupported by the approbation of others*" (*T*, 264; my emphasis). Readers of this representation of a fall have, notoriously, not responded sympathetically. I noted earlier the *History of the Works of the Learned*'s sneering mock sympathy; other eighteenth-century readers tended either to take Hume's melancholy seriously as evidence that skepticism was a species of gloomy enthusiasm, and hence atheistical and evil, or else accused Hume of being sensationalist, viewing the passage as evidence that Hume was simply pretending to be skeptical for effect. Thomas Reid took the latter position, arguing that Hume's gloom was assumed, and claiming that Hume "could hardly, for half a dozen pages, keep up the sceptical character." He insinuates that if Hume were really as despairing as he sounds, he would have committed suicide: "Nor did I ever hear him charged with doing any thing, even in solitude, that argued such a degree of scepticism as his principles maintain. Surely if his friends apprehended this, they would have the charity never to leave him alone."[25]

Modern readers have also tended to question the authenticity of the feelings the philosopher expresses. His interruption of his philosophical argument to confess his own feelings has been called a youthful indiscretion, "a philosophical and emotional extravaganza," "melodrama," "a kind of schizophrenia." One critic has characterized the conclusion as "profound ditherings," "self-dramatized storm and stress," a "*jeux d'esprit*," Hume "not on his best behavior."[26] Critics find it easiest to take the conclusion seriously by arguing that Hume does not mean us to take his feelings seriously but rather as strategic, comic, and ironic. John Richetti has most successfully argued that the "mock terror" that the speaker passes through is a "largely rhetorical means of staging uncertainty, demolishing metaphysics," and revealing the essential "neutrality" of Hume's philosophical position. It thus describes Hume's ironic project as a whole, "the displacement of philosophy by philosophical writing, which is not truly skeptical as such, but is a literary deployment of skepticism to place thought in psychological and moral reality." Annette Baier and Raymond Williams are notable among modern readers for attributing some authenticity to the feelings expressed. For Williams, Hume's confessional turn humanizes his skepticism; for Baier, Hume's turn to his own feelings prepares us for his analysis of the passions in books 2 and 3.[27]

Why has Hume's expression of his own feelings met with such disparate and largely unsympathetic responses? Is not Hume acting for his readers precisely as the ideal of which he speaks, the person who "communicates to us all the actions of his mind; makes us privy to his inmost sentiments and affections; and lets us see, in the very instant of their production, all the emotions, which are caus'd by any object" (*T*, 353)? I will not present here a complete reading of the conclusion; nor will I seek to adjudicate between philosophical accounts of its place in Hume's argument. Rather, I'd simply like to comment on what these passages suggest about the relationship between persons and their passions. A brief look at the language of the conclusion may suggest why it has been possible for responses to differ so wildly. The writer's account of his emotions does seem to teeter on the brink between calculation and helplessness. It may be in part Hume's modulation into the present tense in the conclusion that puts some readers off, leading them to feel that Hume's "sudden view" of his predicament is staged: "This sudden view of my danger strikes me with melancholy; and as 'tis usual for that passion, above all others, to indulge itself; I cannot forbear feeding my despair with all those desponding reflections, which the present subject furnishes me with in such abundance" (*T*, 264). His observation on the "usual" course of melancholy can sound ironic and detached, as can his claim that his predicament reduces him "*almost to despair*" (my emphasis). But if we can put our finger on the language here that makes the feelings seem staged, we should also note that the language of this "melodrama" has an easily locatable source. Using images of light and dark, shipwreck and shoals (see *T*, 263–64), Hume describes his experience in the language of Protestant spiritual autobiography:

Where am I, or what? From what causes do I derive my existence, and to what condition shall I return? Whose favour shall I court, and whose anger must I dread? What beings surround me? . . . I am confounded with all these questions, and begin to fancy myself in the most deplorable condition imaginable, inviron'd with the deepest darkness, and utterly depriv'd of the use of every member and faculty. (*T*, 269)

If Hume can be accused of writing his memoirs in the *Treatise*, as the early reviewer claimed, it is a particular genre of memoir that he draws on here.[28] Appearing a third of the way into his story, the conclusion to book 1 is analogous to the dark moment at sea before conversion. If we read the conclusion's valley of despair ironically, the atheistical philosopher's use of Protestant language (a language that in its own context emphatically refers to authentic personal experience) can seem like the most fitting irony of all. There is no revelation, no breaking in of the light here; if there is a conversion imminent, it is at best a conversion to nature and to common life.

There are, however, some strange logical consequences to interpreting the feelings Hume exposes here as in some sense not his, as ironic or staged. If one reads Hume's gloominess as a mock despair he didn't feel, then how does one read the astonishing passage that follows it?

Most fortunately it happens, that since reason is incapable of dispelling these clouds, nature herself suffices to that purpose, and cures me of this philosophical melancholy and delirium, either by relaxing this bent of mind, or by some avocation, and lively impression of my senses, which obliterate all these chimeras. I dine, I play a game of back-gammon, I converse, and am merry with my friends; and when after three or four hour's amusement, I wou'd return to these speculations, they appear so cold, and strain'd, and ridiculous, that I cannot find in my heart to enter into them any farther. (*T*, 269)

If one takes the melancholy as false, one necessarily commits oneself to taking this account of the "cure" as a return to reasonableness and normality; mock terror could indeed be cured by a game of backgammon. However, Hume does not end his discourses here but returns to philosophical speculation, and we are equally likely to hear the insouciance of this paragraph's advice—just eat and play backgammon—as ironic. Yet if we insist on the irony in Hume's suggestion that the way out of philosophical difficulty is as easy as a game of backgammon, then we are necessarily admitting that, at some level, the agonies this witty passage abruptly cuts off are indeed genuine, if not insurmountable. Taken together, the agony and the cure, the tonal ironies we hear in both passages tend to undo one another.

While I believe we must disagree with M. A. Box's notion that whether we hear the feelings of the conclusion as ironic or melodramatic or genuine, Hume's or not Hume's, is a matter of "personal taste," I think we must concur that it is ultimately very hard to say.[29] We may be more willing to credit Hume's claim that "all . . . passions I feel more from communication" from other people "than from my own natural temper and disposition" when we realize how much trouble we have crediting his "own" emotions. While empiricist philosophy may privilege or authenticate individual feeling as a basis of social and aesthetic experience, Hume's understanding of the relationship between passions and persons, his emphasis on sympathy and the passage of feelings, makes the expression of one's "own" feelings a hard thing to render authentically. Hume seems paradoxically most ironic and distanced when he refers directly to himself: "I cannot forbear"; "I . . . fancy myself." The problem is specifically that he is claiming the feelings are his.[30]

Readers' responses to the figure of Hume confessing his vertigo and distress in the conclusion are thus quite different from our responses to the men who flee sympathy or even the unbalanced figure in the painting in the discussion of the rich and powerful. Readers seem not to have fallen into Hume's despair, catching disagreeable sensations of pain and harm; nor have they commiserated with his plight. Rather, they have cast the feelings expressed as false—as either strategically ironic or unwisely melodramatic and exaggerated. Perhaps Hume's lesson about emotion is indeed that to be found in the example of the fleeing men or in his comments about our sympathy for those murdered in their sleep: sympathy is most forthcoming when the object in question seems most oblivious, when the feelings in question are the imaginary feelings that we—or a narrator—attribute to the object. The difference between the conclusion and the story of the men who flee is the difference between a text that confronts the reader with an authorial figure who directly expresses his feelings and a text in which both reader and author together are involved in speculation about another figure in the text. This speculation, I argued earlier, consists of sympathetically attributing feeling to a figure to whom we have special access, a figure who is unaware of our sympathy. The lesson about the relationship between persons and passions in the

Treatise is that feeling may always be vicarious, something we generate in attributing it to another figure. Our sense that the fleeing men may indeed be blood relatives of the figure in the conclusion—that the fleeing men's story is Hume's story—would only strengthen our sense of the overlapping identities between reader, writer, and characters. The wavering of pronouns—from a vast category of men to a single individual, from I to we to he—that I noted earlier may be seen as symptomatic of the movement of Hume's self-dispersal. Hume's pronomial "fall" into the story he tells is related to the viewer's response to the falling figure in the painting, and to the vertigo Hume expresses in the conclusion to book 1. The wavering of pronouns makes possible the inclusive structure of the example, in which readers, author, and characters all fall in with each other, seemingly sharing and producing each other's feelings.

For Hume, persons feel most the feelings they catch from others, as if by contagion. Their ability to do so is the basis of all social relations. The force of this process—called "sympathy"—by which another's feeling is converted into something we feel, is the force that links impressions and ideas, mind and world. The preceding section of this chapter argued that Hume's empiricist conception of how ideas are derived from experience depends on the notion of liveliness and, moreover, that this force cannot be understood in Newtonian terms as a purely physical property of impressions. I'd like to return briefly to the falling figure in the painting one last time; but first I must correct myself: this is not a "falling figure," merely a figure "not justly ballanc'd," off its "proper center[s] of gravity" (*T*, 364). It is the viewer who makes the figure fall: "A figure, which is not justly ballanc'd, is disagreeable; and that because it conveys the ideas of its fall, of harm, and of pain: Which ideas are painful, when by sympathy they acquire any degree of force and vivacity" (*T*, 364–65). In this respect, the viewer is to the figure as Pygmalion to his statue: the viewer's or reader's fall into sympathy with a falling figure is also a bringing to life. In this instance, the force of gravity is truly inseparable from the force of sympathy.

Coda: Personification and the Epistemology of Emotions

Hume's discussion of our sympathetic responses to a painting amidst his argument about our esteem for the rich and powerful, like his tendency to advert to the example of seeing a play in his discussion of our compassion for the poor and the suffering, is symptomatic of the extent to which aesthetic response and moral relations between persons were theorized together in the eighteenth century.[31] For eighteenth-century writers on aesthetics, the notion that our feelings may be derived from works of art as well as from other people raises a host of new questions about the nature of emotion and the nature of aesthetic objects. Are the feelings raised by art the inevitable effects of the sensory impressions of the objects themselves, as in Burke's *Enquiry Into the Sublime and Beautiful*, or are they effects of associations in our minds?[32]

Eighteenth-century aesthetic theorists are preoccupied by and at the same time strangely unconcerned about the question of *where* feelings come from: whether one is responding to a person or to a representation of a person suffering seems, in many cases, ultimately not to make any difference to the emotional experience itself. These writers also concern themselves, though less explicitly, with the epistemology of emotions: how does one know *what* feeling one is having, or describing, or rejecting? We can see signs of an epistemology of the emotions in discussions of the relationship between language—especially figurative language—and feeling. In this chapter's discussion of Hume's *Treatise*, we noted how the passions, and the meta-passion of pride in particular, perform a kind of personification, making possible the notion of self or person and disseminating figures of persons throughout the text's account of mental operations. It may not be surprising, then, to find a corollary in rhetorical analyses of personification. Personifications of emotions, as they appear in poetry and other elevated discourses, are justified with implicit claims about the knowability of emotions.

What does it say about a culture's relation to feeling that its poetry represents feelings as persons? That "Envy wan, and faded Care," and "Grim-visaged comfortless Despair" are said to work their way through people's lives (Gray, "Eton College")? That a person is said to "fill Affection's eye," or visit where "hopeless Anguish poured his groan" (Johnson, "On the Death of Dr. Robert Levet")? To personify a feeling—to prefer (to borrow an example from Anna Seward) "Pleasure shed all her lustre over the scene" to "We feel pleasure in contemplating the lovely scene" is in a significant sense to endorse an *impersonal* way of expressing a feeling.[33] It removes the feeling from the subject who presumably feels it and gives the feeling the autonomy of a person. Critics of the 1940's characterized the impersonality of eighteenth-century personification as a fulfillment of the values of neoclassicism, giving feelings public and general rather than personal expression. In a 1947 *ELH* article, "Personification Reconsidered," Bertrand H. Bronson hypothesizes a two-step process in which eighteenth-century writers first generalize and abstract their own feeling, then "recapture" the personal element by personifying the abstraction:

> Personification allowed them to recapture the most valuable part of the immediacy of personal statement. It allowed them to make the best of both worlds, the public and the private, to be at the same time general and specific, abstract and concrete. Thus, they first translated personal experience into decorous generalization; and then, without surrendering the general, reparticularized it by means of personification.[34]

This rather contorted account reveals the extent to which twentieth-century discussions of neoclassical feeling depend on a postromantic notion that feelings are, in their origins, at "first" personal; there is twentieth-century nostalgia for the personal even in this celebration of the "neoclassical." This nostalgia, the fear that "surrendering" to the heroics of impersonal neoclassical feeling may involve a loss, might suggest to us that our understanding of the neoclassical is trapped in an opposition between the personal and the general: it cannot admit the possibility of feelings that are genuinely transpersonal.

While the personification of emotion may seem a supremely conventional mode of conveying feelings, the trope of personification itself was thought by eighteenth-century theoreticians to be the natural expression of emotion. Personification or prosopopoeia (the two are discussed together) is central in eighteenth-century poetic theory to the understanding of the relationship between affect and language. Following Cicero, Quintilian, and Renaissance rhetoricians, writers such as Richard Stack asserted that "almost all the passions, if carried to excess, naturally fall into the use of the prosopopoeia, one of the boldest figures of speech, and the sublimest expression of passion."[35] James Beattie claimed that "violent passions are peculiarly inclined to change things into persons."[36] Personification was figurative language *par excellence*, happening spontaneously and demonstrating the capacity of language itself to become animate. According to Joseph Priestley, in a "*serious* personification, . . . the mind is under a temporary deception, the personification is neither made nor helped out by the speaker, but it obtrudes itself upon him; and, while the illusion continues, the passions are as strongly affected, as if the object of them really had the power of thought."[37] Insisting that personifications are "neither made nor helped out by the speaker," Priestley betrays the notion that passions—and hence figurative language—are beyond will and intention. The evacuation of the speaker's agency is accompanied by imagining that there is another person who can will and think: "the passions are as strongly affected, as if the object of them really had the power of thought." An encounter with figurative language really could be like an encounter with a rude person who "obtrudes" him or herself upon us.

Personification's tendency to turn things into *persons* is what makes it the most exemplary instance of the autonomous, spontaneous, and affective nature of figurative language. The relation between language and affect in personification is circular: "Personification is the child of passion, which it serves again to increase," wrote John Donaldson. This circularity takes on an added dimension when the personification in question is *of* an emotion. Donaldson's explanation of why we personify emotions exemplifies the extent to which eighteenth-century writers saw feeling both as strongly originating in an external object, and as something that eclipses the object:

Passion, or sentiment being originally the effect of external sense, cannot be conceived to exist in absence of the material images or impressions of substance; since we cannot conceive the passion of love to be other than a quality belonging to some being or person who loves, or is capable of loving. Neither can we suppose passion to be impassioned, or affection itself to be affected. In order to extend our powers of affection, therefore, we materialise and personify the very affections themselves.[38]

The personification in this case seems to stand in for the "substance" of the object. Allowing passion itself to be impassioned, the form of the personification positions emotion as standing warily between being a subjective and objective experience; the personification is both subject and object.[39] As in Hume, passion creates a person. According to Donaldson and others, personification serves to "extend our powers of affection." Communication of feeling from one person to another, from writer to reader, is facilitated by bodying forth feeling in the form of a person. Despite its "impersonality," late eighteenth-century discussions of feelings in literature can't do without the category of the person: if feelings seem detached from actual persons, the notion of a bounded, self-enclosed entity for feeling seems indispensable.[40]

To late eighteenth-century poetic theory, passion prompts personifications, turning feelings themselves into persons. This practice carries consequences for how this period conceives of the knowability of both emotions and persons. Discussing Wordsworth's well-known objections to personifications, Frances Ferguson has pointed out:

> Personification in its simplest forms fails to recognize the difficulty of comprehending humanness. While seeming to adduce an increment of splendor to the real subjects of admiration, both anthropomorphism and personification can easily become evidence of deity and of humanity. Both assume that there is a stable form to be projected on the world of abstractions, and through their implicit countermovement they thus borrow a specious stability for man from those abstractions.[41]

Personifications can suggest that we know what a person is. In an example of the countermovement Ferguson describes, John Donaldson praises personification for according precisely this stability to the form of personhood: "The mind never more nearly arrives at an image of a person," he asserts, "than when it attempts a moral abstraction." Donaldson also suggests how, through a similar countermovement, emotions themselves become knowable through this form: "Anger, Revenge, Despair, Hope, & c. can be distinguished from each other almost as easily when they are copied by the pen, as when we feel their influence on our own minds, or make others observe it in our actions."[42] It seems more intuitive to us to say that Anger, Hope, Revenge, and all their train are *more* easily distinguished from each other when personified through either verbal or pictorial art than they are in real life, where knowing exactly what feeling is influencing the mind is often a murky matter. To say that personifications are as knowable as feelings are is in fact a way of *attributing* knowability and self-evidence to feelings.

Personification thus can both stabilize and clarify the notion of the person and present us with feelings in knowable forms. Such accounts suggest that knowing one's feelings may always involve recognizing them through conventions or forms. The history of the study of feelings consists of a constant oscillation between recognizing feeling as form, and seeing feeling as the animation of form; attitudes toward personification exemplify this oscillation. From our perspective, we are more likely to see a preference for personification or for any other figure of speech as a conventional preference. We'd like to say, the late eighteenth century used personifications and found them beautiful and powerful because it was conventional to do so. Late eighteenth-century aesthetics, however, appeals to affect as that which authorized a poet's or reader's investment in, or "animated," the repetition of trope or literary convention. Personification itself, moreover, is the trope *of* animation. The vacillation between recognition of personification *as* convention and as the animation of the literary emerges in Wordsworth's well-known prohibition of personification in the 1800 Preface to the *Lyrical Ballads*. Seeking to distinguish the style of his poems from late eighteenth-century "poetic diction," Wordsworth singles out personification as the most conventional of all conventions: "The Reader will find that personifications of abstract ideas rarely occur in these volumes; and are utterly rejected as an ordinary device to elevate the style, and raise it above prose." Wordsworth wishes, he says, to keep his readers "in the company of flesh and blood"; but pages later, in order to buttress an assertion that prose and poetry are made of essentially the same substance, he personifies poetry itself in order to capture its affective and expressive nature: "Poetry sheds no tears 'such as Angels weep,' but natural and human tears; she can boast of no celestial ichor that distinguishes her vital juices from those of prose; the same human blood circulates through the veins of them both."[43] This is personification with a vengeance: the only flesh and blood here is that of a tearful, expressive "Poetry." Feelings may belong no more certainly to real persons in romantic poetry than in eighteenth-century philosophy.

This discussion of personification has tried to show that when we say feelings are personal, we are invoking categories—the "personal" and its opposite, the "conventional"—that are in a shifting, dialectical relationship, that are derived from each other and often collapse into each other. Feelings can either seem conventional themselves, or be seen as that which animates, or makes meaningful, conventions. Interestingly, virtually everyone in the eighteenth century who writes on the topic argues that personification is especially suited to English writing because of a convention of the English language: the absence of gender. Kames claimed that "the chastity of the English language, which in common usage distinguishes by genders no words but what signify beings male and female, gives thus a fine opportunity for the prosopopoeia; a beauty unknown in other languages, where every word is masculine or feminine."⁴⁴ To introduce a gendered pronoun is to personify. Indeed, we can say with Hume that in this case the question of personal identity may be grammatical rather than philosophical. The next chapter will discuss the relations between feeling and gender, between the personal and the conventional, in late eighteenth-century women's poetry.

Chapter 2

Sentimentality and Experience in Charlotte Smith's Sonnets

In the first of his *Essays, Moral, Political, and Literary* (1742), Hume brings his philosophy of feeling to matters of polite conduct, advising his readers on the management of the passions. He identifies two kinds of emotional extravagance, which he calls "delicacy of passion" and "delicacy of taste."[1] People suffering from the first respond with the strongest feelings to "all the accidents of life," feeling both the liveliest joys and the most "pungent sorrows." People of "such lively passions are apt to be transported beyond all bounds of prudence and discretion," liable to suffer more and be dangerous to both themselves and others (91). People blessed with a delicacy of taste, however, feel with a heightened sensitivity not the accidents of life but the beauties of art and manners. A delicacy of taste has the same effects on a person as a delicacy of passion—"it enlarges the sphere both of our happiness and misery, and makes us sensible to pains as well as pleasures, which escape the rest of mankind"—but in this case these feelings are limited to poems, paintings, and polite conversation.

Though the delicacy of passion and the delicacy of taste are, according to Hume, at bottom so similar, and act upon people in such similar ways, the latter is infinitely to be preferred. The reason for this is that "the good or ill accidents of life are very little at our disposal; but we are pretty much masters [of] what books we shall read, what diversions we shall partake of, and what company we shall keep" (92). It is much better to have one's presumably uncontrollable emotional extravagances tied to aesthetic objects we choose than to the accidents of life that we don't. Moreover, Hume contends, in spite of the fundamental similarities between these two propensities, the cultivation of a delicacy of taste can "cure" people of the excesses and miseries of a delicate passion. The cultivation of taste can improve and educate the passions, weaning us of our susceptibility to all kinds of stimuli and channeling our feelings toward aesthetic objects. If put into practice, Hume's lesson about the education of passions would bring about the society his *Essays* as a whole address. The goal is ultimately an exclusive society of cultivated individuals who throw off their indiscriminate pleasure in vulgar company in favor of close attachments to a small band of like-minded lovers of art, polite conversation, and polite letters (see 93–94).

Hume's essay is an ingenious example of eighteenth-century social thinking about emotional extravagance in that it simultaneously posits an area of emotional response *as* extravagant, *and* sees that extravagance as being in the service of its opposite—the cultivation of judgment and moderation. Excess and order work together: Hume's notion of feelings' contribution to a polite and regulated society is predicated on the notion that feelings are fundamentally ungovernable. It is a good thing that "we are pretty much masters [of] what books we shall read" and so on because, Hume's logic suggests, we are not masters of our feelings. The realm of the aesthetic, moreover, is defined as both emotional excess and control. Like almost all of late eighteenth-century aesthetic theory, Hume's essay defines the aesthetic, or the opposition between art and life, not in terms of a difference between real and fictitious objects but in terms of the kinds of feelings it creates. Yet, suggesting that the passions caused by the "accidents of life" can be educated into aesthetic response, Hume's argument depends as much on the confusion between art and life as it does on their separation.

This is especially evident when Hume points, as proof of a fundamental connection between the operations of taste and passion, to their proximity in women: "We may observe that women, who have more delicate passions than men, have also a more delicate taste of the ornaments of life, of dress, equipage, and the ordinary decencies of behavior. Any excellency in these hits their taste much sooner than ours; and when you please their taste, you soon engage their affections" (92). This proof of the common genealogy of taste and passion may seem to veer toward a trivialization of the aesthetic as a feminine fondness of ornament. It is important to note, however, that elsewhere in the *Essays* Hume lauds women's aesthetic sensitivity (see "Of Essay Writing," for example). For Hume as for many eighteenth-century writers, women's talents and sensibilities were crucial to the refinement of English society. Discussions of women's role in society typically put forth the view that "it is an indisputable truth, that the art of refining and polishing the manners and taste in society, is exclusively possessed by the fair sex: and that the further any country advances in, and becomes distinguished for, civilization of sentiment, and elegance of manners, the more the prevalence of female influence is discovered amongst them."[2] Women's association with the realm of taste and the aesthetic was generally seen, by Hume and by others, as having very serious consequences for society as a whole. The philosopher's analysis of the proximity of taste and passion in women, however, expresses a sentiment that can be found throughout eighteenth-century discussions of women's special sensibilities: the concern that women's feelings do not discriminate between appropriate and inappropriate objects (as for example in the conventional fear that a woman may be as alive to a seducer's charms as to a landscape or a poem, as in Austen's *Sense and Sensibility*). Here, in his discussion of the relationship between delicacies of taste and passion, Hume suggests that for women, the "accidents of life" and the aesthetic may become indistinguishable as sources of emotion.

꒜

A similar confusion between matters of taste and the accidents of life has persisted in discussions of eighteenth-century women's lives and especially of eighteenth-century women's writings. Literary critics no longer treat women's literary writings as being fundamentally or exclusively about women's experience—about their lives as women. Feminist theorists and historians have scrutinized the always shifting nature of "experience" both as an explanatory category for literary or historical analysis and as a basis for political claims. For Joan Scott, for example, it is by studying what comes to count *as* experience, rather than by simply recovering what women of the past have experienced, that scholars can understand how gender has worked as a discursive system. Feminist critics have also explored the ways in which women writers have self-consciously mediated between material experience and aesthetic concerns.[3] When women write about emotion, however, it appears to be especially difficult, and especially necessary, to scrutinize the relationship between aesthetics and experience: emotion often appears to us to belong definitively to the realm of experience. It appears as the subjective point at which women can testify to difference and oppression as material facts. This is true in part because of the important role that emotion has always played in feminist politics. Nineteenth- and twentieth-century feminisms have a long tradition of emphasizing women's emotional lives, either seeing women's emotions as repressed in a sexist society and in need of expression, as devalued and in need of revaluation, or as the means by which women can become conscious of their oppression and mobilize for change.[4]

Late eighteenth-century texts are central to the history of the role of emotion in bourgeois feminism. We may no longer insist on claiming Mary Wollstonecraft's *Vindication of the Rights of Woman* as the founding, originary text of this tradition, and we may argue about whether it is in fact anachronistic even to speak of "feminism" in the eighteenth century. However, Wollstonecraft's treatise definitively established the role of feeling in feminist discourse. Elaborating the victimization of women at the hands of their own feelings, Wollstonecraft makes their subjective suffering a crucial aspect of her testimony against inequality, a key exhibit in her argument for extending rights to women.[5] In her chapter entitled "Observations on the State of Degradation to Which Woman Is Reduced by Various Causes," she details the extent to which women have been taught to overvalue and cultivate their emotional sensitivities—their sensibility—and the extent to which they are thus "ever restless and anxious," "blown about by every momentary gust of feeling." "Miserable, indeed, must be that being whose cultivation of mind has only tended to inflame its passions," writes Wollstonecraft: "It would be an endless task to trace the variety of meannesses, cares, and sorrows, into which women are plunged by the prevailing opinion, that they were created rather to feel than reason, and that all the power they obtain, must be obtained by their charms and weakness."[6] An emphasis on how inequality makes women feel is part, though it is not all, of what is at stake in the slogan, the personal is political.

Wollstonecraft's emphasis on feeling simultaneously indicts the "false system of manners" that overvalues women's feelings, *and* itself values those feelings as grounds for political claims. This double valuation of feeling has led both historians of the period and feminist critics to take two different approaches to a historical question: What was the relationship between the culture of sensibility in late eighteenth-century England and the emergence of feminism? Was sensibility, as Wollstonecraft explicitly argued, damaging to women's interests? Or did the culture of sensibility, its ideologies and its literary genres—the sentimental novel, the poetry of sensibility—enable a feminism based on feeling? The best discussions of the period have insisted on the complexity and contradictions of this question.[7] It has been possible to argue that in spite of her attacks on sensibility, Wollstonecraft's writings were fundamentally indebted to a political and literary culture that emphasized feelings. The historian G. J. Barker-Benfield contends that feminism emerged out of the culture of sensibility because of that culture's potential for voicing women's sufferings. Surveying the range of literary writing—both fiction and poetry—by women in the late eighteenth century, he argues: "When women first gained the opportunity to publicize their awakening to self-consciousness as a group, they made their suffering at the hands of men a central focus. If feminism was in part born in women's 'awareness of their mistreatment by men,' of 'felt oppression' and victimization, then it was born in the culture of sensibility."[8] In order for the historian to make this argument, however, he must assume that women's writing is about women's experience: when women wrote, it was of their sufferings as women. The attempt to answer a historical question has brought us back to the fundamental confusion about women's feelings that lurked in Hume's formulation: that in the case of women's feelings, matters of aesthetics and the accidents of experience are the same.

This chapter seeks to clarify our understanding of the relationship between sensibility and feminism by focusing on what women's sentimental literature has to say about the expression of feeling. The poetry I will discuss is Charlotte Smith's gloomy *Elegiac Sonnets* (first edition, 1784). Representing Smith as a perpetual slave to despondency, regret, and grief, these poems raise some crucial questions about where feelings come from. What does it mean for women to write about their own feelings? What exactly does it mean to say that feelings are personal? And what does it mean to call women's poetry "sentimental"? I have focused this investigation on poetry, rather than the sentimental novel, because—as I will sketch briefly at the beginning of the next section—poetry had come, by the end of the century, to have a special relationship to the cultural prestige of feminine feeling. I hope to show that we only know how to call feelings "sentimental" when it becomes possible to find feelings' origins in experience.

The late eighteenth-century link between taste and women to which Hume's essay alludes can be seen in discussions of the reading and writing of poetry. This was a period of expansion in poetry reading and writing—in Robert Mayo's words, "a period of poetic inflation." To his evidence—the existence of poetry departments in periodicals of all kinds, the legions of amateur poets who filled their pages—we might add that in the middle 1780's the poetry departments in the major general periodicals such as the *Gentleman's Magazine* and the *European Magazine* expanded dramatically in length. In the 1760's and 1770's, poetry readings and declamations by fashionable actors had become a popular society entertainment. Changes in copyright law made it possible to reproduce poems endlessly: anthologies and poetic miscellanies were, in the words of one reviewer in 1789, "prodigiously multiplied."[9] Anthologies not only proliferated but also changed in character: they often consisted of either selections from the period's canon of modern (post-Miltonic) British poets or works by contemporary authors, often organized thematically, and directed toward either the leisure or the education of particular audiences: the middle class, children, and women. In anthologies such as the popular *Elegant Extracts*, the terms in which the "influence" of poetry were discussed were not unlike those in which the influence of women was described. Poetry is said to "have drawn the minds of savage men to knowledge, and to have polished human nature"; "minds which are dull, and even brutally insensible, may be penetrated, sharpened, softened, and vivified, by the warm influence of Poetry."[10]

While many treatises for women advised their female readers against novel reading, they often approved the reading and memorizing of poetry. If the novel is a pernicious influence, the reading of poetry has its uses: "The mind is thus stored with a lasting treasure of sentiments and ideas," remarks the author of *The Female Aegis*.[11] Anthologies of poetry directed specifically at women took this as their mission. In the preface to his *Poems for Young Ladies* (1767)—which went through several editions in the last quarter of the century—Oliver Goldsmith wrote that "poetry is an art which no young lady can, or ought to be wholly ignorant of.... The necessity of knowing enough of it to mix in modern conversation, will evince the usefulness of my design."[12] Poetry anthologies and miscellanies directed at women were not entirely new in the late eighteenth century; but a comparison between two "ladies' miscellanies" will make clear the character of the later anthologies. A collection entitled *The Ladies Miscellanie* published in 1718 consists of light pieces centered on female dress: "The Art of Dress," "The Petticoat," "The Fan." In 1793, however, *The Lady's Miscellany, or Pleasing Essays, Poems, Stories and Examples for the Instruction and Entertainment of the Female Sex* is, as its title suggests, a didactic collection that addresses itself to a woman's morals and sentiments, rather than to her love of finery. *The Lady's Poetical Magazine, or Beauties of British Poetry*, which came out in four volumes in 1781–82, combines conduct book with poetry anthology. The editor's introductory poem explicitly links poetry itself to femininity. Women may yield the scepter and the sword, "the rougher arts," to men, but "in those arts which humanize the mind / They boast an equal pow'r with mankind." Poetry, in particular, has its source in the love and influence of women:

> Then why refuse them to an equal share
> In arts which owe their being to the fair?
> Say, canst thou meanly think that science strives
> To taint the female breast where most it thrives?[13]

When he speaks of poetry thriving in the breast of the fair, the editor may seem to be talking about women poets, but in fact there are few poems by women in *The Lady's Poetical Magazine*. The volumes contain selections representative of late eighteenth-century taste: Milton, Dryden, Pope, Gray, Warton, Young, Beattie, Collins, and Akenside appear here. The editor is addressing himself to feminine readers, but he makes a generalized link between femininity and poetry that women writers could exploit.

Woman poets were conscious of the extent to which they could both take advantage of and be limited by their culture's association of women with sensibility. In a period that placed poetic value on "natural genius," on the inspired and authentic rather than on the learned and the cultivated, women's natural sensibility gave them an equal, if not greater, qualification for writing poetry. Discussing the current sentimental trend in poetry, Mrs. Thrale remarked in 1789, "this fashion makes well for us Women however, as Learning no longer forms any part of the Entertainment expected from Poetry—Ladies have therefore as good a chance as People regularly bred to Science in Times when *fire-eyed Fancy* is said to be the only requisite of a Popular Poet."[14] Both female poets and male reviewers knew that "convention" and "the popular" were becoming synonymous with "femininity" in literary discourse. A reviewer of Helen Maria Williams's *Poems in Two Volumes* remarked in 1786 upon the "*tears*, and *love*, and *sounds of woe*" which he called "those eternal topics of female poetry."[15]

Charlotte Smith's poetry meditates on the relationships between literary convention and the sounds of woe, revealing the unpredictable results that could ensue from late eighteenth-century culture's associations between femininity and poetry.[16] Her most important poetic work was her *Elegiac Sonnets*, which first appeared in 1784 and went through nine increasingly expanded editions during her life. She played a major role in reviving the sonnet from the comparative disrepute into which it had fallen in the eighteenth century and thus enabled the romantic poets' further use of the form. Coleridge acknowledged Smith along with William Bowles (whose sonnets were largely imitations of the kind Smith had invented) as a preeminent reviver of the sonnet, and Wordsworth called her "a lady to whom English verse is under greater obligations than are likely to be acknowledged, or remembered."[17] Early reviews coupled extravagant praise of her sonnets with reiteration of the eighteenth-century view that the sonnet form had proven itself, until now, fundamentally incompatible with English poetry: "A very trifling compliment is paid Mrs. Smith, when it is observed how much her Sonnets exceed those of *Shakespeare* and *Milton*. She had undoubtedly conferred honour on a species of poetry which most of her predecessors in this country have disgraced."[18] Reviewers and contemporary readers singled out her sensitivity to the beauties of nature, her elegant use of sonnet form to "shape" a poignant emotion, and above all her emotional tone. Though he goes on to lament Smith's "infection" with "the Gallic mania," the comments of Richard Polwhele in "The Unsex'd Females" are typical of contemporary reception of her work: "The Sonnets of Charlotte Smith, have a pensiveness peculiarly their own: it is not the monotonous plaintiveness of Shenstone, the gloomy melancholy of Gray, or the meek subdued spirit of Collins. It is a strain of wild, yet softened sorrow, that breathes a romantic air, without losing, for a moment, its mellowness."[19]

As Polwhele's comment suggests, Smith bears comparison to the sensibility poets of midcentury. Her sonnets are elegiac in a generalized sense, melancholy meditations of a speaker who typically mourns the loss of past happiness, or the disjunction between the repose and renewal of nature and her gloomy internal state. They are morbid poems; death seems to the speaker the only source of tranquility. In this respect they resemble the poetry of the graveyard poets. However, sonnet 44, "Written in the Church-yard at Middleton in Sussex," dramatically revises the topos of the tranquil country churchyard:

> Press'd by the Moon, mute arbitress of tides,
>   While the loud equinox its power combines,
>   The sea no more its swelling surge confines,
> But o'er the shrinking land sublimely rides.
> The wild blast, rising from the Western cave,
>   Drives the huge billows from their heaving bed;
>   Tears from their grassy tombs the village dead,
> And breaks the silent sabbath of the grave!
> With shells and sea-weed mingled, on the shore
>   Lo! their bones whiten in the frequent wave;
>   But vain to them the winds and waters rave;
> *They* hear the warring elements no more:
>   While I am doom'd—by life's long storm opprest,
>   To gaze with envy on their gloomy rest.[20]

The poem would seem to break down the distinction between the busy, fractious world and the silent grave upon which the musing poet can philosophize. Here, the dead are not immune to the turbulence of the world: they rise up from their graves, exposed to the elements. This graveyard poem indeed suffers a sea change. In the end, the poem threatens the repose of the dead only to further emphasize their utter remoteness from strife and pain. While we may find the final couplet's analogy trite, there is something savage about gazing enviously at storm-battered, seaweed-entangled bones.

Though the sea in sonnet 40 (also from the fifth edition) is considerably calmer, it serves in this poem as in sonnet 44 as a figure for poetic revisionism. In this seashore poem, it is the waves, not the graves, that are silent:

> Far on the sands, the low, retiring tide,
>   In distant murmurs hardly seems to flow;
> And o'er the world of waters, blue and wide,
>   The sighing summer-wind forgets to blow.
> As sinks the day-star in the rosy West,
>   The silent wave, with rich reflection glows:
> Alas! can tranquil nature give *me* rest,
>   Or scenes of beauty soothe me to repose?

> Can the soft lustre of the sleeping main,
>   Yon radiant heaven, or all creation's charms,
> "Erase the written troubles of the brain,"
>   Which Memory tortures, and which Guilt alarms?
> Or bid a bosom transient quiet prove,
> That bleeds with vain remorse and unextinguish'd love!

The sense of spatial distance in the scene described in the first six lines becomes a psychological distance between the speaker and the scene. By vaguely anthropomorphizing the natural elements—the wind, for example, "forgets" to blow—Smith makes the stasis that this normally active seascape displays resemble a kind of unconsciousness. The scene's inertia is repeated in the sonnet's form by the almost identical "b" rhyme of the first and second quatrains, as if the form itself had forgotten to flow. Our attention may have been arrested, however, by the line in quotation marks—which comes from *Macbeth*. Why does this line wash ashore at this point? Is Smith truly comparing herself to Lady Macbeth? Does Smith's literary inheritance—her capacity to revise and to quote other texts—appear as an inherited guilt?

We could perhaps best approach the meaning of this line by considering Smith's practice of quotation. Smith's propensity to quote can help us understand both her relation to eighteenth-century poetry and the status of emotion in her poems. Smith's sonnets are like echo chambers, in which reverberate direct quotations, ideas, and tropes from English poetry. The fundamental unit around which Smith's sonnets seem to be built is not so much the image, or even the individual word or line, but rather the artful, pathetic phrase. It is a poetry of sound bites, noun clusters which describe emotional states or the afflicted, such as "sad children of Despair and Woe" (sonnet 4), "the tortured bosom's pain" (8), "Passion's helpless slave" (21), "Affliction's sharpest dart" (28), "Sorrow's cypress shade" (29), and so on. Many of Smith's expressions of woe are quotations from other poets, especially Shakespeare, Milton, Pope, Young, Gray, Collins—precisely the poets of late eighteenth-century anthologies. As is often the case in the mid- to late eighteenth-century poetry in which this kind of echolalia reigns, it usually does not make sense to try to interpret Smith's echoes of other texts thematically. It may seem odd, for example, that in the eighth sonnet she asserts that the beauties of spring "have power to cure all sadness—but despair" with an echo of book 4 of *Paradise Lost* (line 155 describes the "purer air" that breathes towards Satan as he approaches Eden, "able to drive / All sadness but despair"); but this echo does not simply signal that there is a Satanic tinge to Smith's despair, evoking her exile and alienation from ordinary human pleasures. It also signals the allegiance of this sonnet to a poetry that is formally made out of other poems. In this instance, for example, Smith mines *Paradise Lost* for what appears as an internal rhyme there (air/despair) to form the rhyme that makes her sonnet's final triplet (fair/air/despair). Most readers did not object to Smith's heavy use of quotation and allusion, though there were exceptions: Anna Seward expressed indignation at what she did not hesitate to call Smith's "plagiarism." She referred to "Mrs. C. Smith's everlasting lamentables, which she calls sonnets, made up of hackneyed scraps of dismality, with which her memory furnished her from our various poets."[21] Smith herself affixed notes to the ends of all editions after the third: "I have there quoted such lines as I have borrowed; and even where I am conscious the ideas were not my own, I have restored them to the original possessors."[22] We must insist not on the scandal of Smith's "plagiarisms" but on the lack of scandal, the sense that her sonnets announce a relationship to poetic language and literary tradition that seemed appropriate. A letter from William Cowper to Smith (which alludes to a letter from Smith to the poet William Hayley) suggests that Smith herself served as the figure of echo in her relations with literary men. "I was much struck," Cowper writes, "by an expression in your letter to Hayley where you say that 'you will endeavour to take an interest in green leaves again.' This seems the sound of my own voice reflected to me from a distance, I have so often had the same thought and desire."[23]

If we sometimes have difficulty making sense of Smith's quotations of others' poems thematically, in other words, we might try to connect them to Smith's position as a woman poet reviving and reinventing the moribund English sonnet. She draws attention to the paradox of this position, reminding us that—Petrarchan sonnets penned by women of the Renaissance notwithstanding—woman's position in the sonnet has typically been that of the object, not the subject, of feelings.[24] For example, the collection contains several poems based on Petrarch, followed by five original sonnets "supposed to be written by Werter," which follow Goethe's popular hero to the brink of suicide. In all of these, Smith transmits a man's voice addressing a woman. The complicated nature of her position emerges in the fourth of the Werther sonnets (sonnet 24), in which Werther contemplates the effect of his death on his beloved, Charlotte:

> The tears shall tremble in my CHARLOTTE's eyes;
>   Dear, precious drops! —they shall embalm the dead!
> Yes! —CHARLOTTE o'er the mournful spot shall weep,
>   Where her poor WERTER—and his sorrows sleep! (11–14)

The fact that Smith is also a Charlotte has the effect of making her appear to be both the transmitter and the receiver of Werther's sentiment. Imagining Charlotte weeping, the sonnet transforms the Petrarchan beloved into the woman of feeling. Moreover, it seems to allow Werther to nominate Smith as the woman who weeps over the sorrows of young Werther, as well as others' sorrows. It suggests that the place of melancholy in Smith's poetry may be linked to her gendered relations to others' literary feelings.

In this context, the sonnet that opens each edition of the collection may be read as a revealing declaration of how Smith's poetry links gender and genre, quotation and feeling. She begins by claiming that the muse of poetry has "smiled on the rugged path" she's been "doom'd to tread," accompanying her in her unhappiness and weaving "fantastic garlands" that decorate her in her misery (2, 4). But in the second quatrain, poetry doesn't *simply* adorn misery:

> But far, far happier is the lot of those
>   Who never learn'd her dear delusive art;
> Which, while it decks the head with many a rose,
>   Reserves the thorn to fester in the heart.

Pain here appears to be coming *from* poetry's thorns themselves. The following quatrain retreats from this position a little, suggesting that poetry merely has the power to make existing pain seem worse; it "points every pang, and deepens every sigh" (11). But the final couplet reinforces the claim that writing itself can make one miserable:

> Ah! then, how dear the Muse's favours cost,
>   *If those paint sorrow best—who feel it most!*

The final line—as a note in the text directs us—virtually quotes the final couplet of Pope's *Eloisa to Abelard*. There, Eloisa looks forward to a time when a poet may put her sorrows into verse:

> The well-sung woes shall soothe my pensive ghost;
> He best can paint them who shall feel them most.

Eloisa is making a relatively conventional claim about the relationship between affect and language: feeling precedes writing; the capacity to feel someone's feelings sympathetically is the condition for persuasively and accurately writing about them. But if feeling precedes writing in Pope's couplet, Smith's sonnet leads precisely to a reversal of that claim. Following the preceding line—"Ah! then, how dear the Muse's favours cost," her final line—even though its syntax is almost the same as the original—asserts rather that those who paint sorrow best feel it most. Here writing precedes feeling. Smith recontexualizes Eloisa's claim to shift it into its opposite, suggesting that the price you pay for the Muse's favor is feeling, and therefore that writing, according to this reversal, makes one miserable.

It seems crucial that this reversal of our understanding of the relationship between feeling and poetic language takes the form of a repetition and reversal of a quotation from another poem: asserting that writing makes one miserable takes the form of quoting someone else. If quotation involves incorporation of someone else's expression, perhaps writing makes one miserable because writing always involves taking in, reproducing, other people's expressions of feelings. However, I do not think we should take the affective dimension of this formulation, this misery, as the sign of a woman poet's defeat at the hands of a patriarchal literary tradition, her depression at being always already written: rather, this gloominess is a sign and medium—as we shall see in a later sonnet—of a successful literary transmission.

Quoting Pope in her first sonnet, Smith takes up where Eloisa, one of the most famous literary suffering women of the eighteenth century, leaves off. There is, however, another crucial difference here. Eloisa's couplet is about finding *someone else* who can feel and write about *other people's* feelings—she is not speaking of personally writing her *own* feelings, whereas Smith, it would seem, *is*. In the context of the passage she quotes, Smith is in the odd position of sympathizing with her own feelings, of being feeling's object *and* subject. Or more accurately, since this is a quotation, the feelings about which she writes are not hers. Eloisa's entire utterance is, in some sense, a quotation by *Pope* of a woman's feeling and language. This poem stems from a long tradition—the heroic epistle—in which male poets give voice to female suffering. It is a genre that operates according to the lesson about passion of Hume's *Treatise*: that feeling is most moving when it is most vicarious. A woman's poetry of feeling necessarily responds to such a tradition; but in doing so it makes strange the assumptions about language and feeling that are the essence of that tradition. If sentimental verse is naturally or inevitably a woman's genre, it is so only by making the feelings she expresses not her own.

The first sonnet's revelations about the status of feelings can serve as a guide to the poetics of quotation throughout the *Elegiac Sonnets*. What seems most interesting about Smith's practice of quotation, from this perspective, is not the particular thematic contents of her borrowings but rather the way her poems draw attention to their quotations as things written, expressed, or felt by others. In sonnet 5, Smith addresses the South Downs:

> Ah! hills belov'd! —where once a happy child,
>   Your beechen shades, "your turf, your flowers among,"
> I wove your blue-bells into garlands wild,
>   And woke your echoes with my artless song.

By quoting Gray's "Ode on a Distant Prospect of Eton College" in the context of a remembered scene, Smith raises questions about whether the object of her retrospection and sentiment is properly the South Downs or the poem by Gray—about whether she is invoking echoes of the landscape or waking literary echoes with her present song. Sonnet 9 also cites the Eton College Ode: when she complains of former friends, who deride "the ills they ought to soothe" and "laugh at tears themselves have forced to flow," the tears Smith weeps in the latter phrase are Gray's tears. The idea that the feelings Smith expresses may come from other writing emerges vividly in the line in sonnet 40, discussed earlier, in which she asks whether "tranquil nature," "yon radiant heaven, or all creation's charms" can, as Macbeth hopes for Lady Macbeth (V.iii.42), "Erase the written troubles of the brain." Just as the final line of sonnet 1 invokes a quotation at the moment it is talking about the effects of writing, so here quotation accompanies an assertion that mental distress may, in fact, be "written." Smith's sonnets contend not simply that literature authorizes the way feelings are expressed, but that literature may be responsible for, may be writing in, the very feelings she expresses.

Sonnet 32, "To Melancholy. Written on the Banks of the Arun,

October 1785," displays especially acutely the connection between melancholy and literary transmission that runs through the *Elegaic Sonnets*. It forms one of a group of poems to the river Arun, which Smith associates with the playwright Thomas Otway, as well as with William Collins and William Hayley. These sonnets thus are all involved in invoking the Genius Loci of the river Arun, translating literary history into the landscape. Sonnet 32 renders the process by which literary voices are naturalized and absorbed into the landscape:

> When latest Autumn spreads her evening veil,
>> And the grey mists from these dim waves arise,
>> I love to listen to the hollow sighs,
> Thro' the half-leafless wood that breathes the gale:
> For at such hours the shadowy phantom pale,
>> Oft seems to fleet before the poet's eyes;
>> Strange sounds are heard, and mournful melodies,
> As of night-wanderers, who their woes bewail!
> Here, by his native stream, at such an hour,
>> Pity's own Otway I methinks could meet,
>> And hear his deep sighs swell the sadden'd wind!
> Oh Melancholy! —such thy magic power,
>> That to the soul these dreams are often sweet,
>> And soothe the pensive visionary mind!

The speaker of this poem is much more palpably present in the scene than in most of Smith's nature sonnets. She asserts her presence not only through personal pronouns—"I love to listen," "I methinks could meet"—but also by referring to herself as "the poet" in line 6, and through the specificity of the scene she describes: she points to "*these* dim waves." The description of the scene progresses from what could be called a natural gothic, which then becomes supernaturalized, then humanized. The speaker moves from perceiving its natural ghostliness, its veil, mists, dim waves, and half-leafless woods, and hearing its natural sighs, to a filling in of that landscape with supernatural sounds and sights in the second quatrain: shadowy phantoms, strange sounds, and mournful melodies. This gothicism is tempered, next, into the image of "Pity's own Otway." The shading of the natural into the gothic seems to enable Smith's imaginary access to Otway: as his "deep sighs swell the sadden'd wind," the sibilance of the verse conspires to turn that poet's voice into a breath on the wind. I am most interested, however, in the way that "Melancholy" enables Smith's encounter with a past poet, allowing her to "hear" him.[25] Imagining another poet's misery, the sonnet concludes, is sweet to the melancholy soul, and soothing to the pensive visionary mind. Melancholy has the magic power to make one imagine other poets' misery in the landscape, and hence allows an imagined relation to other poets.

⁂

Smith's sonnets, then, highlight the *literariness* of the melancholy they express.[26] From the first sonnet onward, they seem to argue that their melancholy may indeed be caused by the strange effects of reading and writing. Smith's poetry suggests the extent to which the culture of sensibility and especially its literary forms may not have naturally given voice to women's feelings. They demonstrate as well the ways in which melancholy functions as a medium for the transmission of poetic convention in late eighteenth-century verse. But though the *Elegiac Sonnets* seem to proclaim the literary origins of their feelings, contemporary discussions surrounding them tended to focus on the specifically personal nature of Charlotte Smith's feelings. A sonnet addressed to Smith in the *European Magazine* praises her poems precisely because the feelings in them spring from "REAL woe." The author of another sonnet explicitly criticizes her for attempting to write about others' feelings, and advises her to stick to writing about her own vague moods: "It ill befits, that verse like thine should tell / Of Petrarch's Love, or Werter's frantic pain." The *Gentleman's Magazine* reviewer ends his praise by raising the "reality" of Smith's feelings as a question: "We cannot, however, forbear expressing a hope that the misfortunes she so often hints at, are all imaginary. We must have perused her very tender and exquisite effusions with diminished pleasure, could we have supposed her sorrows to be real."[27] The status of the feelings expressed in Smith's poems—whether they are real or fictive, where they come from, to whom they belong—struck some readers as uncertain.

Most important, Smith herself insisted on the personal, lived nature of the feelings her poems express. In the preface to the sixth edition of the *Elegiac Sonnets*, she recounts a "dialogue" with a friend, who has suggested that she write some more cheerful poems for her new edition. Smith claims that this would be impossible, asserting that the melancholy of her verse has always been the effect of her personal unhappiness: "When . . . I first struck the chords of the melancholy lyre, its notes were never intended for the public ear! It was unaffected sorrows drew them forth: I wrote mournfully because I was unhappy—And I have unfortunately no reason yet, though nine years have since elapsed, to *change my tone*."[28] While the poems themselves define one etiology for feelings, the claims for "experience" need to be argued from the outside. Indeed, we might locate a parallel between Smith and the Hume of the conclusion to book 1 of the *Treatise* in this respect: like Hume, Smith seems to generate an epistemological uncertainty about the status of feeling in her writing precisely when she makes empirical claims about her feelings—that they are derived from her own experience.

Smith's life was indeed awful. Married off at the age of fifteen, Smith had a husband who was perpetually unfaithful to her, possibly violent, and chronically in debt. She accompanied her husband to jail for debt for seven months in 1783, as well as to France in exile, also for debt. After she left him in 1787, Benjamin Smith refused to give any money to their twelve children and would not even allow Smith the interest on her own fortune. Recognizing his son's untrustworthiness, Benjamin Smith's father created a trust fund for the Smith children in his will. But the will proved faulty, and from his death in 1776 until 1798, the estate was in the hands of trustees or the court, and Smith was involved in perpetual legal battles over her children's money, in addition to endless struggles with her estranged husband. Smith supported herself, her children, and occasionally her husband—even after their separation—with the money she made on her novels and volumes of poetry. Cowper described Smith as "chain'd to her desk like a slave to his oar, with no other means of subsistence for herself and her numerous children."[29] In her correspondence, Smith wrote incessantly—and often, in the very style of her poems—of her economic and emotional straits, frequently describing her abuse and victimization not only by her husband but also by the booksellers on whom she was often dependent, as well as the men who had the trusteeship of her children's estate: "It is impossible to guess what purpose such a man has to answer in thus oppressing me," she writes of one of the trustees.[30] In one letter she complains of the seeming endlessness of her plight:

—For two, three or four years the burthen of so large a family whose support depends entirely on me, (while I have not even the interest of my fortunes to do it with) might be undertaken, in the hope that at the end of that period their property might be restored to them—But when above seven years have pass'd in such circumstances—that sickening of the Soul which arises from Hope long delay'd—will inevitably be felt—the worn out pen falls from the tired hand: and the real calamities of life press too heavily, to allow the powers of evading them by fictious detail—Another year however is coming when I must by the same motives, be compelled to a renewal of the same sort of Task.[31]

Smith's image of herself in this passage—the Soul sickening, the worn pen falling from her hand—is echoed in sonnet 36 (the final poem of the third and fourth editions) which ends with "sickening Fancy" throwing her pencil away. Her representations of her sufferings in poems and in personal correspondence are often very close.

Smith's preface to the *Elegiac Sonnets* goes on to detail the current state of her battle with the trustees of her children's estate. She alludes to this matter, she says,

as an apology for that apparent despondence, which when it is observed for a long series of years, may look like affectation. *I shall be sorry*, if on some future occasion, I should feel myself compelled to detail its causes at more length; for, notwithstanding I am thus frequently appearing as an Authoress, and have derived from thence many of the greatest advantages of my life. . . . I am well aware that for a woman—"The Post of Honor is a Private Station."[32]

There are several things that strike me about this preface. Of course this gesture—"I wrote because I was unhappy"—is itself conventional; and I hasten to add that my argument here is not concerned with the true nature of Smith's poems—whether they are more related to reality or to literature—but rather with the poems' self-understanding, how they account for the origins of their feelings. There is something about this preface that makes the idea of advertising that she really feels the feelings expressed in the poems seem gimmicky (as, for example, when she admits that such prolonged despondence may "look like affectation"), an idea invented to make her poems more valuable. Once Smith insists that the poems, with their canniness about the otherness of feelings, are really expressions of her own misery, the sonnets in fact begin to become—in Seward's words—"hackneyed scraps of dismality." Once Smith claims, "I wrote mournfully because I was unhappy," in other words, her sonnets begin to seem lugubrious and "sentimental."

The sentimentality that we may hear in between Smith's claims for her personal experience in her preface and her poems themselves may stem in part from questions of genre, shifts in what kind of poem the sonnet was thought to be. To Charles Lamb writing in the 1790's, the sonnet was precisely a "personal poem"—too personal to be altered by anyone but the poet. He wrote in jest to Coleridge: "Tho' a Gentleman may borrow six lines in an epic poem (I should have no objection to borrow 500 and without acknowledging) still in a Sonnet—a personal poem—I do not 'ask my friend the aiding verse.'"[33] What Lamb means by "personal" in this context would seem to be, precisely, "intimate," referring to one's exclusive private life. The realm of the personal has a self-referential authenticity: persons refer to their personal feelings or experiences as their own essences. Lamb confided, "I love my sonnets because they are the reflected images of my own feelings at different times." Lamb's use of "personal" is hard to find before this period; the *Oxford English Dictionary* records no usages that have this particular shade of meaning in the eighteenth century, when the word tends either to refer to the body (as in "personal charms") or to have a legal meaning (as in "personal injury"). That the *sonnet* could be thought to be the genre of the personal (rather than as, say, the genre of the highest formal restraint) was certainly due to Smith's influence. Yet at the same time Smith's sonnets, as we have seen, practice precisely the kind of borrowing from "friends" that Lamb disavows. Smith's accomplishment may well have been to construct the "personal" with respect to poetry through the very derivativeness and conventionality her poems announce. (A related instance of the way in which the "personal" and the "conventional" may come to be synonymous rather than opposed is the "personalized" cards of greeting or condolence one can buy at the drug store.)

Smith's "personalization" of her conventionalized expressions of woe reminds us that the sentimental involves the sense of a disproportion between an occasion for feeling and the way in which that feeling is expressed. We often feel that people are being sentimental when they appear *really* to be feeling emotions that themselves seem hackneyed, conventional—when the terms in which they express those feelings seem to come not from the situation at hand but rather from some place beyond real life, from the realm of representation. Sentimentality involves moments when the issue of whether feeling is authorized by literature or by life becomes a problem. Smith's poems—which make strong claims that both literature and personal experience authorize their feelings—could make us realize that the notion that feeling is the substance that would glue together, provide interface between, personal experience on the one hand and literary form or convention on the other may be working with realms that don't sit easily with one another; that "feeling," surprisingly, renders it impossible rather than natural to try to reconcile writing and experience. Hence, we could see what I'm calling sentimentality as that which reveals the *arbitrariness* of the distinctions with which we (or Anna Seward, for that matter) discriminate inauthentic from "appropriate" emotional expressions. Such a definition of sentimentality, in other words, would counter the view that the etiological alterity of feeling is, once demonstrated, sufficient to discredit it.[34] Smith's predicament thus suggests the link between empiricism and sentimentality: it is only when empirical claims can be made for feelings' origins—that they come from experience—that the kind of confrontation I am describing as the sentimental can emerge. Sentimentality is the affective dimension of an epistemological conflict over the origins of feelings.

What might a historian of feminism make of Smith's double, overdetermined relation to feeling? How could we place her sentimental, literary sufferings in relation to the witnessing of women's suffering in feminist writing? At the end of the preface to the *Elegiac Sonnets*, Smith apologizes for intruding her "private" matters upon the public: she places her miseries in a private realm, which defines her as a woman: "Notwithstanding I am thus frequently appearing as an Authoress, . . . I am well aware that for a woman—'The Post of Honor is a Private Station.'" Quoting Addison's Cato here, Smith appears to be enacting a personalization of expression in a way that glaringly reveals the costs of such a strategy. I could argue that Smith's claim in the preface thus seems to deny her grievances rather than to give them adequate public expression, that the unsettling yoking of the private and the conventional that I've called sentimentality effectively undercuts any possibility for her poems to assume the status of protests. Smith's work could be seen as an instance of a genre Lauren Berlant has described as "the female complaint." She identifies a tradition of women's writings which simultaneously gives voice to women's suffering and reveals the dependence of that voice on traditional forms: "The female complaint is thus an aesthetic 'witnessing' of injury. Situated precisely in the space between a sexual politics that threatens structures of patriarchal authority and a sentimentality that confirms the inevitability of the speaker's powerlessness, the female complaint registers the speaker's frustration, rage, abjection, and heroic self-sacrifice in an oppositional utterance that declares its limits in its very saying."[35] Smith's volumes seem designed to produce precisely the response she got: they made her a perpetual victim, a universal object of pity.

It would be misguided to see Smith's poetry as even proto-feminist, though her often explicitly political novels, such as *Desmond* (1792), may be. However, I'd like to suggest an alternative point of view. If we define sentimentality not as a failure to assign feelings their true causes and expressions but rather as that which renders questionable the possibility of ever doing so, the contradictions within Smith's etiologies of feeling—her canny understanding of the relationship between misery and literature on the one hand, and her claims to misery's private causes on the other—need not be seen as negating each other, as either inauthenticating or ghettoizing her claims for her own experience. In these poems, as in the other accounts of emotion this book studies, the claim that "these are my feelings" is met with a countermovement that suggests that "these are not *my* feelings"; in so doing they challenge our sense of what the authenticity of a feeling would consist of. I have argued through Smith's poems that the culture of sensibility and its literary genres did not seamlessly accommodate women's interests. While we may be tempted, as eighteenth-century culture often was, to solve the problems of extravagant emotions—where they come from, to whom they belong, what they mean historically—by calling feelings feminine, the gendering of feelings may make feelings harder to place, rather than giving them a clearer meaning. However, feminism may perhaps benefit from the sentimental demonstration that the etiological alterity of feeling is not sufficient to discredit feeling's force. We cannot assert a simple continuity between the expression of misery in women's sentimental literature and the expression of political grievance in late eighteenth-century feminist writing. The formal and epistemological dimensions of a literature of feelings must be taken into account. But doing so may in fact make it possible to see sentimental poetry as *enabling* a political discussion about personal feelings. That is, we might view Smith's poetry as an occasion for seeing "experience" as a strategic, explanatory political category, being constituted within late eighteenth-century women's discourse in dialectical relationship to the wandering feelings of poetry, which know no person.

Chapter 3

Female Chatter
Gender and Feeling in Wordsworth's Early Poetry

For many of his early readers, the problem with Wordsworth was the disproportionate nature of his emotions. Anna Seward, who accused Charlotte Smith of writing "hackneyed scraps of dismality," met Wordsworth's *Poems in Two Volumes* (1807) with mingled "admiration," "astonishment," and "disgust." Of the poet's heart dancing with the daffodils in "I wandered lonely as a cloud," she exclaimed, "Surely if his worst foe had chosen to caricature this egotistic manufacturer of metaphysic importance upon trivial themes, he could not have done it more effectually!" Lucy Aikin remarked in her review of the same volume upon the poet's "unfortunate habit . . . of attaching exquisite emotions to objects which excite none in any other human breast." For another reviewer, Wordsworth's emotional extravagances required gendered terms: "Mr. Wordsworth . . . gave considerable testimony of strong feeling and poetic powers, although like a histerical schoolgirl he had a knack of feeling about subjects with which feeling had no proper concern." The consensus that Wordsworth was a man given to strange fits of passion was corroborated by Coleridge, who admitted that Wordsworth demonstrated "an intensity of feeling disproportionate to *such* knowledge and value of the objects described, as can be fairly anticipated of men in general, even of the most cultivated classes; and with which therefore few only, and those few particularly circumstanced, can be supposed to sympathize."[1] What we hear in some of these comments is in part a moral judgment: the writers express a distaste for enthusiasm, for breaches of decorum that may indicate an ethical inability to discriminate. However, taken together with the Wordsworth poems that prompted them, these comments also reflect a broader debate about whether passion ever does fit, exploring the questions about how one determines the causes of passions that played a crucial role in eighteenth-century philosophy and aesthetic theory.

"To value Wordsworth's emotions is sometimes hard," Geoffrey Hartman remarks at the beginning of his reading of "The Solitary Reaper." Twentieth-century readers are in general less comfortable passing judgment on Wordsworth's emotions themselves than were his early readers, and even less likely to see those emotions as girlish. However, the problem of Wordsworth's emotions has remained central to interpretations both of his character and of his poetry. His excessive investment in his own emotional responses has led somewhat paradoxically to the assessment of his character—present in Hazlitt and De Quincey but elaborated by mid-twentieth-century critics—as cold, inhuman, and indifferent to the sufferings of others.[2] Wordsworth's disproportionate acts of attention and emotion are at the center of Wordsworthian egotism and Wordsworthian apocalyptic self-consciousness. "The heart's response," Hartman argues, "is always too great or too small; and since without this disproportion there is no such thing as a man conscious of himself, we see how precarious Wordsworth's condition is, how inevitably linked to a self-consciousness that may seem egotistical."[3]

While it may be difficult to value Wordsworth's emotions, readers generally have had no trouble taking the Wordsworthian fits of passion they have known to be his. In this chapter I would like to displace the question of the "egotism" of Wordsworth's emotional extravagance, precisely by taking seriously the remarks of his contemporaries: what *was* the poet doing when he attached feeling to objects "with which feeling had no proper concern"? Wordsworth elicited these charges, I would argue, just as his own writing was traversing the borders of empiricist and individualist thinking about emotion. He sets out in the *Lyrical Ballads* to write a poetry in which feeling is not to be judged by its empirical causes: "The feeling therein developed gives importance to the action and situation and not the action and situation to the feeling," the Preface claims.[4] His early writings reflect on transindividual aspects of emotion: on feelings' origins in words and in literary form; on the transferences of feelings between persons; on how "fond and wayward thoughts will slide / Into" a poet's or reader's head.[5] Wordsworth's most philosophical and extended accounts of feelings' origins—of how the love of nature can lead to the love of man, or how a babe can gather passion from his mother's eye—are to be found in *The Prelude*. We can frame that work, however, by situating Wordsworth's understanding of feeling within the context of late eighteenth-century sensibility discussed in the preceding chapter, and thus recovering the meaning of the gendered charges that inflect early accounts of the poet's emotions.

Wordsworth's adolescence coincided with the heyday of poetical femininity. He later recalled a poem by Mrs. Barbauld as one of the first he took pleasure in, and he knew well the work of Charlotte Smith, Helen Maria Williams, and other woman poets. Wordsworth's engagement with women writers, however, was not merely an adolescent fancy, a schoolboy's infatuation with popular literary stars. Later in life he carried on an extensive correspondence with Alexander Dyce, editor of *Specimens of British Poetesses* (1825), in which he expressed interest in compiling an anthology of women's poetry of his own. He commiserates with Dyce that the works of the "Poetesses" are not more readily available, lamenting that the contents of his library—"the two volumes of Extracts of Poems by Eminent Ladies, Helen Maria Williams's Works, Mrs. Smith's Sonnets, and Lady Winchelsea's Poems"—constitute a "scanty" base for such a collection.[6] Eventually, Wordsworth did produce an anthology of his own: in 1819, he compiled a poetry album as a gift for Lady Mary Lowther. Though not devoted exclusively to the poetry of women, more than half the volume consists of the poems of Anne Finch, countess of Winchelsea; it also includes texts by Anne Killigrew and Laetitia Pilkington, clearly drawn from *Poems by Eminent Ladies* (1755), a popular anthology of women's poetry. Pilkington is best known now for her notoriously scandalous *Memoirs* and her friendships with Swift and Pope. The poem by Pilkington that Wordsworth reproduces is called "Sorrow." In it she complains both of public slander and of her divorce by her husband, a divorce, she intimates in the *Memoirs*, that was partially brought on by her insatiable passion for reading and writing ("I was most incorrigibly devoted to versifying, and all my Spouse's wholesome Admonitions had no manner of Effect on me"). Wordsworth excises most of the poem's autobiographical content, leaving a vague, excerpted lament that alludes only generally to her plight, "lost to the soft, endearing ties of life, / And tender names of daughter, mother, wife." Wordsworth's editorial extraction of lyric lament from a longer poem that details a woman's predicament reproduces the fact that Pilkington's lament is itself predicated on her own extraction—or removal—from the realms of the feminine, the realms of "daughter, mother, wife." To Wordsworth, one senses, Pilkington's lament seems paradoxically most feminine when she is lamenting an exile *from* the feminine. His text transforms the woman whom Swift had called "the most profligate Whore in either Kingdom" into a disembodied voice of pathos. Wordsworth's editorial practice suggests that for the poet and his contemporaries, what motivated the anthologizing of women's poetry was a desire to represent women's voice as the production of a certain kind of lyric feeling predicated on women's suffering.[7]

This chapter will look at the roles that gender plays in the production of emotion in Wordsworth's early explorations of poetry as "the history or science of feelings." It does so by situating his writings of the 1780's and 1790's within the context of late eighteenth-century discourses on feelings, focusing not only on poetry by women, but also on some of the feminine figures he borrowed from the culture of sensibility. Earlier commentators on the poet's relationship to late eighteenth-century sentimentality tended to see these figures as vestiges of conventional, popular material that the poet successfully humanizes, purifies, and transcends.[8] We will see, however, that conventional images of women's suffering provide the poet with a medium through which the transmission of feeling and the transmission of poetic language produce and reproduce each other. Wordsworth's ambivalent fascination with how feelings can extravagate from feminine figures to masculine poets and readers takes on special meaning in the context of his explorations of the relationships between language and feeling, especially as they are explored in the *Lyrical Ballads*.[9] The Preface of 1800 suggests that literary feelings are always extravagant, both poetic form and words themselves causing dangerous conjunctions of pleasure and pain. The gendered dramas of several of the ballads illustrate, enact, and resolve some of the Preface's lessons about the passage of feelings. This chapter's attempt to understand the relationship of Wordsworth's ideas about pleasure and pain to those of eighteenth-century empiricism will include a comparison between Wordsworth and Freud. This comparison, paradoxically, can make visible Wordsworth's relations to his late eighteenth-century context.

In the first section, I will be discussing Wordsworth's sentimental education: I'd like to consider what he learned about reading, writing, and feeling from the sentimental women poets he read with pleasure and sought to emulate at the beginning of his poetic career. This investigation takes as its starting point Wordsworth's first published composition, "Sonnet on Seeing Miss Helen Maria Williams Weep at a Tale of Distress"; the title alone is suggestive of the position of the woman poet in English culture, her assimilation to the other pathetic feminine figures that populate sentimental literature. The sonnet raises questions about what it might mean for a poet to initiate his career by fantasizing an encounter with a weeping, reading woman writer.

Sentimental Education

SHE wept.—Life's purple tide began to flow
In languid streams through every thrilling vein;
Dim were my swimming eyes—my pulse beat slow,
And my full heart was swell'd to dear delicious pain.
Life left my loaded heart, and closing eye;
A sigh recall'd the wanderer to my breast;
Dear was the pause of life, and dear the sigh
That call'd the wanderer home, and home to rest.
That tear proclaims—in thee each virtue dwells,
And bright will shine in misery's midnight hour;
As the soft star of dewy evening tells
What radiant fires were drown'd by day's malignant pow'r,
That only wait the darkness of the night
To cheer the wand'ring wretch with hospitable light.

"On Seeing Miss Helen Maria Williams Weep at a Tale of Distress" appeared pseudonymously in the *European Magazine* of March 1787; it was never reprinted during the poet's lifetime, and he acknowledged it only once.[10] It is in some respects a hopelessly conventional poem, an exercise in a certain style of late eighteenth-century poetic diction. The critic who gives attention and significance to this marginal poem in Wordsworth's canon may risk losing her sense of proportion; but to give importance to the insignificant is to participate in a strategy of sentimentality itself, which often involves finding pathos and significance in the disproportion between an object and its effects.

A species of this excessiveness of attention inhabits the sonnet itself. The octave consists of a response to another person's emotion, though it is difficult to characterize the nature of that response: the beholder's emotion is neither wholly an imitation or reproduction of Williams's nor entirely a turn away from it. The beholder's emotion seems in fact both continuous with and detached from Williams's, just as his body seems both continuous with and distinct from hers: this is affect reduced exclusively to bodily response. The simple, epitaphic predication that begins the poem—"she wept"—initiates a descent into the poet's own body. This swift flight from poetic object to emotional response could warrant the charges of egotism, or narcissism, that have often so attached themselves to Wordsworth's poetry. He begins his account of his own bodily response, however, in terms so impersonal that they suspend the identity of the body in question:

> SHE wept.—Life's purple tide began to flow
> In languid streams through every thrilling vein;
> Dim were my swimming eyes—my pulse beat slow.

Until we reach the possessive pronouns of line three, we are likely to assume that the bodily functions described by the first two lines are Williams's. The speaker's detachment from his object, his leaving her spontaneously and immediately to retreat into his own response, is balanced by a blurring of the boundaries between his body and hers, as if his feelings were physically propped upon hers, rather than reflecting or imitating them. The physiological effects described here, moreover, are so contradictory that they hardly seem to belong to a single coherent body. It is hard to imagine blood flowing languidly through veins which are said simultaneously to be "thrilling"; this experience seems to both heighten and extinguish animation, to both thrill the veins and slow the pulse.

The affective experience of the octave is also characterized by the autogenerative quality that Michael Tanner ascribes to sentimental feelings, the tendency of the sentimentalist to stage for him or herself the occasion for feeling.[11] The poet willingly submits himself to this delicious pain. The autogenerative quality of this experience is also foregrounded by the second quatrain, where the poet, peculiarly, twice describes a passage from and return to consciousness:

> Life left my loaded heart, and closing eye;
> A sigh recall'd the wanderer to my breast;
> Dear was the pause of life, and dear the sigh
> That call'd the wanderer home, and home to rest.

The last two lines of the quatrain repeat the "pause of life" described in the first two as if to repeat its pleasures, as if that pause and return could be "call'd" and "recall'd" at will. As in the first quatrain, the experience of the body is told in both intensely personal and strangely impersonal terms. The sigh that recalls the poet's body to life is presumably Williams's, but the speaker's relation to his own body's activity is so estranged and periphrastic that it is again hard to distinguish between the two of them. When he notes, "dear was the pause of life, and dear the sigh / That call'd the wanderer home," both the sigh and the speaker's own fluctuations are equally dear, and equally abstract. The poem gives the impression of someone who is both oppressively close to his own bodily and affective experience and strangely distanced from it. "Life" is not something that is proper to him but is rather a "wanderer" that comes and goes. And if the speaker takes pleasure in his own sensations, he seems also to revel in absences of sensation. The "pause of life" is related to the many blank states, trances, and suspensions that form a topos in Wordsworth's poetry, from *Salisbury Plain* to *Tintern Abbey*.

The peculiar blend of crisis and complacence that characterizes the sonnet's octave makes it difficult to talk about what the function of this affective expenditure is. We might speak of the action of the octave—with its heightened rhetoric of life and death—as a crisis of some sort, but it is a crisis in which both climax and resolution occur almost simultaneously, in which both crisis and resolution are equally pleasurable. This in part gives the action of the octave its peculiarly erotic quality. It ends, moreover, on a very conclusive note: the cadence of "home, and home to rest" brings the poem to a resting point of such finality that it must labor to leave the home of that pause. "That tear proclaims" returns us to the weeping Miss Williams whom the poet abandoned so quickly in the first line. From the undifferentiated, overlapping bodies and emotions of the beginning of the poem, Williams and Wordsworth have become more distinct: Wordsworth's life comes home to rest, while in Williams, each virtue *dwells*.

The sestet does not simply pay Williams the conventional compliment of sensibility that equates feeling with absolute moral value ("*each* virtue dwells"). As James Averill has noted, Wordsworth's early poetry is surprisingly unconcerned with the moral aspects of literary sentimentality, and this poem is no exception.[12] The conventional compliment to the virtues of Williams's sympathy ushers in a simile that claims misery as the condition for the visibility of Williams's virtue:

> That tear proclaims—in thee each virtue dwells,
> And bright will shine in misery's midnight hour;
> As the soft star of dewy evening tells
> What radiant fires were drown'd by day's malignant pow'r
> That only wait the darkness of the night
> To cheer the wand'ring wretch with hospitable light.

More than the visibility of Williams's virtue is at stake here; the visibility of Williams herself depends on "misery's midnight hour," for it is her tear that brings her to Wordsworth's attention. There must always be some misery, perhaps a wandering wretch, for Williams to respond to.

In this respect "On Seeing Miss Helen Maria Williams Weep at a Tale of Distress" is similar to other contemporary poems addressed to women poets—Anna Seward, Charlotte Smith, and Williams—that populated the poetry sections of the magazines in the 1780's. The poetry sections of the more prestigious magazines such as the *Gentleman's Magazine* and the *European Magazine* often housed ongoing dialogues within a coterie of celebrated poets and poetesses who exchanged poems in praise of each other. But since the magazines also depended heavily on contributions, often anonymous or pseudonymous, from their readers, the poem addressed to an author also provided a new writer a means of entering the poetical arena. Of the many panegyrics on contemporary authors, those addressed to sentimental women writers share a distinctive characteristic. They tend to address the woman writer's emotional state rather than her poetry, casting the woman writer as herself an object of pity. A poem "To Miss Helen Maria Williams: On her Poem of *Peru*" signed "Eliza" in the *Gentleman's Magazine* in 1784 ends by imagining Williams "with sad affliction . . . oppresst" in order to express hope that someone will be there "to blend with thine the sympathetic tear." As we saw in the preceding chapter, Charlotte Smith was frequently subject to addresses to her emotional life. Both a "Sonnet to Mrs. Smith, on Reading her Sonnets Lately Published" and "To the Muse, on Reading Miss Smith's Sonnets" perform the double gesture of both insisting that Smith retain her miseries and expressing hope for their amelioration while admitting of its impossibility. The latter paradoxically invokes the muse to soothe Charlotte's woes while hoping that "still in sweet strains may she her sorrow sing," and it ends by implying that her misery is central to the economy of both the production and the reception of Smith's sonnets. The sonnet to Smith in the *European Magazine* of August 1786 explicitly names Smith's unhappy emotional state as the condition for her writing, contrasting the adage, "Fiction's the properest field for Poesy" with Smith's verse—of which "no tenderer plaints the heart can move, / More rouse the soul to sympathetic love"—and which "spring from REAL woe."[13]

Wordsworth's "On Seeing Miss Helen Maria Williams Weep at a Tale of Distress" goes even further than some panegyric verse on women poets; it does not address Williams as a writer at all. The occasion named in the poem's title is a fantasy (though Wordsworth did actually see Williams much later). The poem is organized around a conceit that figures the affective experience of reading Williams's poems as an experience of seeing her reading and weeping. Conceits that represent an experience of reading as an experience of seeing often serve to express the power of the text as having the immediacy of pure perception, a sense-certainty beyond the shifty influences of a text. In Keats's "On First Looking into Chapman's Homer," for example, the trope seeks to stress the transparency of Chapman's translation. What Wordsworth sees when he looks into Williams's poems, however, is Williams herself. The voyeuristic premise of the poem, its claim to be privy to the sight of a woman who is absorbed in a presumably involuntary experience (weeping at the tale of someone else's distress) is intimately linked with the poem's erotic tinge.

This appeal to a visual fantasy of a woman weeping is the trope that enables Wordsworth's apprenticeship to the literary: he imagines Williams weeping in order to respond to her, transposing a response to a text into an emotional, interpersonal encounter with its author. "On Seeing Miss Helen Maria Williams Weep at a Tale of Distress" is Wordsworth's first appearance in a literary culture saturated with feminine sentimentality. If we conceive of Wordsworth's sonnet as a scene of instruction, as an apprenticeship, then perhaps what this transposition of poem to poetess effects is the transmission of poetic conventions and tropes. When Williams weeps, not only "life's purple tide" begins to flow; it is also "life's purple prose"—as I am always tempted to misread this line—that begins to flow—or more accurately, the tropes and conventions of late eighteenth-century sentimental verse: the responsiveness of the body, the pleasure of pain, as well as the stylistic conventions that inform the poem's diction, personifications, periphrases, and its predilection for the fluid and the dewy, the dimming and the swelling. The poem uses the fiction of the immediacy of sympathy, the extravagance of feelings across persons, bodies, and genders, as a medium for the transmission of figurative language. Its conceit provides a solution to the question, how are impersonal, conventional tropes made meaningful, invested with significance? How do figures get from one person's poem to another's? If the peculiar quality of the body in the sonnet's octave, the blurring of the boundaries between Williams's body and Wordsworth's, makes sense, it is because this is a body that is not proper to anyone; it is rather a body of shared convention, which only becomes animate in affective exchange. This is a profoundly unnatural body, a Frankenstein monster of physiological clichés.

Writing his first public poem to a woman weeping, Wordsworth uses his period's sentimental investment in women's emotional life to effect a conversion of an intertextual relationship into an interpersonal one. The poem draws upon an eighteenth-century myth of origins in which feelings are learned from women. In the *Tatler*, for example, Steele describes learning to feel by seeing his mother weeping:

There was a Dignity in her Grief amidst all the Wildness of her Transport, which, methought, struck me with an Instinct of Sorrow, which, before I was sensible of what it was to grieve, seized my very Soul, and has made Pity the Weakness of my heart ever since. . . . Having been so frequently overwhelmed by her Tears before I knew the Cause of any Affliction, or could draw Defences from my own Judgement, I imbibed Commiseration, Remorse and an unmanly Gentleness of mind.[14]

"Overwhelmed" by the spectacle of his mother's tears before he could "know" their cause, Steele conceives of the transmission of emotion as a spontaneous, precognitive process that seems to preclude the possibility both of ever deriving a feeling directly from a real "cause," and of ever making feeling itself an object of reason. Steele "imbibes" emotions from the sight of his mother's tears as if it were mother's milk, figuring, as Wordsworth's sonnet does, the transmission of affects as having the continuity of bodily substances. In his poem on Williams, we are also likely to hear precursors to Wordsworth's account of the origins of feelings in *The Prelude*, the Blessed Babe passage of book 2. There, the babe "doth gather passion from his mother's eye," as here Wordsworth derives affect from Williams's tear. Gathering passion from his mother's eye is said to animate the babe ("Such feelings pass into his torpid life / Like an awakening breeze") just as seeing Williams awakens and animates the poet's body (1805 2.243–45).

Wordsworth's poem conceives of the production of emotion in terms of a response or a relation to another's feelings. Williams's tears not only cause Wordsworth's heart to swell, his eyes to dim, with an excess of feeling; they are also, according to the fiction of the poem, responsible for the very condition of feeling, for "life" itself. Seeing Miss Helen Maria Williams weep is what animates the poet's body: if life's purple tide begins to flow only at the sight of her tears, then the poem must imagine the state before this encounter as one of lifelessness and stasis. Animating, making personal, an encounter with a text is what animates its reader. But if the poem sees emotion as that which animates the literary, it also reveals the fundamentally literary character of affect: Williams is weeping at a *tale* of distress; the feelings that create Wordsworth's feelings are themselves responding to a narrative, a "tale." In the world of this poem, it seems, there's no escaping the realm of representation when accounting for the generation of affect. The "Sonnet on Seeing Miss Helen Maria Williams Weep at a Tale of Distress" suggests that Wordsworth complicates a commonsense epistemology of the emotions that conceives of affects as fundamentally prelinguistic but knowable only in their representations.[15] The poem insists, on the one hand, on the separate and autonomous existence of the affective and the linguistic and, on the other, on an inextricable, dynamic relationship between the two orders. In his most radical assertion about the relation between affect and language, Wordsworth conceives of "words, not only as symbols of the passion, but as *things*, active and efficient, which are of themselves part of the passion." In "On Seeing Miss Helen Maria Williams Weep at a Tale of Distress," words do not merely represent feelings, they also call them into being; the order of affect and the order of language and representation are mutually constituting, propped on each other.[16]

Female Chatter

> Though in the higher forms at school the children were no longer beaten, the influence of such occasions was replaced and more than replaced by the effects of reading, of which the importance was soon to be felt.
>
> Freud, "A Child Is Being Beaten"

We could pursue further the associations of gender, affect, and language in Wordsworth's poetry by situating his poetics most broadly within a tradition that begins with Locke and ends with Freud. Claiming that books could "replace and more than replace" beatings, my epigraph suggests that one thing Freud and Wordsworth may share is a highly affective conception of "the effects of reading," an understanding of reading as an experience that can be as painful, or as pleasurable, as bodily sensation. In this respect they both demonstrate a debt to associationist psychology. Locke, for example, laments the following instance of the association of ideas: "Many Children imputing the Pain they endured at School to their Books they were corrected for, so joyn those *Ideas* together, that a Book becomes their Aversion, and . . . thus Reading becomes a torment to them, which otherwise possibly they might have made the great Pleasure of their Lives." Locke expresses sadness that our intellectual or at least our private pleasures are hemmed in by the vagaries of experiences beyond our control. While he asserts that an aversion to reading is grounded in the actual experience of being beaten at school, associationist logic attributes to such connections a double relation to empirical events. An unintended, freakish childhood association such as this one, which can have such lamentable and unalterable effects on the subject's later life, happens by definition when he or she is not watching, is unconscious of the connections forming in his or her mind. Locke notes that a grown person who surfeits on honey may afterward experience an aversion to it, "but he knows from whence to date this Weakness, and can tell how he got this Indisposition." Had the honey-eater had his overdose as a child, "all the same Effects would have followed, but the Cause would have been mistaken, and the Antipathy counted Natural."[17] Locke's tormented reader cannot tell how he or she became indisposed to reading; there is a breach between the child's experience and the reader's aversion which requires the intervention of a narrative of the accidental displacements and substitutions that constitute the associations of ideas.

Both Wordsworth and Freud are indebted to this tradition, though Freud's investigations of the workings of sexuality and the unconscious also constitute a radical break with associationist psychology. In "A Child Is Being Beaten," for example, the mental life of Freud's child is substantially less tied to physical sensation than that of the tormented reader in Locke. Freud posits an essential continuity between reading about beating and fantasizing scenes of beating: reading provides a "stimulus" to beating fantasies, and the child begins to produce its own fantasies about beating in order to "compete with . . . works of fiction."[18] He stresses, however, that both the pleasure of reading about beating and an erotic attachment to fantasies about beating are only tenuously connected to actual experience of corporal punishment: the pleasures of the mind follow a logic of their own. Moreover, both Freud and Wordsworth demonstrate how gender might shape the relationship between a reader and the associations that determine his or her affective response to literary form. For Wordsworth and Freud also resemble each other in the central role that investigations of the sufferings of women play in the production of lyric and psychoanalytic authority.[19] Of the masochistic fantasies of "A Child Is Being Beaten," Freud says, "It would have been quite impossible to give a clear survey [*Beschreibung*] . . . if I had not limited it . . . to the state of things in females" (17.195). Wordsworth's early ballads about abject, suffering women, particularly those that give voice to women, such as "The Mad Mother" and "The Complaint of a Forsaken Indian Woman," were the poems that struck Hazlitt, among other early readers, with "that deeper power and pathos" he associated with Wordsworth.[20]

It may seem strange to compare romantic aesthetic theory with psychoanalytic theory: these two kinds of writing are separated not only by a century but also by their vast differences in genre and contexts, and it is important to respect those differences. Yet reading them together can isolate the extent to which both romantic and psychoanalytic approaches to emotion share common assumptions and problems with—as well as constitute departures from—eighteenth-century accounts. It may seem even stranger to compare Freud's female masochist with Wordsworth's forsaken Indian woman: the masochist enjoys her own fantasies of abuse, while it is only the reader who takes pleasure in the forsaken woman's pathos. This conjunction, however, raises questions that are of concern to readers of both Wordsworth and Freud. Who is enjoying, or benefiting from, whose feelings? To whom do feelings really belong? What kinds of pleasure can be derived from the representation of others' pain?

Comparing Wordsworth's relation to his representations of feminine suffering with Freud's relation to the masochistic woman, that is, can demonstrate how attention to gender could illuminate the broader question of how other people's suffering functions in Wordsworth's early poetry. One suspects that earlier critics tended to avoid the gender of Wordsworth's principal sufferers in order to persist in trying to dignify or to distance Wordsworth from a sensational engagement with others' suffering, as if it were indeed "a wantonness" (to quote the Pedlar of *The Ruined Cottage*), a morally suspect sexual pleasure, to write about suffering. This perspective implies that persons in poems are subject to the same moral violations as people in real life, that engagement with literary suffering would be like a form of personal violence; and it grants an autonomy to both poet and poet's "victim," each inhabiting a fixed position of subject or object.[21] Reading Wordsworth's poems about suffering with Freud's "construction" of the female masochist's inner life can complicate this polarity, while a Freudian understanding of sadomasochism will allow us to explore what it means to say that a response to another's suffering is "sexual."

These two things that Wordsworth and Freud have in common— their conceptions of the powerful effects of reading and their investments in the sufferings of the women they represent—can be seen working together in texts that describe how certain formal questions involve gender, questions concerning how we are affected by the form of a fantasy, or the formal properties of a poem. This section will discuss masochism and meter in the *Lyrical Ballads* in order to approach the role of gender in the production of readerly pleasure, both as it is described in Wordsworth's Preface and in the ballads themselves. It takes as its starting point the problematic relationship between pain and pleasure that emerges through Wordsworth's emphasis on poetic production as a process of "producing immediate pleasure" for readers, through his imperative to "produce excitement in co-existence with an overbalance of pleasure," while negotiating the "danger that the excitement may be carried beyond its proper bounds" (140, 147). It proceeds through a discussion of some passages in the Preface, a reading of "Goody Blake and Harry Gill," and a brief consideration of Freud's "A Child Is Being Beaten."

⁂

Both the affective nature of reading and the power of words themselves constitute the sources of the literary pain that Wordsworth attempts to negotiate in the Preface; for both, meter and the invocation of sexual difference provide partial solutions. Following the work of eighteenth-century associationists such as David Hartley, Wordsworth's conception of "pleasure" often depends on "excitement," on sheer affective expenditure. Thus one's affective response to a representation of feeling—which for romantic theorists as for eighteenth-century philosophy consisted of "sympathy"—will always be unstable, producing a species of pleasurable excitement that threatens to spill over into pain.[22] Wordsworth claims that by identifying his feelings with even the painful feelings of others, the poet aspires to the "freedom and power of real and substantial action and suffering"; however, the poet must modify his reproductions of suffering if they are to be pleasurable, "removing what would otherwise be painful or disgusting in the passion" (138–39). He describes the kind of identification that the poet must perform as a process of slipping into "an entire delusion" (138). If the poet must modify his reproductions of passions in order to make them pleasurable for the reader, it must be because the reader risks slipping into the same delusion: literary affects threaten to enter the reader immediately and entirely.

A reader's response to a representation of feeling, however, involves more than a repetition of that feeling. Wordsworth sometimes suggests that "reproducing in our minds the feelings of another" is in itself pleasurable: "in describing any passions whatsoever, which are voluntarily described, the mind will upon the whole be in a state of enjoyment" (148). But he also describes that experience as invariably unpleasurable: there is a "painful feeling which will always be found intermingled with powerful descriptions of the deeper passions" (150). What is striking about both these passages is the arbitrariness of the original passion: it is the act of reproducing them itself which is said to be alternately always pleasurable or always painful.

Wordsworth also worries that words themselves can be the messengers of pain. Like the late eighteenth-century critics discussed in

Chapter 1, he conceives of figurative language as the natural expression of passion. Both the Preface and the appendix of 1802 admit, however, that figures can become detached from affects, mechanically repeated, "applied . . . to feelings and thoughts with which they had no natural connection whatsoever" (160). Thus the power of words to cause pain, autonomously, seems at times located in what Wordsworth calls poetic diction, which leaves readers "utterly at the mercy" of a poet's decision to connect words with feelings at will (144). But he also articulates the danger of the always unpredictable relationship between feelings and words, "those arbitrary connections of feelings and ideas with particular words, from which no man can altogether protect himself" (152).

Both these sources of literary excitement—the reproduction of powerful feelings and the power of words themselves—need to be carefully monitored: "If the words by which this excitement is produced are in themselves powerful, or the images and feelings have an undue proportion of pain connected with them, there is some danger that the excitement may be carried beyond its proper bounds" (146). The language of sex enters Wordsworth's discussion of pain and pleasure when he introduces meter as that which can protect men from literary pain. While he declares that to renounce the power of identification is "to encourage idleness and unmanly despair" (139), he also suggests that to identify too sympathetically with a representation is to be unmanned. Arguing for the need to maintain a "manly" style for "tempering and restraining" overexcitement, Wordsworth claims that "more pathetic situations and sentiments, that is, those which have a greater proportion of pain connected with them, may be endured in metrical composition . . . than in prose," and he appeals to the unendurable pathos of prose fiction: "This may be illustrated by appealing to the Reader's own experience of the reluctance with which he comes to the re-perusal of the distressful parts of Clarissa Harlowe" (147, 146). Sentimental prose narrative is too immediately exciting; to insure that representations of pain do not "act upon us as pathetic beyond the bounds of pleasure," a work needs meter. Meter provides pleasure not through excitement but through the reduction or regulation of excitement, and Wordsworth links meter to sex. He describes the "pleasure received from metrical language" as "the pleasure which the mind derives from the perception of similitude in dissimilitude. This principle is the great spring of the activity of our minds and their chief feeder. From this principle the direction of the sexual appetite, and all the passions connected with it take their origin" (148). If, in this curious passage, the pleasure of meter is allied to sexual pleasure, it seems to be because the principle from which the pleasure of meter is derived is related to the heterosexist principle that holds that sexual difference, or "dissimilitude," is a necessary condition for attraction, or the "perception of similitude."[23] The operation of the pathetic "beyond the bounds of pleasure" visits the reader with an affective invasion he dreads to repeat; the maintenance of gender boundaries, the preservation of manliness, serves as a reminder of that which would guarantee the autonomy and integrity of the reader before a representation.

Meter reduces to a regular, pleasurable level the excitement caused both by sympathetic identification with representations and by the ambushes of affective language, and it also makes things more readable.[24] The reader is reluctant to reperuse the distressful parts of *Clarissa*, read again the distresses he already knows are there. Meter, on the other hand, makes a representation inexhaustibly rereadable: "Of two descriptions either of passions, manners, or characters, each of them equally well executed, the one in prose and the other in verse, the verse will be read a hundred times where the prose is read once" (150).

The connections among meter, sexual pleasure, and sexual difference are corroborated when Wordsworth curiously singles out, as an example of the powers of meter to confer iterability on a representation, the poem "Goody Blake and Harry Gill": "In consequence of these convictions I related in metre the Tale of GOODY BLAKE AND HARRY GILL, which is one of the rudest of this collection. I wished to draw attention to the truth that the power of the human imagination is sufficient to produce such changes even in our physical nature as might almost appear miraculous" (150). This "truth," he claims, is an important one, one that "has been communicated to many hundreds of people who would never have heard of it, had it not been narrated as a Ballad, and in a more impressive metre than is usual in Ballads" (150). There are traces here of the rhetoric of a social reformer such as Hannah More, for whom ballad form serves as a vessel for the transmission of "truths" to the "many hundreds" of the semiliterate who might otherwise never hear them, reminding us that the passage is situated in a period in which popular literature and mass communications were often sites of political and cultural conflict.[25] That this "truth," moreover, about the susceptibility of the body must be impressed upon the reader through a rude and "impressive" ballad meter suggests that, for Wordsworth, the effects of meter upon the reader's attention are not unlike the effects of the imagination on the body of Harry Gill.

The slight metonymic drift that associates Harry Gill with the reader of the Preface encourages me to press the analogy further—to see, that is, the poem's encounter between the "lusty" Harry Gill and the miserable, impoverished Goody Blake as a dramatization of the relationship between the masculine reader of the Preface and the pathetic, feminized text. In the Preface meter is said to have powers to assuage the pains of affective language, prevent overidentification, maintain manliness. But the poem Wordsworth singles out to illustrate the powers of meter tells the story rather of a man who becomes a victim not only of words' power to wound but also of an invasion by feminine suffering. Reading the thematic content of Wordsworth's illustration of a formal property of poetic language (meter as pleasurable repetition) suggests that Wordsworth's aesthetic theory involves a thinking beyond the pleasure principle.

The encounter between Goody and Harry manifests a violence tinged with sexuality and masculine panic. The vulgar narrator's verbal excesses—a tendency to hyperbole, enumeration, repetition, and homely detail—produce a ballad of proliferating and interchangeable body parts, sticks, and limbs. Harry Gill is a "lusty drover," "stout of limb," whose "voice was like the voice of three"; Goody Blake is an isolated, impoverished spinner whose "old bones . . . shake" in the winter when she is scarcely able to keep warm for "three days" with the "lusty splinters" she steals from the more fortunate.[26] Harry shouts and springs upon Goody when he catches her filling her lap with sticks from his hedge:

> And fiercely by the arm he took her,
> And by the arm he held her fast,
> And fiercely by the arm he shook her,
> And cried, 'I've caught you then at last!' (89–92)

Goody drops the sticks and utters a curse:

> She pray'd, her wither'd hand uprearing,
> While Harry held her by the arm—
> 'God! who art never out of hearing,
> O may he never more be warm!'

> The cold, cold moon above her head,
> Thus on her knees did Goody pray,
> Young Harry heard what she had said,
> And icy-cold he turned away. (97–104)

In this strange scene, it is hard to tell whether the hand Goody raises is attached to the arm Harry holds. This confusion of body parts, this exchange of sticks and limbs, seems appropriate, for Goody's utterance—an association of "feelings and ideas with particular words and phrases" from which Harry cannot protect himself—turns his body into hers. The power of Goody's curse thus dramatizes the affinities between Wordsworth's understanding of the autonomous affective powers of language and the associationism of David Hartley, for whom sensations of heat and cold serve as primary examples both for his theory of vibrations itself and for the process through which words can become repositories of sensations of pain "which exceed ordinary actual Pains in Strength." What distinguishes Wordsworth from Hartley is that for Wordsworth, it is the unpredictability of associations between words and feelings that makes words dangerous.[27] Under the force of Goody's words, Harry's flesh withers away, and he is paralyzed by her cold even when he is buried under "coats enough to smother nine." Though once he had "the voice of three" Harry now becomes uncommunicative:

> No word to any man he utters,
> A-bed or up, to young or old;
> But ever to himself he mutters,
> 'Poor Harry Gill is very cold.' (121–24)

His body, however, makes up for this taciturnity, becoming an uncontrollable source of percussive, meaningless sound: "Yet still his jaws and teeth they clatter, / Like a loose casement in the wind" (115–16). Harry's relentless "chattering," which the poem repeats like a refrain ("evermore his teeth they chatter, / Chatter, chatter, chatter still") both testifies to the transformation of Harry's body into an old woman's and marks out the rude meter of the poem: the onomatopoetic line—"Chatter, chatter, chatter still"—approaches sheer rhythm as it describes the repetition of unintelligible sound located in the body.

Rather than converting pain into pleasure by reducing excitement to a regular level, meter here enacts what would seem to be a painful disintegration of a man into a chattering old woman. Pursuing our reading of "Goody Blake and Harry Gill" as an encounter between reader and literary form, what if we were to suggest that meter mediates between pain and pleasure not through an economic regulation of tensions but as an instance of the noneconomic relation of pleasure and unpleasure that characterizes masochism? Abandoning a purely economic or quantitative model of excitation in his own attempt to account for the paradox of masochism, or how it is that we can find pleasure in pain, Freud himself appeals wistfully to something like meter: "Perhaps it is the rhythm, the temporal sequence of changes, rises and falls in the quantity of stimulus. We do not know" ("The Economic Problem of Masochism," 19:160). Masochism and meter—as a principle of repetition—would also be linked in Freud's metapsychology through a common affiliation with the death drive. According to Wordsworth, meter could make distressing representations of pathos rereadable: one thinks of the child in *Beyond the Pleasure Principle* who wishes to have the same story read over and over (18:35).

Perhaps, if we think of "Goody Blake and Harry Gill" as enacting a transaction between subject and representation, we should think of it as describing a masochistic relation to a representation. I am thinking primarily of Jean Laplanche's discussion of masochism as that which reveals the fundamental role of representation in sexuality. For Laplanche, the very *emergence* of sexuality involves acts of representation: sexual feelings emerge out of nonsexual impulses when a nonsexual activity has lost or become detached from its object, and that object "has been replaced by a fantasy, by an object *reflected* within the subject." Sexuality emerges in a turn away from a natural object, a turn into the self and into representation. Although Freud hypothesized, after he introduced the death drive, that aggression directed against the self is the originary form of aggression, masochism only emerges as a sexual drive when aggression directed toward an object is turned inward upon the self; thus masochism is for Laplanche a fundamental instance of the turning into the self that constitutes sexuality. Acts of fantasy or mental representation are themselves, moreover, experiences of psychic pain: "We are obliged to admit that a fantasy, the introjection of the object, is a perturbation and, in its essence (whether its 'content' be pleasant or unpleasant), a generator of autoerotic excitation.... The fantasy is the first psychical pain and is thus intimately related, in its origin, to the emergence of the masochistic sexual drive."[28] This understanding of fantasy intrigues the reader who wishes to pursue that aspect of Wordsworth's aesthetic which affirms that taking in "descriptions of the deeper passions," whether they be passions of love, hate, or intense joy, is always attended by a "painful feeling." It suggests, as does Wordsworth's Preface, that when we reproduce in our minds the feeling of another, what we feel is never simply a repetition of that feeling but an excitement beyond its proper bounds.

Laplanche argues that all Freud's discussions of the vicissitudes of sadomasochism point to the primacy of masochism. Masochism represents for Laplanche not a perversion but a structure: as originary aggression or as primary sexual drive, masochism inhabits and structures all relations to others. Sadism (the drive that seems at least superficially to describe the impulse behind Harry's assault on Goody) is derived from masochism and "implies an identification with the suffering object; it is within the suffering position that the enjoyment lies."[29] To the poem's urgent opening question—

> Oh! what's the matter? what's the matter?
> What is't that ails young Harry Gill?
> That evermore his teeth they chatter,
> Chatter, chatter, chatter still. (1–4)

—perhaps we could answer, Harry Gill is suffering from the excitation of a masochistic introjection of a woman's suffering. Read as an identificatory encounter with poetic form, the poem could suggest that Wordsworthian pleasure in representations of suffering is always tinged with masochistic excitation. Following Laplanche, Leo Bersani has suggested that all relations—including sympathy—to the sufferings of others contain traces of masochistic sexuality, a sexuality that is fundamentally "shattering" to the subject:[30] Harry's chattering would be the symptom of that "shattering."

But to "chatter" is also to go on speaking. Wordsworth's poetry suggests how a masculine relation to feminine suffering could, in addition to shattering the subject, be in this instance productive of a lyric voice.[31] A "sadist" not only experiences pleasure by identifying masochistically with his victim's suffering; he also aspires to the authenticity of his victim's involuntary expressions of pain. For Wordsworth, the "freedom and power of real and substantial . . . suffering" to which the poet aspires lie in the unquestionable immediacy and authority of the language uttered "under the actual pressure of . . . passions" (138). Real suffering puts "pressure" on utterance, rendering the sufferer's words an "emanation" beyond the "slavish and mechanical" character of willed or imagined speech which attempts merely to describe passions (138). The idea that poetic authority may depend on the suffering of others also haunts Wordsworth's early, gothic *ars poetica*, *The Vale of Esthwaite* (1787). An exploration of the sources of lyric voice, it represents voice as variously disruptive, unlocatable, ghostly groans and sighs. In this poem, the minstrel's harp registers the cries of others' pain:

> Spirits yelling from their pains
> And lashes loud, and clanking chains,
> Were heard by minstrel led astray
> Cold wandering thro' the swampy way,
> Who, as he flees the mingled moan,
> Deep sighs his harp with hollow groan.[32]

Hearing others' cries of pain produces spontaneous music independent of the minstrel's will. The vicissitudes of sadomasochism conspire closely with the vicissitudes of ventriloquism, often involving processes of speaking through or being spoken through by an other, under the pressure of suffering. Identifying masochistically with another's suffering, the subject is "shattered" into a voice not properly his own, a voice beyond the deceptions and disappointments of ordinary speech.

In "Goody Blake and Harry Gill," a man's masochistic introjection of a woman's suffering takes place in relation to the effects of a woman's voice. While the Preface claims that the poem illustrates the power of the *imagination* to produce miraculous changes in our physical nature, the poem represents those changes as the effects of a woman's curse. Wordsworth's source for the poem, Erasmus Darwin's *Zoonomia*, likens the Goody Blake figure to "a witch in a play"; Southey worried that the poem itself might "promote the popular superstition of witchcraft."[33] This ambiguous, bifocal attribution of agency—imagination? or woman's curse?—represents perhaps a successful instance of what Coleridge said Wordsworth's contributions to the *Lyrical Ballads* were to achieve: "to excite a feeling analogous to the supernatural, by awakening the mind's attention from the lethargy of custom, and directing it to the loveliness and the wonders of the world before us."[34] But to figure the power of the imagination as the power of a woman's utterance is also to raise crucial questions about the role of gender in the production of literary power. "Popular superstition" confers on woman the power of impressive utterance; in the Preface Wordsworth speaks of his satisfaction at the popular transmission of the "truths" of "Goody Blake and Harry Gill" to the "many hundreds of people who would never have heard it."[35]

For Wordsworth, representing the power of the imagination as the power of a woman's voice also represents a search for poetic power without agency, for affective lyric voice unhindered by the labor of its own production. Goody's curse represents the authenticity of her suffering as a source of imaginative power, as a source of inspiration so irresistible that it would bypass the will, seizing and entering the body. However, the wounding, prophetic force of Goody's utterance is disarmed when it speaks through Harry. The effect of her curse, the miraculous transformation of Harry's body into a woman's, transforms him into an automatic, seemingly agentless generator of metrical sound—female "chatter." Female ventriloquism (etymologically, "speaking through the stomach, torso") in this poem is a speech literally routed through a feminized body. The involuntary voice of the body is a voice beyond the deceptions of willed speech, but it is the voice only of the body, no more capable of producing meaning than the clattering of "a loose casement in the wind." Here, an assumption of femininity to produce voice renders audible the ways in which lyric voice is implicated in the nonsignificative aspects of poetic form. It reveals that what we think of as voice, as pure articulation of meaning, depends on the effects of the formal properties of poetic language, such as meter.

So far I have explored the extent to which contemporary psychoanalytic discussions of sadism, masochism, and representation can help us understand Wordsworth's affective aesthetics. While Laplanche's reading of Freud on masochism and Leo Bersani's reading of that reading may offer a useful way to think about the paradoxes of a Wordsworthian economics of readerly pleasure, they do not help us think about why letting *feminine* suffering inhabit and speak through one would be a source of poetic pleasure and power. It would be a mistake to expect psychoanalysis to explain Wordsworth's poetics. However, I would like to conclude this section by looking briefly at Freud's own essay on female masochists, "A Child Is Being Beaten," to show how it is constructed *like* a romantic text. In it, Freud's account of how feelings wander from one person to another, one fantasy to another, is as much shaped by both gender and literary form as Wordsworth's. In this essay, Freud characterizes a series of fantasies reported to him by his female patients through a sequence of three sentences. He charts the transition from the second phase of the masochistic girl's fantasy, the unconscious "I am being beaten by my father" (which represents for Freud the "essence of masochism") to its conscious substitute, the highly pleasurable "a child is being beaten" (17:189, 180). In this third phase, which no longer represents the girl but rather anonymous boys being beaten, the fantasy "seems to have become sadistic" (190). But it only "seems" to be so: "only the *form* of this phantasy is sadistic; the satisfaction which is derived from it is masochistic" (191).

Freud has opened up a space between the form in which the fantasy is represented and the feelings attached to it, a space Eve Sedgwick has described as an effect of the work of form itself. The "framing" of the fantasy, its "contraction" to a bare predication such as "a child is being beaten," opens up the possibility of a multiplicity of relations between the subject and the scene of her fantasy: "The redrawing of the frame in such a way as to banish the other characters of the drama," she writes, "reunites them . . . on the hither side of the viewer's or imaginer's own gaze: the decontextualized, legless, and often headless figure of di/s/play creates in turn a free switchpoint for the identities of subject, object, onlooker, desirer, looker-away."[36] The fantasist's mobile relationship to her own fantasy, her ability to have a fantasy that looks one way but feels another, is determined by the formal properties of fantasizing itself.

It is, moreover, an act of gender identification that defines the particular relation between form and mode of gratification in this instance. Freud asserts that the fantasy "a child is being beaten" gratifies masochistic rather than sadistic desires because the children it represents are substitutes for the feminine subject. He is led to this interpretation through an asymmetry in his observations:

The children who are being beaten are almost invariably boys, in the phantasies of boys just as much as in those of girls. This characteristic is naturally not to be explained by any rivalry between the sexes, as otherwise of course in the phantasies of boys it would be girls who were being beaten; and it has nothing to do with the sex of the child who was hated in the first phase. But it points to a complication in the case of girls. When they turn away from their incestuous love for their father, with its genital significance, they easily abandon their feminine role . . . and from that time forward only want to be boys. For that reason the whipping-boys who represent them are boys too. (191)

Freud's need to explain the "complication in the case of girls" leads him to give girls a strange power: "Between the second and third phases the girls change their sex, for in the phantasies of the latter phase they turn into boys" (196); hence, "a child is being beaten" is a fantasy of masochistic identification with the victims of the tableau, rather than one of sadistic spectatorship. At the end of the essay, Freud will reinterpret the female masochist's fantasy as an "escape" from "the demands of the erotic side of her life," effectively cutting her off from the pleasure of her own fantasy while maintaining his own access to it (199). But at this point, the female masochist who enjoys her own pain is, oddly, a girl with the power to redefine her own gender in fantasy. The relationship between the form in which a fantasy is represented and its affective significance is determined by the fantastic nature of sexual difference. "Masochism" is the name for a structure that involves not only an identification with suffering ("it is within the suffering position that enjoyment lies") but also an identification across gender boundaries.

Reading "A Child Is Being Beaten" alongside Wordsworth's ballads of female suffering and female ventriloquism brings to light the roles of form and voice in Freud's essay. The role of the female masochist in "A Child Is Being Beaten" is related to the presence of her voice. There's a certain "confusion of tongues" between Freud and the female masochist, raising further questions about Freud's own fantastic relation to the exciting representations of the female masochist's fantasy life, about who is deriving pleasure from her psychic scenes of violence. He justifies the need to "construct" his patients' fantasies as a form of ventriloquism: while the "later impressions of life speak loudly enough through the mouth of the patient," it is "the physician who has to raise his voice on behalf of the claims of childhood" (183–84). But if Freud speaks *for* his patient, he also borrows her voice to structure and elaborate his argument: the essay is punctuated by the female masochist's utterances, which Freud repeats, in quotation marks, throughout the text like a refrain. In the essay's only other appeal to quotation, Freud articulates his sense of the female masochist's first fantasy in the voice of "a witch in a play." Paraphrasing the weird sisters of *Macbeth*, he says, "So perhaps we may say in terms recalling the prophecy made by the Three Witches to Banquo: 'Not clearly sexual, not in itself sadistic, but yet the stuff from which both will later come'" (187). That the masculine theorist should cast his thesis about the emergence of sexuality as the prophecy of a dangerous feminine authority suggests that female ventriloquism—female "chatter"—plays a role in the production of psychoanalytic theory as well as poetic pleasure. Masculine poets' and theorists' investments in representing the suffering or masochistic woman are neither merely "sadistic" nor "really sexual" but are mediated by identifications, ventriloquizations, and a relay of fantasies.

๛

The following anecdote suggests what a feminine reader's identification with the gendered dramas of the *Lyrical Ballads* might look like. Joseph Cottle records reading aloud some of the *Lyrical Ballads* to Hannah More, apparently an early admirer: "Producing the book, she requested me to read several of the poems, which I did, to the great amusement of the ladies. On concluding, she said, 'I must hear "Harry Gill," once more.' On coming to the words, 'O, may he never more be warm!' she lifted up her hands, in smiling horror."[37] The loosely placed participial phrases of Cottle's last two sentences—"On concluding," "On coming to the words . . . "—have the curious effect of rendering him invisible, making More appear to be the author of her own unmediated encounter with the poem. The poem seems, moreover, in this instance to be subject to the kind of iterability Wordsworth claims for verse ("the verse will be read a hundred times . . . "). Not only does More insist on hearing more, on having the poem repeated; she also, as if on cue, mimics Goody, who "upraise[s] her withered hand" as she utters these words. Hannah More, antifeminist and enemy to popular culture, is enacting some kind of identification with the figure of a witch, though what that identification might mean is fascinatingly unclear. She may not merely be raising her hands in righteous indignation, gesturing that Harry Gill deserves what he gets: "smiling horror" suggests the dawning of some awful—if spurious—pleasure. With "smiling horror," More perhaps recognizes through her own playacting the power of a woman's curse to engender poetic pleasure.

True Colors: "Poor Susan"

In the encounters between the young Wordsworth and the weeping Helen Maria Williams, between young Harry Gill and the shivering, impoverished Goody Blake, the transmission of feeling from suffering female figure to her masculine observer serves as a fantasy for the passing on of poetic convention: in the first case, poetic diction, in the latter, meter. In "Poor Susan," Wordsworth confronts one of the most conventional of the figures from the literature of sensibility that he borrows for his *Lyrical Ballads*: the unhappy fallen woman. "Poor Susan" may remind us of Hume's lessons about the epistemologies of sympathy: her poignant inner life is accessible to us only through the speculations of a narrator, and, moreover, Susan's *own* relationship to her inner life is tenuous at best. "Poor Susan" herself deserves the pitying epithet of the title first of all because she's a displaced person, a country girl unreconciled to London life, homesick for "a single small cottage, a nest like a dove's / The only one dwelling on earth that she loves."[38] Susan, perhaps, is also "poor" because she is subject to nostalgic delusions. Like "Goody Blake and Harry Gill," "Poor Susan" seems to ask us to diagnose its subject; it asks "what ails her?" and describes her symptoms:

> At the corner of Wood-Street, when day-light appears,
> There's a Thrush that sings loud, it has sung for three years:
> Poor Susan has pass'd by the spot, and has heard
> In the silence of morning the song of the bird.
>
> 'Tis a note of enchantment; what ails her? She sees
> A mountain ascending, a vision of trees;
> Bright volumes of vapour through Lothbury glide,
> And a river flows on through the vale of Cheapside. (1–8)

Susan's unhappiness, however, involves not her susceptibility to nostalgic reverie but rather her inability to sustain her fantasy. The fourth stanza, which was the poem's last after Wordsworth's 1802 revisions, describes the disappearance of Susan's vision:

> She looks, and her heart is in Heaven, but they fade,
> The mist and the river, the hill and the shade;
> The stream will not flow, and the hill will not rise,
> And the colours have all pass'd away from her eyes. (13–16)

The poem's pathos lies here, in Susan's inability to control or to enjoy, except fleetingly, the colors of her fantasy life. One critic finds "uncertainty" in the stanza's last line; to him the present perfect of the verb connotes that "the colors have passed away, but implicitly something remains."[39] But I'd argue rather that the last line rings of an overdetermined finality: that the colors have *all* passed away from her eyes suggests that all color has passed away from Susan's eyes for all time. The present perfect is the tense of choice for the elegist of the recently dead ("he has returned to his maker"); more poignant than a simple past tense can be (because it implicitly puts the action into a closer relation to the present of the speaker and audience), it suggests that nothing remains, and nothing will return.

If the essence of Susan's relationship to her fantasy life lies in her inability to sustain or to enjoy it, we might ask, who *is* enjoying her inner life? Critics who write about "Poor Susan" tend to rely on the "dramatic" model for reading the *Lyrical Ballads*, treating both Susan and the poem's narrator as characters, both separate from Wordsworth himself. Two examples demonstrate the assumptions that underlie this approach. Heather Glen asserts that Susan is not "simply . . . a figure of pathos. She is seen as a person, with a personal history in which the speaker is sympathetically interested, and a fantasy-life which he finds imaginatively compelling." James Averill also treats narrator and Susan as persons, separated by distinct personal identities but linked through the bonds of sympathy and surmise: "Susan's melancholy in what ought to be a pleasant situation causes the narrator to guess what troubles her. In this case, the surmise is expressed by a shift to the woman's perspective: we see what she sees and presumably identify with her feelings."[40] Both Glen and Averill conceive of the narrator and Susan as minds "other" to each other, his knowledge of her mediated by surmise and an affective investment of "sympathy" or "identification" that presupposes an otherness to be breached.

But what is striking about the narrator's knowledge of Susan's inner life is its absoluteness. The peculiar present perfect verbs of the first stanza connote a continuity of action that transcends personal observation. The introduction of Susan's hallucination, the "shift" to her perspective, is utterly unlike the Wordsworthian mode of surmise, the mode in which the speaker of "The Solitary Reaper," for example, guesses what the highland girl sings. The lines in which this shift from observation to surmise, from outside to inside, supposedly occurs, moreover, are genuinely disorienting: "'Tis a note of enchantment; what ails her? She sees / A mountain ascending, a vision of trees." The difficulty of these lines lies in the relationship between "enchantment" and ailment, for how we weight each term determines when or where exactly a shift from outside to inside would occur. We can read "enchantment" and "ailment" as opposites: a voice "outside" Susan is asking perplexedly—the song is lovely; so what is Susan's problem? In this case the voice that resumes ("she sees . . . ") is a radically different voice, a voice "inside" Susan that seeks to explain why she ails at this note of delight. However, we can also read "enchantment" and "ailment" as continuous with each other. If a strong "enchantment" by bird song is a kind of ailment, then the question "what ails her" becomes more rhetorical, and the narrator is "already with thee" with Susan, describing symptoms of an enchantment rather than diagnosing an ailment. Both the rhythm of the line and the fact that the line ends after "she sees" rather than before stress the continuity of seeing with both enchantment and ailment. The proximity of these two terms and the shiftiness of their relation to one another (aided by the ambiguous perspective of the pair "a mountain ascending, a vision of trees"—are we seeing *with* Susan or being told she's having a vision?) provoke a kind of Keatsian disorientation if we persist in conceiving of the poem as a "dramatic" encounter between sympathetic individuals, trying to determine where the narrator ends and Susan begins.

In the Preface to the *Lyrical Ballads*, Wordsworth cites "Poor Susan" as an illustration of the characteristic that "distinguishes these Poems from the popular Poetry of the day": "The feeling therein developed gives importance to the action and situation and not the action and situation to the feeling" (128). If the poem's feeling is not given importance by the situation it is attached to, where does the feeling's importance come from? His suggestion that "feeling" takes precedence over "action and situation" suggests the inadequacy of an approach to this poem that stresses character and dramatic situation. We should rather see its figures as productive of the forms that allow for the representation of feeling. In the Fenwick note of 1843, Wordsworth claimed that the poem "arose out of my observation of the affecting music of these birds hanging in this way in the London streets in the freshness and stillness of the Spring morning."[41] In this commentary he remembers the poem as a kind of reverie inspired by the "enchanting" song of the bird; Susan would in this case stand as a surrogate for the poet. The Wordsworth who wrote "Poor Susan" was also remembering hearing—or reading—Cowper's self-elegiac "The Poplar Field," which was surely his model for the elegiac use of anapestic meter. Not only is "Poor Susan" in the same meter as "The Poplar Field"; it is the same number of stanzas and uses a number of the same rhymes, words, and images. Cowper gazes at the field where the poplars once stood, and muses on his own mortality:

> 'Tis a sight to engage me, if anything can,
> To muse on the perishing pleasures of man;
> Though his life be a dream, his enjoyments, I see,
> Have a being less durable even than he. (20–24)

We could see "Poor Susan" as a remembrance of Cowper's poem, Susan herself as a conduit for a literary relationship to another poet's melancholy reflections.

Conceiving of "Poor Susan" as the staging of another's feeling confirms one's sense that the poem's most intense passages are those that describe the rising and fading of Susan's vision. The modulations of the poem's intensity are effected through shifts in verb tense. What is striking, for example, about the shift from the first stanza to the second is not so much a shift of point of view but rather the suggestiveness of the present perfect opening onto the brightness of the simple present. In the fourth stanza, too, it is the shifts in verb tenses—from simple present to future ("the stream will not flow, and the hill will not rise") to present perfect—that give the simple language its elegiac intensity. The fade/shade rhyme constitutes a conventionally, inevitably elegiac pair: Susan's vision dies a natural death, seeming simply to "fade" of its own accord. The implications of the present perfect tense of the last line differ from those of the beginning of the poem. There, it connoted continuity and repetition; here, it sounds like the end of all things.[42] This difference is brought into sharper focus by the repetition of the verb "to pass" in lines 3 and 16: "has passed by" suggests mundane routine, while in "have all passed away," we can't help hearing echoes of the euphemism "to pass away."

After the death of Susan's fantasy—after the colors have all passed away from her eyes—what does remain is Wordsworth's poem, and, before 1802, the poem's concluding stanza:

> Poor Outcast! return—to receive thee once more
> The house of thy Father will open its door,
> And thou once again, in thy plain russet gown,
> May'st hear the thrush sing from a tree of its own. (17–20)

It is primarily the poem's last stanza, as well as Wordsworth's decision to excise it, that has determined one of the main concerns of critical commentary on this poem: whether or not "poor Susan" is a prostitute, a true "outcast" from her father's home, who wears instead of a "plain russet gown" the tawdry rags of a London streetwalker. This stanza leads us in two directions. On the one hand, it rescues Susan from the desolation of the preceding line, promising her a restoration to the land of bird, and mist, and stream. On the other hand, however, it reveals her true colors, rendering her loss more irrevocable by implying that she has lost not simply her vision but also her virtue. The implications of this stanza color the poem even after its excision, as the poem's readers speculate upon Susan's sexual state. Two examples will demonstrate that readers' speculations about Susan's sexual character mimic the narrator's relationship to her. The speculations, moreover, suggest the cultural politics at issue in Wordsworth's borrowings of the suffering figures of sensibility.

Charles Lamb opened the debate over Susan's sexual character by pretending to close it. Writing to Wordsworth in 1815, he declared:

> The last verse of Susan was to be got rid of at all events. It threw a kind of dubiety on Susan's moral conduct. Susan is a servant maid. I see her trundling her mop and contemplating the whirling phenomenon thro' blurred optics; but to term her a poor outcast seems as much as to say that poor Susan was no better than she should be, which I trust was not what you meant to express.[43]

Lamb clearly assumed Susan was a prostitute; writing to Wordsworth *after* he had excised the offending stanza, his comments form an ironic ventriloquism of the prudish response that presumably dictated Wordsworth's decision. Lamb puts his response to Susan in the form of a doubling or repetition of the structure of her experience. He represents his reading of the poem in a present-tense vision: just as Susan "sees" things that are not there, so Lamb "sees" Susan trundling her mop and contemplating the whirling phenomenon. Lamb's vision, moreover, is as fantastic as Susan's. What he sees is not in the poem;

what he sees is closer, in fact, to a fantasy colored by other poems. While Wordsworth may have been feeling the feelings of a Cowper poem through Susan, Lamb may be pointing out that we necessarily see the phenomenon of Susan herself through the "blurred optics" of literary history. I would point to Swift's "A Description of Morning," where "*Moll* had whirl'd her Mop with dextr'ous Airs / Prepar'd to Scrub the Entry and the Stairs." Peter Manning cites Swift's "A Description of a City Shower":

> Brisk *Susan* whips her Linen from the Rope,
> While the first drizzling Show'r is born aslope,
> Such is that Sprinkling which some careless Quean
> Flirts at you from her Mop, but not so clean,
> You fly, invoke the Gods; then turning, stop
> To rail; she singing, still whirls on her Mop.[44]

In this passage the distinction between servant maid and prostitute that Lamb's vision is ostensibly trying to maintain collapses: Swift's mop-trundler is already a mischievous "Quean" who flirts and provokes. Lamb has already perceived Susan as being "no better than she should be" and suggests that it may be impossible to see her otherwise.

In an essay called "What Bothered Charles Lamb About Poor Susan?" David Simpson repeats the fantastic nature of Lamb's commentary, but perhaps without all of Lamb's irony. Simpson collapses the distinction that Lamb maintains between the servant maid who innocently trundles her mop and a Susan who is no better than she should be, by constructing a narrative of causality between the two: the former is always on its way to becoming the latter. Drawing on late eighteenth-century accounts of female domestic servants and debates about prostitution and vice in the city, Simpson situates the poem within contemporary anxieties about the social and economic status of single working-class women. To late eighteenth-century narratives about "the domestic servant slipping into prostitution," Simpson adds his own narrative, a present-tense vision of Susan as imaginary as Lamb's:

Suppose our country girl—let's call her Susan—makes it through the moment of arrival, and has an honest employer to go to. She then faces two new threats, different but mutually enforcing. First, there is the appeal to her vanity. Discarding the "plain russet gown" of her rural companions, she puts on (if she has a good place) the fine clothes in which her mistress likes to read a reflection of her own image; or at least, she finds herself in the presence of conspicuous consumption for the first time. The chances are that her head will be turned. . . . The second, and related threat [is] sexual desire.[45]

For the critic sympathetic to historicist criticism, it is strange to sense that Simpson has crossed over from historical reconstruction to the construction of a fantasy. It is not simply that the familial, present-tense "you are there" form ("our country girl") of Simpson's reverie repeats Lamb's move; we should also notice how close he comes to attributing an inevitable vanity and desire to *his* servant girl: faced with a new dress and surrounded by conspicuous consumption, "chances are" that she will fall. If Lamb's vision of Susan was based on Swift, Simpson's is novelistic, a *Pamela* gone wrong.

This fantastic narrative reminds us that the prostitute and her inner life are always objects of fantastic speculation. We can hear, I would suggest, the logic and the affect that attend the story of the fall in the overdetermined finality of the line, "And the colours have all pass'd away from her eyes"; for it is the irrevocable loss of virtue that casts a definitive pall over the prostitute's inner life. Simpson's construction should also make us wary of any discourse—whether late eighteenth-century poem or contemporary historicist criticism—that maps the ideologies of country versus city onto the figure of a woman. The developments of early industrial England—the capitalization of agriculture in the country and the growth of an urban underclass in London—furthered the economic marginalization of working-class women and contributed to an increase in prostitution. But to use a woman to protest the social and economic conditions that produced the corruptions of Lothbury and Cheapside is inevitably to make her sexuality the register of those conditions; just as to make woman the subject of pastoral nostalgia is to make visible the paternalism ("return to thy father's house") that implicitly governs social relations in the pastoral world.[46]

Moreover, as Simpson discusses the prostitute option for Susan, the prostitute shifts slightly but tellingly from being a sympathetic victim of social ills to becoming a dangerous social threat herself. Discussing Wordsworth's critique of the theater in book 7 of *The Prelude*, he remarks, "Is not prostitution a further example, with a quite precise empirical identity, of this dangerous metropolitan culture of surfaces and facsimiles?"[47] This association of prostitution and representation—a "culture of surfaces and facsimiles"—suggests that readers' interest in Susan's sexual colors may have something to do with the fact that she *is* part of a culture of facsimiles—that she's a representation. If Susan seems like she has been around, it is partly because she has circulated as a conventional literary figure. Susan has literary antecedents much closer than Swift or Richardson. As Robert Mayo noted, prostitutes were among the "species of unfortunates" that populated magazine poetry of the 1780's and 1790's.[48] But Susan is related not only to the figure of the prostitute; more generally she belongs to the class of variously fallen, displaced, disconsolate, penitent, sometimes dead women that were the poetic objects of choice during this period.

There is nothing new in pointing out that in the *Lyrical Ballads*, Wordsworth attempted to distinguish his poetry from "the popular Poetry of the day" not by rejecting but by using its figures. We are all familiar with the argument that Wordsworth sought to combat the "degrading thirst after outrageous stimulation" to which the popular literature of his time had conformed itself by renovating its forms, turning the sensational against itself. But the figure of the haplessly fantasizing prostitute displays especially vividly both Wordsworth's use of and violence toward the popular. I have described the pathos of "Poor Susan" as the pathos of the tenuousness of fantasy: her pathos is her inability to escape through the imagination the "real" social conditions of her life. Indeed, in spite of the promise held out to her in the last stanza, the implications of the stanza itself, the history of its excision, and the poem's critical reception all suggest that she *can't* escape her determination as a socially scripted sexual character. Not only does her very literariness conspire to make us read her as a prostitute, but, as we've seen, the historicist literary critic identifies her, as a prostitute, *with* the very social threats—commodification, overpopulation—that determine her.

The conflation of the prostitute with her material context can be compared to Wordsworth's tendency to merge popular literature with *its* social conditions in the Preface. Wordsworth's cultural politics are, on the one hand, resolutely materialist,[49] reducing popular literature—the "frantic novels, sickly and stupid German Tragedies, and deluges of idle and extravagant stories in verse"—to the social conditions he claims produced them: "the great national events which are daily taking place, and the encreasing accumulation of men in cities" as well as "the uniformity of their occupations" (128). Conforming to and reproducing a "degrading thirst after outrageous stimulation," popular literature—like the prostitute—lacks autonomy, is both a mere effect of the social and its dangerous co-conspirator. Wordsworth's cultural politics also involve, however, a claim to "counteract" this taste with a literature that would have escaped these material determinations: a literature of the imagination? If Susan is a prostitute, perhaps it's because she's a common figure whom Wordsworth could "use," staging feeling through her. As a cultural fantasy herself, "Poor Susan" is an appropriate figure for an investigation of the fleeting forms and colors that fantasies take, while Susan herself is doomed, like the "popular Poetry of the day," to return to the realm of the social.

Coda: "Fond and Wayward Thoughts"

I conclude by returning to the problem of gender and emotion in the early responses to Wordsworth's poetry with which I began. Early reviewers and readers were perplexed by what seemed to be disproportionate intensities of feeling, habits of attaching emotions to objects that excite none, and feelings about subjects with which feeling had no proper concern. These emotionally extravagant habits seemed to at least one reader to be those of a hysterical schoolgirl. Yet for Hazlitt, it was Wordsworth's access to feminine feeling that gave the *Lyrical Ballads* their characteristic power. He singled out "the *Thorn*, the *Mad Mother*, and the *Complaint of a Poor Indian Woman*" as the poems in which he "felt that deeper power and pathos which have since been acknowledged . . . as the characteristics of this author."[50] Hannah More's highly participatory response to "Goody Blake and Harry Gill," recorded earlier, documents another reader's recognition of the power of Wordsworth's female figures of woe. We might find a useful allegory for the debate over the value of Wordsworth's emotions in the erotic anxieties of "Strange Fits of Passion." Like many of the writings I have been discussing in this book, this poem stages a debate over the origins of emotions and their appropriateness to their causes. It features a speaker who seems as perplexed by his own wayward emotions as some of Wordsworth's readers were with his. In this poem, the debate over how to know feelings' true proportions takes the form of a difference between a man and a woman.

"Strange Fits of Passion" is a poem of misfittings. As readers have pointed out, it seems to suffer from a "mismatch" between the speaker's opening, portentous promise of mysterious events and its oddly anticlimactic ending; between the speaker's representation of himself as a romantic knight errant and the rather plodding and mechanical quality of his moonlit journey; between fixity and vagary; between the potential sublimity of the experience and the poem's comic air.[51] Seemingly mismatched as well are the poem's mood of deep inwardness and the conventional materials out of which it is made. Like "Poor Susan," "Strange Fits" communicates a very private experience of a solitary individual, an individual absorbed in reverie. As he posts along to his beloved's house, the rider recounts, "In one of those sweet dreams I slept, / Kind Nature's gentlest boon!"[52] Here Wordsworth enters not into a woman's feelings but into the experience of a masculine "I" who lets us in on a secret:

> Strange fits of passion I have known,
> And I will dare to tell,
> But in the lover's ear alone,
> What once to me befel. (1–4)

The opening stanza frames the self-enclosedness of the speaker's perplexing experience by restricting its audience; by the end of the poem, the speaker seems to be his only audience, as he winds up talking to himself. Unlike the self-absorbed trance states of "Poor Susan" and the sonnet to Helen Maria Williams, this one is shattered not by a return to the real but by a deeper delusion: watching the progress of the moon across the sky as he rides to Lucy's house, the speaker is startled, by the moon's seemingly precipitous descent behind the house, into a paroxysm of anxiety:

> What fond and wayward thoughts will slide
> Into a Lover's head—
> "O Mercy!" to myself I cried,
> "If Lucy should be dead!" (25–28)

What causes this fit of passion? Does it fit its occasion? How would we know? Ending here, the poem throws us back on its narrative for an explanation it never quite yields: we are left trying to figure out the relationship between Lucy and the dropping moon, a relationship that the bare narrative doesn't resolve for us. This final stanza reveals that the speaker considers his experience to be "strange" not only in the sense of "odd" but also in the sense of "foreign," or "alien": the poem thus confirms that dilemmas about the proportions of a feeling are inseparable from questions about its origins, either within or without a person. These fond and wayward thoughts "slide" into the head: an odd word here, where "glide," perhaps, might do (as in "bright volumes of vapour through Lothbury glide"). "Slide" imparts to these thoughts a more exteriorized, agentless quality, a viscous quality, like that of medicine sliding down a throat.[53] It gives them the concrete character of things that exist in the world, and thus come from somewhere. Thus as personal and inward as this experience—and Wordsworth's account of it—seem, this fit of passion is an extrapersonal one.

Meanwhile, the echo of the speaker's opening promise to pour what befell him "in the lover's ear," in the line "into a Lover's head" at the end of the poem, puts this narrative itself into circulation. The echo constitutes the "strange fit" as a kind of open secret, something that gets passed along, as in a game of telephone, from lover's ear to lover's head and so on. It orbits like the moon itself. This effect is heightened by the speaker's self-quotation: he reports his panic to himself, telling it to his own ear. That there's something circular about the relationship between the strange fit and the account of the strange fit—that a strange fit might be induced by the experience of hearing about strange fits—is confirmed by a look at the poetry that circulates through here. The moon, for example, on which the speaker is "fix'd"—as often have been critics, wishing to determine whether it is a symbol for Lucy herself—may be most noteworthy for rhyming with "June":

> When she I lov'd, was strong and gay
> And like a rose in June,
> I to her cottage bent my way,
> Beneath the evening moon. (5–8)

This is a cliché-ridden poem, one in which a self-styled lover travels along well-worn "paths" (12). Since the optical illusion that makes the moon seem to drop so fast is caused by his own desirous motion up the hill (21–24), we could say that the anxiety here is that love equals death; or rather, that the intentionality of romantic clichés can be deadly.

That the speaker's panic is induced by poetic feeling could be further confirmed by its proximity to Wordsworth's own poems. Susan J.

Wolfson has pointed out that the speaker's delirium is not unlike the madness of some of Wordsworth's deranged female speakers, noting out that the speaker's "to myself I cried" echoes the description of Martha Ray in "The Thorn": "to herself she cries." (Perhaps even his "O Mercy!" is akin to her "oh woe is me! oh misery!") The spontaneous cry in "Strange Fits," she suggests, is akin to Harry Gill's spontaneous, uncontrollable chattering.[54] Like Harry Gill, in other words, this poem's speaker may get both his strange fit and his automatic speech from the feminized literary world of the *Lyrical Ballads* that this chapter has focused on. The poem takes up the collection's concern with what happens when men meet with sudden influxes of (literary) pain. We might connect the speaker uttering "O Mercy" to Wordsworth's warning in the Preface that poetry can leave us "utterly at the mercy" of "those arbitrary connections of feelings and ideas with particular words, from which no man can altogether protect himself" (145). What is striking about "Strange Fits of Passion," and many of the *Lyrical Ballads*, is their ability to (mis)fit together poetry that shows the strangeness—in the sense of idiosyncratic, unyielding, and alien— of that which comes too close. They are like the speaker's self-quotation, for self-quoted words are both familiar and estranged.

"Strange Fits of Passion" thus records an experience that poses the dilemma of Wordsworth's early poems. Our interpretive activities— our hunch that intertextuality gives us a way to know the emotional excess of the speaker—might be brought up short by the earliest version of the poem that Dorothy Wordsworth sent to Coleridge in 1798. Like "Poor Susan," "Strange Fits" presents the reader with an excised final stanza to contend with, one that tells of the woman's fate. Here, there is another ear for this story, and the speaker has more than a "Lover's" tales in *his* ears:

> I told her this: her laughter light
> Is ringing in my ears:
> And when I think upon that night
> My eyes are dim with tears.[55]

In this stanza, the debate over emotions' proportions to their occasions takes the form of a debate between the speaker and Lucy; and Lucy appears to take the position of some of Wordsworth's early female readers, such as Anna Seward and Lucy Aikin. Her lover's strange fit is laughable, perhaps even "histerical." The speaker's last lines may give him the last word, in that they suggest that his intimation of Lucy's mortality was well-founded. In excising this stanza, Wordsworth indeed gave the speaker the last word, hastening Lucy's disappearance by removing her voice from the poem. However, in deleting this stanza, he also renders her death less certain, putting into play a fundamental uncertainty about the basis for the speaker's fit. "Strange Fits" demonstrates how poetically productive Wordsworth found it to cast feelings as wayward and difficult to know. Yet the gendered debate of the final, excised stanza confirms that for Wordsworth, his admirers, and his detractors, gender difference served to "fix" the meaning and the value of extravagant feeling.

Chapter 4

Phantom Feelings
Emotional Occupation in
The Mysteries of Udolpho

The gothic novel is the genre that is most devoted to exploring and adjudicating the proportions of emotional response. This is especially true of Ann Radcliffe's novels, for her notorious eleventh-hour "natural" explanations of supernatural appearances imply that her characters' emotional responses—to the pile of old clothes they mistake for a ghost, for example—are disproportionate to their causes. Disciplining and demystifying her characters' terrors, Radcliffe's novels suggest that there are ultimately standards of suitable emotional response. At the same time, of course, her novels glorify and cultivate all kinds of excessive feeling in both her characters and her readers.

The Radcliffean gothic's double-edged attitude toward extravagant feeling—both indulgent and disciplinarian—reminds us that the politics of feeling in the gothic decade of the 1790's often turned on precisely such claims to distinguish excessive from "natural" feelings. Every participant in the great debate over the French Revolution accused his or her opponents of exhibiting either too much emotion or not enough. Burke distinguished between the "natural" feelings that bind a country to its past and the unnatural "enthusiasms" of his republican opponents. Pondering the revolutionary sermon of the dissenting Dr. Price, Burke reflects upon his own emotions:

Why do I feel so differently from the Reverend Dr. Price, and those of his lay flock, who will choose to adopt the sentiments of his discourse?— For this plain reason—because it is *natural* I should; because we are so made as to be affected at such spectacles with melancholy sentiments . . . ; because in those natural feelings we learn great lessons; because in events like these our passions instruct our reason.

In this passage from his *Reflections*, Burke asserts that a political vision is underwritten by standards of suitable emotional response, which are personally verifiable; at the same time, this passage leaves Burke vulnerable to the charge that he glorifies passion over reason. Thus, while Burke, like other anti-Jacobin writers, found his opponents alternately to be dangerous enthusiasts or fundamentally unfeeling, writers sympathetic to reform and revolution turned their response to Burke in the same terms. In *A Vindication of the Rights of Man*, Wollstonecraft finds Burke's own feelings false, referring ironically to the "compassionate tears" he "elaborately laboured to excite": "You foster every emotion till the fumes, mounting to your brain, dispel the sober suggestions of reason." She denounces his "sentimental exclamations," his "pampered sensibility," and the sentimental nostalgia of his political vision: his "gothic" view that "our *feelings* should lead us to excuse ... the venerable vestiges of ancient days." But Burke's feelings are not only false and regressive; they also fail where real feeling is due: "Your tears," Wollstonecraft admonishes, "are reserved ... for the declamation of the theatre, or for the downfall of queens ... whilst the distress of many ... were vulgar sorrows that could not move your commiseration." For all sides of the revolution controversy, both the naming of feelings and the naming of feelings' sources—as an excess of sensibility, perhaps, or a false theatricality—carried great ethical weight.[1]

The novels of Ann Radcliffe take the judgment of passion as their territory, giving philosophical scrutiny and narrative form to the ethics and politics of the naming of feelings. Thus in the decade in which the stakes of declaring feelings to be either extravagant or natural responses to political "terrors" were high, her long, complex plots told stories about the philosophical and aesthetic discussions of feelings' origins we have been tracing in this book. Her novels question how one might verify the claims of emotional rhetoric.

We might find an example of *The Mysteries of Udolpho*'s accounting for emotion in its most canonical image, the black veil. (For the heroine of Austen's *Northanger Abbey*, the pleasures of reading the novel and the mystery of the black veil are almost synonymous. "While I have Udolpho to read," she explains, "I feel as if nobody could make me miserable. Oh! the dreadful black veil!")[2] A black veil hanging in the castle of Udolpho is thought to cover a painting. In a brave moment, Emily lifts the veil but drops it when she realizes it hides something else: "—perceiving that what it had concealed was no picture, and, before she could leave the chamber, she dropped senseless on the floor."³ This brief encounter prompts one fainting fit, several close calls, a "thousand nameless terrors" (240), and a chain of mysterious, affectively charged associations that recur to Emily throughout the novel. Conditioned to presume that something which is "no picture" must be the opposite—something "real"—Emily concludes that the veil conceals the corpse of the murdered Lady Laurentini. We can bracket temporarily the hypothetical contents of the veil: as a figure for the unveiled, the thing behind the veil stands throughout most of the novel as an empirical cause for an authentic, reverberating emotional shock. It stands as an example of an object that naturally causes terror, according to the sensationalist reasonings to be found, for example, in Burke's earlier treatise, the *Philosophical Enquiry into the Origin of Our Ideas of the Sublime and Beautiful*. In that treatise, Burke rejects the view that the feelings occasioned by a sublime object are the result of associations in our minds and locates them instead "in the natural properties of things." Thus Burke's position in the *Enquiry*—that emotional responses to objects are the effects of the natural properties of objects— might be seen as laying down a foundation for his later certainties about melancholy "spectacles" that naturally affect us. Burke explains, moreover, that in confronting such an object the self aspires to the object's power, as our feelings follow the principles of ambition and self-preservation. The black veil's associations between terror, nature, and the real are thus corroborated by the Burkean thinking that accompanies Emily's approach to the dreaded veil: "But a terror of this nature, as it occupies and expands the mind, and elevates it to high expectation, is purely sublime, and leads us, by a kind of fascination, to seek even the object, from which we appear to shrink."⁴ A strong emotion, such as a sublime terror, seems to be not only a natural response to the real; it also enables an approach to the real, a lifting of the veil.

At the end of the novel, the mysterious object behind the veil is disclosed, famously, to be not a corpse but only a wax representation of one. Emily's responses are inauthenticated: her willingness to find Montoni capable of the most horrid crimes is blamed for her delusion; and, as in other instances of Radcliffean demystification, the episode teaches a lesson about both the fallibility of individual senses and the need to discipline the emotions. The narrator affirms that experience can indeed instruct one how to feel: "Had she dared to look again, her delusion and her fears would have vanished together" (662).

Once one knows what something is, Radcliffe implies, one's feelings will be appropriate to it. However, while most of her demystifications work by revealing the "real" behind the deluded impression that caused the reaction—the ghost was only a bandit, the clothes belonged to a perfectly real person, the knock on the door was really a servant's—here, in the space of the real, is another veil of illusion. The object is not exactly "no picture." Unlike the other demystifications that replace the object of terror with a natural object and thus reduce the object of terror to a "nothing," the scary thing in this case turns out to be a replica of a scary thing, naturalistically rendered. Thus this object and its effects require a different kind of explanation.[5] Had Emily "dared to look again" and perceived the object to be an imitation, what should have been her response? Does a picture of something horrible lie somewhere between a "something to be scared of" and a "nothing"? Does the object behind the veil confirm that emotions are proportionate to their empirical objects, or does it scramble the narrator's ability to deauthenticate Emily's feelings?

Udolpho's adjudication between spurious terrors and authentic emotions thus takes it into the realm of aesthetic theory's views of its objects. Late eighteenth-century aesthetic theory frequently pondered how an emotional response to an image of a thing should be like and unlike a response to the thing itself. For Hume, the "*feelings* of the passions" caused by poetical fictions are fainter than those caused by the same objects in reality: the passion "feels less firm and solid"; it is but a "mere phantom" of the passion caused by reality. Frequently, however, imitation itself is seen as adding an emotional power all its own. In Hume's discussion of tragedy, for example, imitation—which is "always itself agreeable"—converts into pleasure the disagreeable emotions we would feel if the objects on the stage were real. For Wordsworth, as we have seen, imitation (especially in the case of another person's feelings) was a repetition that threatened to take an original feeling beyond its proper bounds; associationist critics also gave privilege to representation as a source of unpredictable associative emotions.[6] Burke questioned the power of imitation itself: the fact that a tragedy "is a deceit, and its representations no realities" could not for him be a "considerable part" of its power.[7] As for a representation of an object, Burke asserts that how much of its power belongs to the object, how much to imitation itself, depends upon the nature of the object:

When the object represented in poetry or painting is such, as we could have no desire of seeing in the reality; then I may be sure that its power in poetry or painting is owing to the power of imitation, and to no cause operating in the thing itself. So it is with most of the pieces which the painters call still life. In these a cottage, a dunghill, the meanest and most ordinary utensils of the kitchen, are capable of giving us pleasure. But when the object of the painting or poem is such as we should run to see if real, let it affect us with what odd sort of sense it will, we may rely upon it, that the power of the poem or picture is more owing to the nature of the thing itself than to the mere effect of imitation, or to a consideration of the skill of the imitator however excellent.[8]

Though Burke admits here and elsewhere that imitation has a power of its own, it is a "mere effect"; the object has the power to dictate how imitation shall affect us. In Burke's analysis, moreover, we will "run to see" all kinds of dreadful objects—a criminal executed, London in ruins.[9] The tendency of the *Enquiry* as a whole is to treat the pleasures and pains caused by things and by representations as equivalent; and the same is true, though for different reasons, of Kames's *Elements of Criticism*. In his discussion of "Emotions caused by Fictions," Kames explains that representations affect us to the extent that the objects of representations take on an "ideal presence" in our minds, affecting us as if we were "spectators" of the things themselves. "The idea of a thing I never saw, raised in me by speech, by writing, or by painting," according to Kames, causes emotion when it produces a species of reverie that places the object before us.[10]

According to late eighteenth-century theorists, then, the emotions inspired by an image or effigy find their causes and their intensities somewhere along a wide spectrum. They are derived from the power of natural objects or the powers of imitation; they either are in excess of real emotions or are real emotions' paler "phantoms." In Kames's formulation, the emotion caused by an image is the same as the emotion caused by real objects, but the image does its work by creating a reverie, a delusion of presence. Seen from the Kamesian point of view, one's response to the horrifying thing behind the black veil would not be qualitatively, or even quantitatively, different from Emily's mistaken response: aesthetic emotions are always delusional. If the emotions caused by images are in Hume's word "phantoms," then the wayward terrors that haunt Emily after she lifts the veil may be fitting. Somewhere between a real cause and a false source of terror, the thing behind the black veil goes some way to question the grounds on which the novel adjudicates questions of emotional response, troubling the line that would separate authentic emotional response from extravagance.

But if at its most canonical moment, *The Mysteries of Udolpho* discloses something that seems to question the notion of a "real" cause, the novel nevertheless repeatedly looks for feelings' empirical origins, hunting after—as Emily poses it—"the remote cause of this emotion" (73). In Radcliffe's inquiries into feelings, appeals to the order of experience and appeals to the order of representation closely accompany each other. This chapter will try to account for why this doubled appeal recurs in the gothic novel. It will consider whether the logic that attributes real causes to emotions in experience can turn out to be just as deluded as that which causes false terrors. I will be focusing less on the properly gothic terrors of the novel than on its gentler emotions, its seductive representations of an ideal world of melancholy, nostalgia, and tearful exchanges.[11] Doing so will affirm that the events of the 1790's elicited other emotional rhetorics as complex as the claims and counterclaims about feeling in the Revolution debates. Gothic nostalgia might seem to locate the origins of emotion in an empirical past—a historical past, or a familial past. However, nostalgia's circuitous narrative paths disclose instead the political, philosophical, and formal benefits of casting the origins of feelings as attenuated and difficult to know. I will begin and end by discussing the naming of feelings.

ॐ

As much as *Udolpho* focuses our attention on the origins of feelings, it expresses special interest in feelings whose sources are remote, attenuated, and diffuse. Radcliffe is lavish in her attentions to feelings that can barely be named: though we think of her work as providing us with a whole taxonomy of emotion—discriminating between "horror" and "terror" for example—the book as frequently engages in a process of *de-naming* emotions. The most glamorous and touching feelings are those which are named negatively, such as that behind the tears Emily sheds on first returning to her family's home, La Vallée, toward the end of the book: "While she contemplated, with tempered resignation, the picture of past times, which her memory gave, the tears she shed could scarcely be called those of grief" (591). This kind of formulation occurs several times at important moments in the text, suggesting that the best emotions are those that can "scarcely" be called anything at all. The relationship between emotion and language here should be distinguished from a gesture toward the ineffable, the more conventional notion that powerful emotions belong to the realm of the unsayable beyond the reach of language. The pleasure in Radcliffe's "gently euphemistic" prose seems to be in endlessly discriminating between fine feelings rather than in pointing to the beyond.[12] To euphemize is to speak not of what one cannot spell out but rather precisely of what one can but would prefer not to. Euphemism pronounces that there are, in fact, words that are unbearably close to the things to which they are attached. Radcliffean melancholy is inseparable from a prose style whose glamour lies in the way it brushes up against the referential status of feelings. Through this naming and unnaming of emotions—through the prose's dramatization of its ability to refer or not to refer to feeling—feeling attaches itself most of all not to persons or to causes but to the novel's language itself.

Melancholy is embodied in a certain kind of language in *The Mysteries of Udolpho*, and it seems as well to be almost literally in the air. After Emily has listened to some songs in Venice,

> she then remained sunk in that pensive tranquillity which soft music leaves on the mind—a state like that produced by the view of a beautiful landscape by the moon-light, or by the recollection of scenes marked with the tenderness of friends lost for ever, and with sorrows, which time has mellowed into mild regret. Such scenes are indeed, to the mind, like "those faint traces which the memory bears of music that is past." (177–78)

This state of mind seems distinguished most of all by its ability to evoke a multiplying chain of associations; Radcliffean melancholy is among other things a medium of metaphorizing, and thus a way (as in Charlotte Smith's poetry) of eliciting remarkably hackneyed poetical phrases, allusions, and quotations. "Melancholy" would seem to function teleologically rather than referentially, to be about recognizing clichés rather than about experiencing the things to which these images refer. The associative drift of the passage ends by coming full circle: the scenes marked by tenderness and sorrow which were at first simply in the service of a comparison become the subject of the next sentence, where they are compared to the original subject, music. Present scenes (a view of a landscape by moonlight) and recollected scenes, music present and music past, are seen as acting identically, leaving the same trace or mark on the mind. The absence or presence of an object of feeling seems immaterial.

As this example suggests, melancholy in *The Mysteries of Udolpho* always reverts to the past. To remember is to feel sad; and if a character is feeling sad it is because she or he is remembering. Objects of nostalgia seem to maintain their melancholic aura of perpetual loss even when they are restored to presence. When St. Aubert moves back to his childhood home, La Vallée, it is already an object thought of with "enthusiasm and regret" (2), and it remains so. Feeling melancholy is the form of cognition where the past is concerned, and the past that is the object of melancholy feelings is not limited to a character's own personal past: memory in this book exceeds personal memories. After their escape from Udolpho, Emily and Du Pont pass by the river Arno and contemplate "the remembrances, which its classic waves revived" (460). Needless to say, neither Du Pont nor Emily has seen the Arno before; the remembrances revived are cultural ones. This nostalgia for a cultural past could provide one way of thinking about Radcliffe's characters' melancholy fixation on all kinds of pasts, personal, fictional, and historical: it could be linked to the gothic novel's nostalgia, as a genre, for an idealized, preindustrial, chivalric past. That the characters' objects of nostalgia are so varied and extrapersonal suggests indeed that their feelings are never simply their own feelings. It is as if the characters were oddly aware of and acting out the book's own generic longings.

It is easy to imagine what a popular novel of the 1790's might be nostalgic for: a landscape different from the changing countryside of agrarian capitalism; a landscape in which peasants danced, rather than a countryside in which relations between classes displaced and threatened many; a world in which one could travel freely (Radcliffe's own journey on the continent in the summer of 1794 was, as we shall see, thwarted and shaped by the Revolution); an idealized, unanxious leisure. It is important, however, to see nostalgia in *The Mysteries of Udolpho* not simply as a conservative, Burkean sentiment (I am thinking of Wollstonecraft's attack on that writer's "gothic" attachment to "the venerable vestiges of ancient days"). Nostalgia is a cultural practice that has no determinate content. A structure that opens up a space between a "once was" and a "now," nostalgia can provide a framework for the making of meanings, a road map for navigating a changing landscape.[13]

One of the ways in which nostalgia may create a possibility of meaning is through its claims to rewrite the contingencies of history. The gothic novel is an instance of what Susan Stewart—preeminent theorist of nostalgia—calls "distressed genres," the archaic genres such as ballad, fairy tale, and romance that were revived and imitated as "new antiques" in the eighteenth century. For Stewart the popularity of the "new antique" is the appeal of a cultural form that invents "its own temporal grounds," that represses its cultural context in order "to conceive of its own context as being encapsulated within the form of representation." She argues that the distressed genre, in looking back, marks the emergence of literary modernity, as changes in literary production, reception, and technology separate literary form from its own temporal moment and spatial position. The creation of the "new antique" is "an attempt to bypass the contingencies of time," to bypass not only an alienating system of literary production, but also the defacing traces of a work's own context and history. "By creating new antiques, the author hopes to author a context as well as an artifact": in doing so, the author's own authority is exposed as embedded in the work's own gestures of legitimation:

> Thus distressed forms show us the gap between past and present as a structure of desire, a structure in which authority seeks legitimation by recontextualizing its object and thereby recontextualizing itself. If distressed forms involve a negation of the contingencies of their immediate history, they also involve an invention of a version of the past that could only arise from such contingencies. We see this structure of desire as the structure of nostalgia—that is, the desire for desire in which objects are the means of generation and not the ends.[14]

Nostalgia poses a circular relationship between event and emotion. It looks back to a lost object in order to generate desire, inventing contexts for its own emotions. At the same time, the nostalgic mode uses the feelings it generates in looking back as evidence with which to canonize the lost object or event as an origin.

We could sharpen our sense of *The Mysteries of Udolpho*'s nostalgic refiguring of its own histories by comparing its characters' sojourns through an idealized Europe to Radcliffe's *Journey Made in the Summer* of 1794 *Through Holland and Germany*. The novelist's debts to the travels of others are well known.[15] Because Radcliffe made her own continental tour within the year of the publication of *Udolpho*, it would be possible to argue only for the influence of the novel on the *Journey*, rather than the other way around. However, the two texts often read quite similarly. In her *Journey*, Radcliffe often stops to ponder the aesthetic dilemmas the genre of travel writing elicits: how the act of describing a place can transform the way it looks (all Dutch towns begin to appear alike); how places of canonical beauty can reduce one's writing to a compulsive stutter (a scene in the Lake District compels attempts at description yet yields only "a repetition of the same images of rock, wood and water, and the same epithets of grand, vast and sublime"); how the travel writer is always losing "the dignity of writing" in her reports of mundane detail.[16] In the *Journey* these aesthetic dilemmas are shaped by the ways in which Radcliffe's European tour of 1794 was marked by the wars with France. She reports conversations with people whose lives have been changed, including an expatriate French royalist who laments that all has been lost. Radcliffe's own remarks express revulsion at the tyranny of the revolutionary leaders, but she also deplores the backward state of the continental nations in general, which, in contrast to England, have been weakened through the "senseless degradation" of their "lower classes."[17] The very landscape Radcliffe seeks to describe has been marked by Revolution as well. In the German town of Goodesberg, which has recently been visited by the French army, they see a procession of wounded French prisoners; they visit the castle of Goodesberg from which the Archduchess Maria Christina has just fled. The castle inspires an apostrophe on the unhappiness of war and the inadequacies of description:

The situation of this house is beautiful beyond any hope or power of description; for description, though it may tell that there are mountains and rocks, cannot paint the grandeur, or the elegance of outline, cannot give the effect of precipices, or draw the minute features, that reward the actual observer by continual changes of colour, and by varying their forms at every new choice of his position. Delightful Goodesberg! the sublime and beautiful of landscape, the charms of music, and the pleasures of gay and elegant society, were thine! The immediate unhappiness of war has now fallen upon thee; but, though the graces may have fled thee, thy terrible majesty remains, beyond the sphere of human contention.[18]

The consciousness of change and loss in the second part of this passage sheds light on the lament about description in the first half. The passage shifts from a complaint about the stasis of description, its inability to grasp change in the object, to a lament about the changes and losses that the place has suffered. Almost everything good about Goodesberg is in the past, altered by the "immediate unhappiness of war": even "the sublime and beautiful of landscape," which one would expect to survive a war, are in the past tense. Goodesberg's majesty consists of the fact that everything about it is in the past; and description, for Radcliffe, is most moving when it points to what is gone. For Radcliffe, historical change is synonymous with the aesthetic: she speaks touchingly of ruins of monasteries and convents, for example, which "though reason rejoices that they no longer exist, the eye may be allowed to regret."[19]

If the 1794 *Journey* bears sentimental witness to historical events, the 1794 novel invents its own events through feeling. Almost any given moment in the novel earns its significance in relationship to other moments, past, future, or both: while sometimes the past or future will seem to be the true origin for the significance of that present, often a series of moments will be linked together through a temporalizing that is purely relational, without a single origin. The death of the mother, Mme St. Aubert, at the beginning of the novel is the occasion for one of these series. After M. St. Aubert's own illness, he spends an afternoon with his wife and daughter at the family's fishing house at the river's edge. Everybody admires the beauties of nature and looks at each other through veils of tears as St. Aubert luxuriates in acute anticipatory nostalgia:

> He felt the tender enthusiasm stealing upon himself in a degree that became almost painful; his features assumed a serious air, and he could not forbear secretly sighing—"Perhaps I shall some time look back to these moments, as to the summit of my happiness, with hopeless regret. But let me not misuse them by useless anticipation; let me hope I shall not live to mourn the loss of those who are dearer to me than life." (8–9)

When Madame is, later in the same chapter, on her deathbed, St. Aubert "remembered the feelings and the reflections that had called a momentary gloom upon his mind, on the day when he had last visited the fishing house, in company with Madame St. Aubert, and he now admitted a presentiment, that this illness would be a fatal one" (18). Looking back to those earlier feelings, in other words, allows him to look forward to the future. And a short time after her death, while nostalgically looking at a landscape that resembles the view from the fishing house, the earliest moment is finally canonized as a premonition: "St. Aubert remembered the last time of his visiting that spot in company with her, and also the mournfully presaging thoughts, which had then arisen in his mind, and were now, even thus soon, realized!" (29). An earlier feeling is now grounded and identified ("premonition of death") not simply retrospectively, at the time of death, but later through nostalgic reminiscence.

Later in the novel, two paragraphs link this kind of temporalizing to an aesthetic dilemma similar to those discussed in Radcliffe's *Journey*. The family that dominates the post-Udolpho section of the novel, the Villeforts, repeat both the St. Aubert family's perpetually nostalgic relation to an old family place and their strange way of relating to each other by imagining each other dead. Like Radcliffe in her *Journey*, they travel to a castle marked by time. Returning to the scenes of his youth at Chateau-le-Blanc in the company of his daughter, the Count ruminates on his own aging, and looks forward to when Blanche will have the same experience of looking back: "The landscape is not changed, but time has changed me; from my mind the illusion, which gave spirit to the colouring of nature, is fading fast! If you live, my dear Blanche, to re-visit this spot, at the distance of many years, you will, perhaps, remember and understand the feelings of your father" (474). This invocation to anticipatory nostalgia of course provokes Blanche to weep as she imagines the death of her father, who in turn must go to the window to conceal his own emotion. Here a present moment of bonding between daughter and father (they join hands) is constituted not simply by looking back or looking forward, but both.

This moment of family sentiment, moreover, is followed by one of cultural nostalgia. Blanche leaves her "fading" father and goes to her antique, tarnished room in the chateau, dwelling in particular on a "faded" tapestry representing the scenes from the Trojan Wars, "though the almost colourless worsted now mocked the glowing actions they once had painted. She laughed at the ludicrous absurdity she observed, till, recollecting, that the hands, which had wove it, were, like the poet, whose thoughts of fire they had attempted to express, long since mouldered into dust, a train of melancholy ideas passed over her mind, and she almost wept" (474). As Eve Sedgwick has noted, the "almost colourless" fabric here is typical of Radcliffe's predilection for the faded, her distrust of color.[20] But this is not simply an aesthetic of pastness: these fading colors take on significance in relation to a more persistently robust and colorful "past," the glowing actions of Troy. The passage reverses the idea that art lives long and preserves human action, which does not last: here art becomes "distressed" by time. The relation between representation and action—really, between representation (the tapestry) and representation (Homer)—manifested here becomes more complicated in the last sentence, in which Blanche recollects that the "hands" who wove the carpet are as dead as Homer. (I will return to the synecdochic hand in the next section.) In one sense this doesn't seem like such a bad way to be dead: to be as dead as Homer is to be memorialized in marble. This passage is indicative of the ways in which almost anything can be made into a memorial in Radcliffe's book. That Blanche's recollection should be a cause for melancholy might perhaps be understood by contemplating her transition from laughter (at the "ludicrous absurdity") to weeping here. The gap between representation and action can seem ludicrous, or it can be tempered and converted into a mourning over the mortality of the anonymous.[21]

The juxtaposition of the fading father with the fading tapestry asks us to try to join the book's obsessive anticipatory nostalgia in human relationships with Radcliffe's meditations on the movingly nonmimetic in art and writing. Each takes meaning from the other: the fading father borrows from the fading tapestry some of its consolatory aura, its capacity to elicit a mourning or commemoration. At the same time, this juxtaposition reveals the extent to which Radcliffe's aesthetic depends on the invention of a temporal gap between artifacts and their origins.

The attractions for Radcliffe of nostalgia, of fading fathers and fading tapestries, are evident in the context of her relationship to the genre in which she writes. Such nostalgia could be seen as an effect of the book's worries about the legitimacy of its own terrifying events. Radcliffe's novels are supremely concerned with their own repetitions. Their most familiar tropes all bespeak the novels' knowledge of their belatedness, their highly formal nature. The novels frequently begin in atmospheres of great self-consciousness about their own return upon the familiar; places their characters think are most their own, as we shall see, bear traces of other inhabitants.[22] Characters hear mysterious yet familiar music coming from unlocatable sources; they return to spots that have meant something in the past; they discover themselves in dramas of recognition: these scenarios constitute the gothic novel's acknowledgment that they—and we—have all been here before.

The fundamental mystery of *The Mysteries of Udolpho* concerns how to explain the repetition of its forms. We can see the book's notorious need for elaborate explanations—how the voice and the music got to be there, for example—as an attempt to wed the book's highly formal aesthetic with a more empiricist one.[23] While the melancholy that frames the book can seem to express the novel's sense of belatedness, the characters' moody nostalgia also invents and canonizes its own origins. The gloomy feelings that frame the novel's gothic terrors may be a symptom of Radcliffe's sense of the illegitimacy of her plots and terrors, but, as I have been arguing, melancholy often plays a teleological role. Nostalgia appears both as a way of representing the conventional gothic plot as a return, and as a way of retreating from its repetitive nature. If extravagant emotion is often, in *The Mysteries of Udolpho*, what needs to be explained, it can also serve *as* explanation.

Meanwhile, it is the gothic heroine who stands as the figure for the recipient of these returns. Robert Kiely has shrewdly remarked of Radcliffe: "What her heroines must do during their ordeals is not simply preserve their lives and their virginity—that they would do so is taken so much for granted it is hardly at issue—but they must 'hold fast' in every way, keep every old idea and emotion intact."[24] Kiely's remark is apt because it links what is most conventional (and hardly worth remarking) in the gothic heroine's plot—her struggle to preserve life, chastity, and love—with what produces some of the novel's most deviant effects. There is indeed a profound conservatism in Emily's emotional life, an effort to preserve former feelings and ideas. She is often returning to places, and "remembering the emotions, which she had formerly suffered there" (501). Emily frequently keeps the idea of the past before her eyes so firmly that she barely sees what is before her. Imagining that she can see into her homeland of Gascony from hundreds of miles away, for example, Emily fixes on the past: "Inattentive to the scene immediately before her, and to the flight of time, she continued to lean on the window of a pavilion, that terminated the terrace, with her eyes fixed on Gascony, and her mind occupied with the interesting ideas which the view of it awakened"

(120). In fact, it would be possible to see the emotional excesses of *The Mysteries of Udolpho* as effects of the gravitational pull of this conservative impulse. Rather than seeing the gothic novel as taking an old plot—the embattled virgin—and adding to it new extremes, we might see its new extremes as the effects of a wholesale effort to preserve, at all levels, the old. The conservatism of the gothic heroine, her efforts to "hold fast," is in fact what produces the most extravagant aspects of the genre.[25]

༒

The phenomenology of feeling described thus far has been associated with the structure of nostalgia, with an emptying out of the present and an attenuation of feelings located in the past. People's affective lives seem emptied of anything proper to the present itself. Concomitantly, another pattern of images in the book depicts characters as *filled in* by feelings that may or may not be theirs. The characters' emotional lives turn out to be occupied territory; and we can begin to establish this pattern by noticing it at all levels.

In *The Mysteries of Udolpho*, the places one thinks are most one's own never are: they always turn out to be occupied by someone else. This is true not only of the variously haunted rooms and recesses of the castle of Udolpho but also of the place that is truly home, La Vallée. The fishing house that is Emily's—and her parents'—"favourite retreat" and setting of the musical and melancholy exchanges that establish the St. Aubert family's identity in the first section of the novel, is from the beginning filled with the traces of an other. A sonnet, addressed to Emily, appears penciled on the wainscot (7); someone plays her lute there (9); the crucial miniature of Emily disappears there (10). This other is revealed to be the insignificant Du Pont, who serves in the book only as a shadow for Valancourt, or later on as an utterly banal source of mysteries. The home's occupation by traces of another, however, is an ontological condition in this novel, essential to the way it represents identities. From this perspective, the typically gothic episodes in which intruders break into one's room at night or find one's secret mountain hiding place (see 596–618) could be seen as illustrations of a self always occupied, rather than as trials and assaults which the inviolate self must resist. Lovers are particularly prone to invading and occupying the home of the beloved.[26] Wandering through the estate at Toulouse that she has now inherited, Emily is mentally occupied with the image of Valancourt: "Sometimes, indeed, she thought, that her fancy, which had been occupied by the idea of him, had suggested his image to her uncertain sight" (586). It turns out that he is, in fact, trespassing on her estate, where he is mistaken by a servant for a common poacher and shot. That Valancourt can be seen as threatening Emily with territorial encroachment makes the lover's approaches seem dangerously close to those of her persecutor, Montoni, who pursues Emily chiefly for her estates.

The feelings the lover expresses, moreover, may be feelings that are not his: indeed it is difficult to know whose language is the language of the beloved's heart. In a crucial scene shortly after Valancourt parts company with Emily and St. Aubert, she begins to think about reading one of her books:

She sought for one, in which Valancourt had been reading the day before, and hoped for the pleasure of re-tracing a page, over which the eyes of a beloved friend had lately passed, of dwelling on the passages, which he had admired, and of permitting them to speak to her in the language of his own mind, and to bring himself to her presence. On searching for the book, she could find it no where, but in its stead perceived a volume of Petrarch's poems, that had belonged to Valancourt, whose name was written in it, and from which he had frequently read passages to her, with all the pathetic expression, that characterized the feelings of the author. She hesitated in believing, what would have been sufficiently apparent to almost any other person, that he had purposely left this book, instead of the one she had lost, and that love had prompted the exchange; but, having opened it with an impatient pleasure, and observed the lines of his pencil drawn along the various passages he had read aloud, and under others more descriptive of delicate tenderness than he had dared to trust his voice with, the conviction came, at length, to her mind. For some moments she was conscious only of being beloved; then, a recollection of all the variations of tone and countenance, with which he had recited these sonnets, and of the soul, which spoke in their expression, pressed to her memory, and she wept over the memorial of his affection. (58)

Emily's experience of finding someone else's book where she expected to find her own is reminiscent of her experiences of finding the fishing house already occupied. The novel's plot encourages us to see these episodes as parallel, insofar as it suggests that Valancourt is also the perpetrator of the fishing house transgressions. As a writer of gothic romance, moreover, Radcliffe knows to what extent books are occupied: we can see this passage as a typically Radcliffean instance of taking a canonical trope—the lovers who fall in love through reading books (Paolo and Francesca)—and temporalizing it, separating the lovers in time and making one already think of the other as an object of nostalgia. The presence of the beloved is once again a violation; and indeed here the language of the passage ("lost" rather than stolen books) and its elegiac tone associate the consciousness of being belovèd with a fall. The funereal language of the passage is unmistakable, from Emily's desire to peruse a page "over which the eyes of a beloved friend had lately passed" to the book as a "memorial of his affection." Emily expects the book she seeks to "speak to her in the language of [Valancourt's] own mind," and Valancourt can read "with all the pathetic expression" characteristic of Petrarch's own feelings. The passage suggests that the language of the heart is never really one's own.

To describe someone as preoccupied is to suggest that he or she is unfit for gothic experience, unreceptive to its terrors. Describing Emily's sensations as she approaches the castle of Udolpho, Radcliffe poses a perplexing question: "From the deep solitudes, into which she was immerging, and from the gloomy castle, of which she had heard some mysterious hints, her sick heart recoiled in despair, and she experienced, that, though her mind was already occupied by peculiar distress, it was still alive to the influence of new and local circumstance; why else did she shudder at the idea of this desolate castle?" (225). In its very gesture of pointing to the obviousness or inevitability of Emily's response to the gloomy castle, the rhetorical question also implies that a mind already occupied by peculiar distresses should *not* be susceptible to new and local circumstances. The double gesture of the rhetorical question I take to be paradigmatic of how the novel articulates connections between one psychological state and a subsequent one. It intimates, first, that the mind can be occupied by only one kind of distress at a time, and that minds are thus preoccupied as a rule; and second, that preoccupation rather leads to or prepares one for new forms of distress. In *The Mysteries of Udolpho*, the relationship between previous states of feeling and new ones tends to lead in two directions: "Emily's mind was even so much engaged with new and wonderful images, that they sometimes banished the idea of Valancourt, though they more frequently revived it" (163).

That people are occupied by alien feelings suggests that they are highly susceptible to catching other people's. A key figure for emotional transmission in *The Mysteries of Udolpho* is the image of someone's tears falling on someone else's hands. Emily's tears fall on her father's hands (67); his "warm tear" falls on hers (46). Emily weeps "over the hand she held there" (78); Valancourt holds Emily's hand, which is "wet with . . . tears" (101). In a characteristic moment (characteristic because in it the novel identifies its own semiotic codes), this exchange—tears falling on hands—is called a language: "Valancourt sighed deeply, and was unable to reply; but, as he pressed her hand to his lips, the tears, that fell over it, spoke a language, which could not be mistaken, and to which words were inadequate" (668). The tear-bathed hand undergoes a kind of baptism: it is the way Emily imbibes her father's melancholy, the way she and Valancourt communicate love. To have feelings transmitted through this bodily exchange of fluids revises the sentimental trope (seen, for example, in Wordsworth's sonnet on seeing Helen Maria Williams weeping discussed in the preceding chapter) in which one imbibes feelings by *seeing* the tears of another. The tears-on-hands trope makes the exchange more magical, immediate, and contagious. In this ambiguously gendered exchange of bodily fluids, moreover, unlike in the sentimental tableau, feeling can flow in both directions.

Why is a hand a receptacle of tears? The trope foregrounds the physicality of emotional exchange, the hand representing the body as a whole. But the hand also especially represents the seat of emotion, the "heart," which itself has only a metaphorical existence. The hand is thus simultaneously more physical and more metaphorical than the eye. Further, the hand as a figure in *Udolpho* is especially susceptible to the ambiguities of synecdoche, which can both connect, and detach, the figure and its referent. In the tapestry scene discussed earlier, for example, the pathos of the pastness of the tapestry-weaver is reinforced by the sense of loss that is built into synecdoche: the weaver is already only a hand, the rest of him or her having faded away, Cheshire cat–like, with the tapestry itself. Hands appear elsewhere in the novel as images of decay, and synecdoches of hands, moreover, are associated not only with the figuration of loss or severing but with figuration and writing itself. In addition to the weaving hand of the tapestry passage, there is the writing hand of the novel's last paragraph: "And, if the weak hand, that has recorded this tale, has, by its scenes, beguiled the mourner of one hour of sorrow, or, by its moral, taught him to sustain it—the effort, however humble, has not been vain, nor is the writer unrewarded" (672). What interests me here is the "weak hand" of the writer. Once again, the structure of synecdoche—a hand detached from, as well as standing in for, the subject—seems to add to the debility of the professed hand (and whose hand wouldn't feel weak after writing *The Mysteries of Udolpho*?). The symmetry between the weak writerly hand and the mourning reader links this passage to the "tears-on-hands" exchanges, suggesting that reader and writer are ideally bound together much as the characters are. However, the mourning reader's tears fall not into an open hand but into an open book, where the hand has disappeared into tiny marks of print.

The conjunction of hands, loss, and figuration can be seen as well in the novel's central figure for representation itself, the wax figure behind the black veil. Located behind the veil, and thus in the space identified as the space of the unrepresentable real, this memento mori—constructed in penance by an earlier inhabitant of the castle of Udolpho—suggests, as we've seen, that it's representation all the way down. Revealed for what it is at the end of the novel, the narrator points out as one of the horrors of the spectacle the "worms" that disfigure the face, "which were visible on the features and hands" (662). Disfiguring markings highlight the most legible features of this image that fills the space where we most expect the real. Because hands have already been linked with tearful exchange, hands such as these (even such grotesque ones) which are associated with loss and figuration are rendered objects of some pathos. But this vacillation of the hand, from organic, living conduit for the transmission of feeling to cut-off figure of decay, can also cast doubt on the tears-and-hands affirmations of the successful, spontaneous transmissions of feeling: the different uses of the hand reveal the hand in the text as precisely a figure, cut off by the movement of synecdoche and proliferating throughout the novel.

☙

It is tempting to see the two directions in which the uses of hands appear to go—the one hand invoking the contagious transmission of feeling, the other hand severed, signifying the detached, figurative repetition of feeling—as pointing to a model for two general modes of emotional transmission in the novel. In the first case a person's feelings have their origins in an observable relationship to another empirical person; in the second, feelings pass to persons in mysterious ways. We could test this hypothesis by focusing on the relationship of Emily and M. St. Aubert, between whom many of these tears-on-hands exchanges take place. The fading father is the novel's primary locus for investigations into the causes of feelings. Recollecting her ailing father's inexplicable response to the environs of Chateau-le-Blanc, Emily feels "strongly interested concerning the remote cause" of his emotions (73). Emily gets her most explicit lessons about emotional susceptibility from her father in his famous deathbed speech about the dangers of sensibility: "Above all, my dear Emily . . . do not indulge in the pride of fine feeling. . . . Those, who really possess sensibility, ought early to be taught, that it is a dangerous quality, which is continually extracting the excess of misery, or delight" (79–81). If, like her fishing house, Emily is persistently occupied by things that may belong to other people, it would make sense to point to the father.

The attractions of seeing "the father"—or "the mother"—as the explanation for Emily's emotions are compelling.[27] We could begin with the scene in which Emily enters her father's room at night and sees him reading and weeping: "She could not witness his sorrow, without being anxious to know the subject of it; and she therefore continued to observe him in silence, concluding that those papers were letters of her late mother." What Emily soon discovers is that her father is weeping and sighing convulsively over a miniature: "She perceived it to be that of a lady, but not of her mother" (26). We could then move to the episode in which Emily returns to the scene and burns—at her father's dying injunction—the papers, but not before she has found the miniature of the lady and seen some dreadful words: "She was unconscious, that she was transgressing her father's strict injunction, till a sentence of dreadful import awakened her attention and her memory together. She hastily put the papers from her; but the words, which had roused equally her curiosity and terror, she could not dismiss from her thoughts" (103). The miniature her father wept over is found at the bottom of a hidden purse along with some coins that Emily now weeps over: "'His hand deposited them here,' said she, as she kissed some pieces of the coin, and wetted them with her tears, 'his hand—which is now dust!'" (104). Here, we could say, we have the coming together of the tears-on-hands trope with the hand as figure for death: the tears-on-hands is mediated by the coin that Emily wets with tears. The transmission of feeling has become the transmission of both paternal responsibility (he leaves her some money) and sexuality. The miniature and the dreadful words awaken memory and canonize the first scene as a primal scene: and behind the vision "my father is weeping over someone who is not my mother" is the fantasy "my father is sleeping with someone who is not my mother."

From this point we could see the novel as telling a certain kind of story, suggesting that Emily's extravagant emotional sensitivity is symptomatic of a returned, repressed fantasy about her father's sexuality, specifically about the classic primal scene, the scene of her own conception. The novel's gothic horrors—the lifting of a veil, the pulling back of bedclothes, anxious bedrooms and anxious nights—can thus be seen as repetitions of the fantasized bedroom scene between the father and "a lady." Emily's progress through the novel is thus a search for her origins, a search that repeatedly casts before her horrifying bedroom images: as one critic has argued, "the more Emily investigates her origins, the more such mementi she comes upon in the form of progressive, replicated corpses"; "behind the veil is an image of the generating marriage bed of her parents, of the violence and 'death' of the sexual act."[28]

But as some of Freud's best readers have pointed out, an original fantasy—especially when it is a fantasy about origins—is a strange kind of origin.[29] Primal fantasies are subject to and constructed by strange chronologies similar to the deferred temporalities surrounding St. Aubert's response to the death of his wife in *Udolpho*. They are never a fixed point of origin but are constructed retrospectively. The original fantasy is neither an empirical event nor wholly an internal affair: Freud was compelled, in his writings about primal fantasy, to conceive of it as a sign of the subject's fundamental preoccupation with something that precedes it, whether we call that something prehistory, phylogenesis (as Freud sometimes did), or structure (as Lacanians do). A fantasy about the father, as an origin for the daughter's emotional life, is both a seductive story of origin and that which suggests an original preoccupation.

What if Emily's feelings were her father's? if the tears he sheds on her hands and those she sheds on his coins were in fact the same? if these scenarios—scenes of seeing the father reading and weeping, for example—had truly involved the transmission of his gloomy preoccupation, his melancholy to her? As we saw in the last chapter's scene of seeing, reading, weeping, and the transmission of feeling (in our discussion of Wordsworth and Helen Maria Williams), it is often difficult to say where one person's feelings end and others' begin. Hysterically seeing women murdered in beds (her aunt at Udolpho, the mysterious figure in the bed at Chateau-le-Blanc), Emily is in fact obsessed with her *father's* secret fear: that his sister has been murdered. We could propose that *The Mysteries of Udolpho* is indeed haunted by a phantom, the kind described by the very gothic psychoanalysis of Nicolas Abraham and Maria Torok. They describe patients haunted in their words and feelings not by the *presence* of a ghost but precisely by a *gap* left within the patient by a concealment or secret not in their own life but in the life of a loved one. They thus propose the possibility of persons being subject to feelings that are fundamentally gratuitous in relation to themselves but rather belong to someone else.

The question of how a secret pain in a father is transmitted to a child—as in a number of Abraham's case studies—is one that, in their analysis, resists being answered by other psychoanalytic explanations. The mode in which the interpersonal phantom passes, for example, is evidently to be distinguished from the dynamics of repression: "The phantom's periodic and compulsive return lies beyond the scope of symptom-formation in the sense of a return of the repressed; it works like a ventriloquist, like a stranger within the subject's own mental topography." The phantom is "radically heterogeneous" in relation to the subject, "to whom it at no time bears any direct reference. In no way can the subject relate to it as his own repressed experience, not even as an experience by incorporation."[30] The result is a subject who—in an earlier formulation—"experienced (unaccountably for himself and, for a long time, for the analyst) affects that were not his own."[31] Abraham and Torok recount, for example, the story of the woman whose father mysteriously disappeared during her childhood and who enacts the father's mourning for *her*, rather than her own for him: "She lived *entirely* on the concealed phantasy of herself *being* the father weeping over her, who suffers because he is bereft of her, and who, forever disconsolate, accuses himself of the worst of crimes since he had to be subjected to the punishment of losing her." She dreams and talks incessantly of cut-off arms and scattered limbs. "Whose are these *scattered limbs*?" ask the analysts. They "represent the dejected suffering of her father: his limbs are as if cut off, not having his little girl to carry."[32]

The theory of the phantom and of endocryptic identification suggests that psychoanalysis makes in itself a place for gothic, uncanny stories about being occupied by feelings that aren't one's own, that belong to another. It is a theory of affective movement that bypasses the subject in order to speak of transgenerational and social practices; of mental processes fixed on words that work *against* oedipal stories;[33] and it is connected, for Abraham, to the theory of the death drive:

> A surprising fact gradually emerges: the work of the phantom coincides in every respect with Freud's description of the death instinct. First of all, it has no energy of its own; it cannot be "abreacted," merely designated. Second, it pursues in silence its work of disarray. Let us add that the phantom is sustained by secreted words, invisible gnomes whose aim is to wreak havoc, from within the unconscious, in the coherence of logical progression. Finally, it gives rise to endless repetition and, more often than not, eludes rationalization.[34]

A theory of emotional occupation—of feelings transmitted not through empirical intersubjective encounter but secretly, through the repetition of words without energy: this sounds more like (to return to the two Radcliffe tropes with which we began this section) the cut-off hand than the transmission of feelings through tearful exchange. My point here is not to offer Abraham and Torok's theory as an explanation of the gothic but to note the similarities between its stories and the gothic's, between its scattered limbs and Radcliffe's weak and faded hands. Readers have often drawn parallels between gothic literature and psychoanalysis: most comparisons between the two modes have focused on their common fascination with the recovery and repetition of primal, illicit, uncanny material.[35] Perhaps these common materials, however, can be seen as effects of psychoanalysis's central debt to the gothic: a compulsion to tell often conflicting stories about feeling's origins in experience.

A turn to the father thus reveals, once again, the gothic novel's conflicted relationship to empirical explanation. Like the other accounts of how people get their feelings that this study has traced, *Udolpho*'s narratives claim conflicting origins. If we ask, is "the father" the origin of the daughter's feelings?, we must also ask, what would it mean to say so? That the daughter's feelings are the return of a repressed primal scene? That they reveal as the daughter's structural prehistory the Law of the Father? Or might "the father" merely serve as a way of naming feelings that seem simply to repeat? Could the story of a father-daughter relationship—or, for that matter, a *theory* of the transmission of the father's affects to the daughter—be a way of structuring the movement of feelings in precisely those contexts in which the movements of feelings appear to become untraceable? Like the nostalgic fading father we examined earlier, St. Aubert and the daughter who is the recipient of his feelings' returns are caught up in the novel's accounting for where its own conventions of extravagant feeling come from. We noted that the fading father of Chateau-le-Blanc derives some of his meaning from the chateau's fading tapestries: he is a figure for the book's aesthetic dilemmas. Emily and St. Aubert too are as figural as the cut-off, synecdochic hands that represent them in their tearful exchanges.[36] It might be useful to consider the final hand of the novel once again. As we noted, *Udolpho* ends by naming as its source the synecdochic "weak hand" of writing: the book claims to be authored only by a figure for authorship. Susan Stewart's remarks on narrative's fundamental inauthenticity, and its fundamental nostalgia, may be relevant here. For Stewart, fictional narrative constitutes itself as a repetition without origin: it advertises itself as an account of "what happened" when in fact there may be no "happened before"; it cuts itself off from the temporality of lived experience by declaring its own beginnings and endings. This disjunction makes fictional narrative impossibly nostalgic for the authenticity it lacks; it "leads to a generalized desire for origin, for nature, and for unmediated experience." For Stewart, "nostalgia is the repetition that mourns the inauthenticity of all repetition and denies the repetition's capacity to form identity."[37] The gothic novel, a highly conventional genre that knows its own lacks, may especially carry out a search for its origins. Embodied in St. Aubert and Emily, this search alternately mourns and reveals its own repetitions in the two narratives we have been tracing: one in which the daughter learns to experience emotions about her father, one in which the daughter is subject to the mysterious repetitions of his feelings. "The father" may be the source of feelings—and of the woman writer's gothic conventions—only insofar as he is a name that reveals the extent to which these things seem unlocatable, without source.

Gothic fiction and psychoanalysis are not alone in naming the father as the source of daughters' affective lives. The politics of feeling of the 1790's, which I invoked at the beginning of this chapter, included, of course, Wollstonecraft's feminism of feeling. For Wollstonecraft—as I discussed in Chapter 2—as for Radcliffe, it was crucial to name feelings as the source of women's suffering. To give an emotion a name is, as the participants in the Revolution debates knew, a highly political act. Emotion words can be used to dismiss another's political position—as when Burke called Price's views mere "enthusiasm"—but they can also call into being a new political landscape. To call a woman's feelings "sensibility," "terror," or—to choose a modern example—"anger" is to change what needs to be explained.[38] Feminism has persisted, since Wollstonecraft, in finding explanations for the affective dimension of women's suffering; and here feminist theory and the gothic novel have conspired together in naming the father. The gothic tells this tale, for example, in Mary Shelley's story of incest, *Matilda* (1819–20), in which the secret that the father bears—of his desire for his daughter—becomes the daughter's identity; while feminism has postulated that in bourgeois society daughters are always occupied and emotionally distorted by the rule of the father and the family he heads. The vicissitudes of the term "patriarchy" in feminism confirm, however, that using the father as a name and explanation for systemic suffering may also involve problems of reference, repetition, and nostalgia such as we've seen in *Udolpho*'s stories of the daughter's feelings. In feminist writing, the word "patriarchy" has often promised a lot: it "promises both to deliver the history of the relations between the sexes and to explain the form and function of male domination."[39] But as many feminist theorists have by now argued, the word is beset by problems. Does it refer to empirical fathers or to a system? Is patriarchy a structure or an event? Where does it come from? What exactly can it explain? Does it determine sexual interests, or is it determined by the interests of the sexes? Is "patriarchy," as many feminist theorists have argued, a highly problematic way of naming a complex system of relations with the single name of the father?

"It has been tempting to think," notes Rosalind Coward in *Patriarchal Precedents*, "that perhaps our inadequate means of understanding sexual relations occurs simply because we have lost or neglected a useful concept."[40] Feminist theory and history, as Coward's remark suggests, may sometimes have been as nostalgic in their search for an answer to the mystery of the persistence of gender inequality as the gothic novel has been in its own dilemmas. Thus, the gothic novel is not alone in coming up against the problem of naming in accounting for the origins of feelings. If the gothic novel suffers from a sense of the *under*determination of its extravagant feelings (the sense that they merely repeat), in psychoanalytic or feminist accounts of social life we may be grappling with feelings' *over*determination, attempting to sort out the multiple social and psychological factors that make family feelings what they are. But if the gothic novel suggests that the naming of feelings is a political gesture, it can also demonstrate that there may be virtue as well in a refusal to name. We might take a lesson from Ann Radcliffe's tendency in *The Mysteries of Udolpho* to discriminate endlessly in naming Emily's feelings that can "scarcely be called" by any given name (591): not because feelings belong to the realm of the unnameable, the unexplainable, but rather because a commitment to understanding daughters' feelings requires endless discrimination, a refusal to name prematurely. We should be wary of allowing the perpetuation of personal life to be explained away as "just feelings," or cast as a mystery that can be solved with a word.

Chapter 5

Lost in a Book

Jane Austen's *Persuasion*

In their accounting for the origins of feelings, several of the writers who appear in this study pondered whether a special source for feeling was to be found in books. The aesthetic theorists discussed at the beginning of the last chapter sought to determine whether the feelings derived from poetical fictions exceed the feelings of real life or are merely their pale phantoms. Charlotte Smith's poetry reveals the extent to which the melancholy passed on through reading and writing competes with the emotions caused by the accidents of life. Wordsworth began his poetic career by recording his emotional response to a woman poet's writing, imagining her, in turn, reading and weeping. *The Mysteries of Udolpho* perceives that the mind may be occupied territory. This perception is corroborated by the advice its gloomy patriarch, St. Aubert, gives to his daughter concerning reading: as the "best security against the contagion of folly and vice," he counsels her to "store" the "vacant mind" with "every part of elegant literature." St. Aubert's words are echoed in countless conduct books for women which, while they warn against novel reading, recommend the reading of poetry: "The mind is thus stored with a lasting treasure of sentiments and ideas."[1] Readers in the late eighteenth and early nineteenth centuries took seriously the emotions derived from books, both taking consolation in and deploring their effects. The notion that literary feelings can enter a reader and substantially disorder him or her can be found in a wide variety of registers—from the theoretical register of Wordsworth's Preface, where the poet worries about the pain of literary possession, to the pervasive, socially conscious concern, found in conduct books, educational treatises, and novels themselves, that novel reading is a seduction that reproduces fictive passions in its female readers' hearts.[2] Ambivalence about the emotions derived from books ran deep, as literary feeling could disappoint by being either too powerful or not powerful enough.

Jane Austen's *Persuasion* is a book that is interested in people's indebtedness to books, in the capacities of books to provide consolation, and in the adequacy of books to consciousness. The novel opens, for example, upon "Sir Walter Elliot, of Kellynch-hall" reading the entry under "Elliot of Kellynch-hall" in his favorite book, the Baronetage:

> Sir Walter Elliot, of Kellynch-hall, in Somersetshire, was a man who, for his own amusement, never took up any book but the Baronetage; there he found occupation for an idle hour, and consolation in a distressed one; there his faculties were roused into admiration and respect, by contemplating the limited remnant of the earliest patents; there any unwelcome sensations, arising from domestic affairs, changed naturally into pity and contempt, as he turned over the almost endless creations of the last century—and there, if every other leaf were powerless, he could read his own history with an interest which never failed—this was the page at which the favourite volume always opened:
>
> ELLIOT OF KELLYNCH-HALL[3]

Austen suggests that Elliot reads this book not only as an amusement, an idle occupation, but as "consolation." Reading the Baronetage can reroute "any unwelcome sensations arising from domestic affairs" into other feelings with other subjects. This paragraph asserts that a book can have such "powers"; but of course in this case those powers are the powers of vanity. Sir Walter is a particularly narcissistic reader, and the book confirms his own social superiority: reading arouses his feelings not into an Aristotelian "pity and terror" but rather into a snobbish "pity and contempt." The page that has the most power bears his own history. However, by presenting Sir Walter not simply with his family name but with virtually the same first words that meet our eyes when we open her book—"Elliot of Kellynch-hall"—Austen broaches the subject of what it is that attaches us to books in a way that embraces her own readers as well. Even in this perfect marriage of man and book, moreover, the adequacy of books is in question. The "book of books," as it is later called, proves insufficient as a record of personal catastrophe: Sir Walter must supplement the printed text of his family history "by inserting most accurately the day of the month on which he had lost his wife" (3).

Persuasion's ambivalent explorations of the powers of books might be situated within the context of debates that take place in England from the mid-eighteenth century on, especially debates about women and reading: about whether and in what ways women are particularly susceptible to the effects of reading, and the extent to which this susceptibility can be either dangerous or beneficial to women's minds. This is an issue that Austen explores, of course, in *Northanger Abbey*. In that novel, the reading of gothic romances often laughably exaggerates Catherine Morland's perceptions of reality, but it also renders her highly sensitive to some real social difficulties. I would like to argue that Austen takes up this issue in *Persuasion* as well, though in more oblique and phenomenological ways. *Persuasion* explores what it feels like to be a reader. It does so by connecting this feeling to what the presence of other people feels like. It explores, that is, the influence reading can have on one's mind by comparing it to the influence of one person's mind over another's.

The question of the influence of other minds figures most centrally in Anne Elliot's great act of submission to duty and propriety, her refusal of Captain Wentworth. She refuses him, persuaded that her "engagement [was] a wrong thing—indiscreet, improper, hardly capable of success, and not deserving it" (27). The duties to which Anne submits herself belong to the scheme of things outlined in the Baronetage her father loves to read—the preservation and perpetuation of the landed gentry through marriage. Anne submits, however, under no terrors, no parental threats and prohibitions. She gives in under the gentler ministrations of a friend, Lady Russell, who compensates for her family's indifference to her. Devoted to registering the repercussions of Anne's act of renunciation, *Persuasion* is about what it is like to be subject to the influences of others, and the novel conceives of this as particularly a women's predicament. (Indeed, one critic has argued that for contemporary readers the word "persuasion" would have resonated specifically with the question of parents' rights over the marriage of daughters.)[4] Concerned with the emotional repercussions of a woman's submission to duty, *Persuasion* thus continues the late eighteenth century's investigation of the origins and meanings of women's feelings. It ends with a famous debate between Anne Elliot and Captain Harville over the comparative strengths of men's and women's feelings, in which Anne links the strength of "woman's feelings" (233) to their social position. "It is, perhaps, our fate rather than our merit" to feel, she says: "We cannot help ourselves. We live at home, quiet, confined, and our feelings prey upon us. You are forced on exertion. You have always a profession, pursuits, business of some sort or other, to take you back into the world immediately, and continual occupation and change soon weakens impressions" (232). Both Anne's argument and her language—as she speaks of women's "fate" to feel, of feelings that "prey"—place this conversation squarely in the tradition of debates over women's feelings in the late eighteenth century, in particular the sensibility debates of women's sentimental poetry.

Austen's interest in the subjects that Anne and Harville debate, however, derives most particularly from the concerns that her genre, the novel of manners, has with the traffic in men's and women's feelings. Austen's novels would seem to announce themselves as enemies of the emotional extravagances of the gothic discussed in the last chapter. Sir Walter Scott, whose 1816 essay on Austen did much to define the novel of manners by heralding a new "style of novel," distinguished the new style from the old romance by contrasting "the difference . . . of the sentiments." While the romance novel propelled its hero or heroine through a series of outlandish adventures and vicissitudes of emotions never found in "ordinary life," the new kind of novel "affords" its readers "a pleasure nearly allied with the experience of their own social habits." For the "excitements" of the "pure, elevated, and romantic" sentiments of the romance, the new novel substitutes "the art of copying from nature as she really exists in the common walks of life, and presenting to the reader, instead of the splendid scenes of an imaginary world, a correct and striking representation of that which is daily taking place around him."[5]

The novel of manners, as Scott intimates, is crucially concerned with the pleasures of its readers' "social habits." The genre's innovation is its microscopic and seemingly realistic attention to behaviors, bodies, and signs of feeling. It imagines a world in which social habits—rather than power, rank, or class—themselves define and delimit the social order. Feelings are the social noise of the novel of manners: they are the environment that makes possible the commerce between people and the relationships that constitute society. This vision of feelings' role in society-making is reminiscent of Hume's essay "Of the Delicacy of

Taste and Passion," which I discussed in Chapter 2. In that essay, Hume encouraged his readers to manage their emotions by channeling a "delicacy of passion," which heightens the emotional vicissitudes of an ungoverned life, into a "delicacy of taste" in which the emotions are roused strongly only by the beauties of art and manners. For Hume, such exercise of the passions improves society by weaning the individual from vulgar passions. An extravagant emotional sensitivity is thus made socially productive, and thus allows society itself to be conceived in a restrictive sense; "society" designates a polite community of people who appreciate manners. The "society" that novelists like Austen, Edgeworth, Inchbald, Brunton, and Burney imagine is often similarly restrictive. That Scott—and other readers after him—takes Austen's novels to be representing "ordinary life" and its "common walks" indicates that he has already assented to the novels' aesthetic and political claims: to make the romantic lives of young women of the lower gentry seem ordinary and common. The promise of such an "ordinary life," in which style and morality come together, was surely an attractive one in early nineteenth-century England, when in public life—as we will discuss in the next chapter—style and morality often seemed at odds. In the novel of manners as in Hume's vision, emotion improves polite society not principally by being restrained but by being trained to flourish in certain domains. In the novel that domain is, above all, romantic love. In the conclusion of his essay on Austen, Scott articulates the productive, "improving" nature of even a strong and unhappy romantic passion, when he worries that the "new style" of novelist has dethroned "Cupid" from his rightful place in the novel. In preferring prudent matches over romantic ones, he suggests, the new novelists may be "substitut[ing] more mean, more sordid, and more selfish motives of conduct, for the romantic feelings which their predecessors perhaps fanned into too powerful a flame." Individuals, he claims, are led to "what is honourable, dignified, and disinterested" by the experience of romantic love, making them fitter members of polite society:

Even the habitual indulgence of feelings totally unconnected with ourself and our own immediate interest, softens, graces, and amends the human mind; and after the pain of disappointment is past, those who survive . . . are neither less wise nor less worthy members of society for having felt, for a time, the influence of a passion which has been well qualified as the "tenderest, noblest, and best."[6]

For Scott as for Hume, a passion is a social good—even when it ends miserably; for Scott the place where the benefits of romantic love are best exhibited is the novel.

If the novels of manners of Scott's contemporaries are concerned with calibrating feelings to "social habits," then, they do so not by discouraging extravagant feelings but by routing them along improving paths. Thus while it may be tempting to stress the "difference of sentiments" between the gothic novel and the Regency novel of manners, both genres—in spite of their different emotional registers—do similar work. If the gothic novel's emotional excesses are linked—as I argued in the last chapter—to its philosophical accounting for feelings' origins, the social form of feeling in the novel of manners is inseparable from those feelings' place at the center of the novels' epistemological dramas. For the novel of manners puts feelings into motion by making them difficult to know. The subject of Austen's novels, for example, is the arduousness of knowing both one's own feelings and the feelings of others—of knowing, as Anne Elliot wonders about Captain Wentworth, "how were his sentiments to be read?" (60). Austen's novels thus put the drive to know feelings that we have been exploring in this book into social circulation. Moments of strong feeling often occasion or are occasioned by moments of certain and sudden knowing: we might think of Elinor Dashwood running out of the room and uncharacteristically bursting into tears she thinks will never cease when she learns that Edward Ferrars is free to love her.[7] Such moments, I would suggest, reveal in Austen a fundamental skepticism about the extent to which her heroines can know their own and their lovers' feelings.

The case of *Emma* is helpful here. Emma believes herself to be "in the secret of everybody's feelings," but she is ignorant and grievously mistaken about everybody's feelings, including her own. Emma has, of course, her moment of revelation in which she realizes simultaneously her love for Mr. Knightley and her error about everyone else's feelings. This moment is astonishing for its speed—it has the speed of an arrow:

Why was it so much worse that Harriet should be in love with Mr. Knightley, than with Frank Churchill? Why was the evil so dreadfully increased by Harriet's having some hope of a return? It darted through her, with the speed of an arrow, that Mr. Knightley must marry no one but herself!

Her own conduct, as well as her own heart, was before her in the same few minutes.[8]

Austen's last sentence confirms her novels' goal of getting matters of the heart and matters of conduct to work in concert: a knowledge of one's passions corrects one's conduct. But why must Emma's knowledge of her own feelings arrive with such unnatural speed? It could be—and has been—argued that the velocity of this moment of revelation suits Emma because it matches the speed with which she invents deluded stories for people: for an imaginative "mind like her's,"[9] the hint of a rival for Mr. Knightley's affections is enough to reveal the truth. However, Austen's language also suggests what an unnatural shock it is for Emma to know her love. The arrow alludes not only to the speed of the revelation but to the very god Cupid whom Scott worried her novels had dethroned in favor of prudence and ordinariness, and Austen's recourse to an outdated and uncharacteristic figure to describe this revelation implies rhetorically that Emma's knowledge of love is alien to her. Emma's new knowledge of her heart and others' must be truth, Austen's arrow seems to say, because it has the rhetorical form of truth. It overturns her experience, rather than being verified by it. Hence the speed and violence of this figure. Emma's arrow is an example of what Martha Nussbaum has described—following ancient Stoics—as a cataleptic impression: it is an impression with the appearance of a soul-wounding certainty, reassuring the skeptic with its seemingly incontrovertible self-evidence.[10] Emma's knowledge is a swift pain that comes from without. That the revelation takes this form reveals how natural it would be for Emma to go on not knowing her own feelings. In a world in which people express their feelings through word games and charades, make love to one woman to conceal their passion for another, a world that simultaneously flatters Emma's opinions and limits her vision, it is indeed easier for her not to know than to know. As Susan Morgan says of some of Austen's heroines, they "cannot be described as making the traditional progressive journey from self-deception to understanding."[11] While the novel of manners would seem to be about learning to make that journey, it dramatizes its difficulties; Emma's experience suggests that there may be no way to "know" her feelings without a swift pain that blanks out everything else she thought she knew: "—Every other part of her mind was disgusting."[12]

Emma's flash of insight illuminates a predicament that almost all Austen's heroines find themselves in concerning their knowledge either of their own feelings or of their beloved's. It focuses our attention on the conjunction in Austen's fiction between a commitment to feelings' social virtues and a skepticism about knowing them. It also makes it possible to see this conjunction as determined by gender, by questions about what, and how, women can know. The woman in the novel of manners must be looking for signs of love and also be blind to them. Blinded by her education, the constraints of courtship, and the constraints of form, she must wish to know feelings without knowing that she knows them. The situation of woman as knower may be exemplified by a conversation in Elizabeth Inchbald's *A Simple Story* (1791). The heroine, Matilda, is hiding out in the house of her estranged and vengeful father. Her advisor, Mr. Sandford, tells her that he believes her father's uncharacteristic good spirits are due to his knowledge of her presence on his estate. Lord Elmwood has allowed Matilda to live there, but he forbids her to come near him: Sandford's point is that if Lord Elmwood's knowledge of his daughter's presence is the cause of his good spirits, he cannot actually know that, or admit it to himself. Matilda declares, "If he does but think of me with tenderness . . . I am recompensed." When Sandford asks "But how are you to know he has these kind thoughts, while he gives you no proof of them?" Matilda answers, "No, Mr. Sandford, but *supposing* we could know them without the proof."[13] Sandford, who is, appropriately, a Jesuit priest, finds Matilda's supposition lacking: he disavows the possibility of such a knowledge of feelings without proof. Two visions of knowledge are thus pitted against one another. This conversation between the Jesuit priest and his youthful female pupil suggests that a conflict between two epistemologies of feeling may correspond to differences in privilege, authority, and gender. Matilda's supposition—being able to know the state of her father's feelings about her without empirical evidence—is a wishful fantasy that is born of an extreme deprivation: she is in her father's house, but she cannot see him. This combination of domestic proximity and inequality, blindness and desire, is paradigmatic of woman's position in the domestic novel of manners, from Inchbald's Matilda to Austen's Anne Elliot.

Persuasion dramatizes the position of the woman as knower in the novel of manners by presenting us with a heroine who seems to resist knowing what she doesn't already know, and who experiences knowledge of others' wishes and desires as a form of oppressive persuasion. If eighteenth-century writers suggested that the name for the state of knowing someone else's feelings was "sympathy," Austen suggests here that it may feel more like persuasion. The treatment of the feeling of knowledge and the knowledge of feeling in *Persuasion* is fundamentally shaped by the aesthetic qualities that seem to set this Austen novel apart from the others, the qualities that make up what is frequently called the novel's lyricism. People are drawn to discussing *Persuasion* in relation to romantic lyric poetry. Its emphasis on memory and subjectivity has been called Wordsworthian, its emotional tone has been likened to Shelley and Keats and its epistemological strategies compared to Coleridge's conversation poems; its modernity has been hinted at through allusions to the lyric fiction of Virginia Woolf.[14] The concept of the "lyric" can usefully describe certain aspects of the novel— its emphasis on loss, its emphasis on temporality and repetition instead of plot, and its interest in voice and in noise. But I will, in addition, be defining the lyric in *Persuasion* as a particular way of rendering consciousness's apprehension of the social.

This discussion of *Persuasion* begins with Austen's treatment of the pressures of other people. It will next consider how she represents knowledge of the beloved, and then the influence of books.

༂

Persuasion is striking for the ways in which the presences of other people are apprehended as insistently sensory phenomena. Anne Elliot's sister, Mary Musgrove, who has more of the "Elliot pride" (88) than does Anne, and who is constantly fretting that her in-laws do not give her the "precedence" that is due to her, registers their claims as a physical pressure. She complains after a dinner party:

It is so very uncomfortable, not having a carriage of one's own. Mr. and Mrs. Musgrove took me, and we were so crowded! They are both so very large, and take up so much room! And Mr. Musgrove always sits forward. So, there was I, crowded into the back seat with Henrietta and Louisa. And I think it very likely that my illness today may be owing to it. (39)

Mary feels the Musgroves' proximity to be a threat, their bodily presence capable of making her ill. Anne, however, also frequently finds herself crowded in by other people, in rooms, on furniture. She feels "astonishment" at finding herself, at the Harvilles' house in Lyme, in "rooms so small as none but those who invite from the heart could think capable of accommodating so many" (98). She is crowded on a sofa by Wentworth and the "substantial" Mrs. Musgrove. Perhaps the best emblem for Anne's tendency to be swamped by family duties is the moment in chapter 9 (to which I will return) in which, as she busily attends to one of her nephews, another one fixes himself upon her back. Her family is literally crawling all over her.

Families, and the Musgrove family in particular, are often represented in terms of the space they take up, the noise they make. Austen describes the Musgroves at Christmas as a collection of noises, a room full of "chattering girls," "riotous . . . boys holding high revel,"

> the whole completed by a roaring Christmas fire, which seemed determined to be heard, in spite of all the noise of the others. Charles and Mary also came in, of course, during their visit; and Mr. Musgrove made a point of paying his respects to Lady Russell, and sat down close to her for ten minutes, talking in a very raised voice, but, from the clamour of the children on his knees, generally in vain. It was a fine family-piece. (134)

The emphasis on family noise may remind us of the representation of the Price family at Portsmouth in *Mansfield Park*. To the "delicate and nervous" Fanny, the noise at Portsmouth is "the greatest misery of all": "Here, every body was noisy, every voice was loud. . . . Whatever was wanted, was halloo'd for, and the servants halloo'd out their excuses from the kitchen. The doors were in constant banging, the stairs were never at rest, nothing was done without a clatter, nobody sat still, and nobody could command attention when they spoke."[15] But in *Mansfield Park*, noise is attached to one particular social sphere: it underlines the novel's need to separate the superior Fanny Price from her distinctly inferior family. In contrast to the heavily weighted description of the Price family noise, Austen's description of the Musgrove noise is rather detached. In *Persuasion*, noise is everywhere, vaguely menacing but at the same time strangely neutral, and even the best of families, such as the Harvilles, are perceived as crowds. Domestic spaces, moreover, have a way of impressing themselves upon us in this novel as containers of bodies as well. Furniture often seems the register of the pressures that the characters tend to feel from other people. The furniture of the Musgroves' drawing room has grown shabby "under the influence of four summers and two children" (37). Mrs. Croft is especially recommended to the Elliots as a tenant because "a lady, without a family, was the very best preserver of furniture in the world" (22). And Anne, using a word that makes several strange appearances in this novel, thinks of her house occupied by others in this way: "All the precious rooms and furniture, groves, and prospects, beginning to own other eyes and other *limbs*" (47).

It is not simply other people's bodily presence that conditions mental life in this novel; mental life seems crowded in by bodily life in general. In chapter 8, we find the estranged lovers Anne and Wentworth, divided from each other by the physical form—"no insignificant barrier"—of Mrs. Musgrove, whose body, Austen declares, "was of a comfortable substantial size, infinitely more fitted by nature to express good cheer and good humour, than tenderness and sentiment" (68). Anne and Wentworth are listening to her "large fat sighings over the destiny of a son, whom alive nobody had cared for." Austen comments: "Personal size and mental sorrow have certainly no necessary proportions. A large bulky figure has as good a right to be in deep affliction, as the most graceful set of limbs in the world. But, fair or not fair, there are unbecoming conjunctions, which reason will patronize in vain,—which taste cannot tolerate,—which ridicule will seize" (68). This passage has baffled readers as a piece of gratuitous viciousness. It is vicious; Austen applies the language of neoclassical aesthetic judgment ("unbecoming conjunctions . . . taste cannot tolerate") to Mrs. Musgrove's expressive body, as if she were a bad poem or book. The result is not far from the physical snobbery of Sir Walter Elliot: deeply offended and disgusted by the weatherbeaten looks of Navy men, Sir Walter deems them "not fit to be seen," and to spare the world the sight of them, opines, "It is a pity they are not knocked on the head at once, before they reach Admiral Baldwin's age" (20). But if extreme physical snobbery has already been represented and ridiculed *within* the novel in the characters of Sir Walter and Elizabeth Elliot, finding the narrator raising similar questions suggests that a serious inquiry of some kind about the relationship between personal form and mental life is taking place here. In spite of the rational disclaimers of the first two sentences, the last seems to be admitting that there are, in fact, "necessary proportions" between body and mind. The notion that there might be *no* connection between body and mind seems a foreclosed option—foreclosed even by Austen's use of metonymy. By the second sentence of this passage, there are no heads, no mental spaces for mental sorrow to take place in: "deep affliction" is located in either a "large bulky figure" or a "graceful set of limbs."[16]

The dislocation of head from limbs here recalls the one-line, one-paragraph verdict on Louisa Musgrove's accident at Lyme: "Louisa's limbs had escaped. There was no injury but to the head" (112). The phrasing of this assertion puts into question our sense of priorities. Again it sounds like something Sir Walter—always more concerned for people's appearances than for their inward states—might say. But, as is often the case in Austen, certain ideas are simultaneously repudiated and raised as serious suggestions; and heads, as in Austen's metonymy, Louisa's accident, and Sir Walter's quip about sailors, seem somewhat cavalierly treated, and perilously at risk in this novel. The humorous Admiral Croft, on surmising that there is some relationship between Wentworth's part in Louisa's fall and his supposed romantic interest in her, exclaims: "Ay, a very bad business indeed.—A new sort of way this, for a young fellow to be making love, by breaking his mistress's head! . . . —This is breaking a head and giving a plaister truly!" (126). And in a strange figure toward the end of the novel Austen comments, on Anne's deferral of making public the crimes of Mr. William Elliot, "Mr. Elliot's character, like the Sultaness Scheherazade's head, must live another day" (229). Austen repeatedly warns that the rights of heads to bear thoughts and feelings of their own may be precarious.

Thus, in *Persuasion*, the spaces, bodily attitudes, and manners that serve as clues and proofs of feelings in the novel of courtship are productive here only of a feeling of claustrophobia. The question of "persuasion," of the pressures that one mind can put on another, assumes, at the phenomenal level, less gentle or at least more physical forms. The novel repeatedly figures an acute awareness of others, an exaggerated sense of the contingency of mind. The cumulative effect of this hypersensitivity to the presence of others makes us aware of the oppressiveness of this social environment. As the presence of others is phenomenalized, it seems to become absolutely pervasive, extending to reach all the ways in which mental life is crowded in by the presence of other people, even by other bodies. The text's emphasis on the phenomenal nature of the pressures of others is naturally accompanied by an emphasis on sensation as the form of apprehension of these pressures. Readers have often pointed out that knowledge of the outside world seems to make its way into *Persuasion* more than into any of

Austen's other novels. There are allusions to specific dates, military events, glimpses of people from all walks of life—farmers, boatmen, and nurses. What interests me, however, is the way in which the novel foregrounds the sensory nature of this knowledge. In the disquisition on noises that Austen interjects right after her picture of the noisy family-piece at Uppercross, she highlights the sensory, and the pleasurable or unpleasurable, aspects of noise:

> Every body has their taste in noises as well as in other matters; and sounds are quite innoxious, or most distressing, by their sort rather than their quantity. When Lady Russell, not long afterwards, was entering Bath on a wet afternoon, and driving through the long course of streets from the Old Bridge to Camden-place, amidst the dash of other carriages, the heavy rumble of carts and drays, the bawling of newsmen, muffin-men and milkmen, and the ceaseless clink of pattens, she made no complaint. No, these were noises which belonged to winter pleasures; her spirits rose under their influence. (135)

In this novel, in which overhearing is such an important way of knowing (in the hedgerow scene, for example, and in the climactic scene at the White Hart), noise and sound have special prominence. Spoken language is often apprehended as sheer sound. This passage is an urban pastoral in the tradition of Swift, where instead of pastoral sounds the ear is met with the sounds of the town, which are ranged in a list, from "the dash of other carriages" to "the ceaseless clink of pattens." Both the listing and the conjunction of sound with the word "ceaseless" (a conjunction that will occur again) evoke an atmosphere of continuous, unhierarchized sound. I will return to the topic of noise later.

જી

The courtship between Anne and Wentworth provides Austen with an especially vivid arena for exploring what the presence of other people feels like. Anne's experience of her gradual reunion with Wentworth takes particularly sensational forms. They are reunited through a series of encounters that Anne experiences as shocks to her consciousness. Their courtship takes its sensuous forms precisely *because* it is a re-courtship: the shocks are not the shocks of newness impressing themselves upon a "virgin" consciousness. Having already "done" this before, and with the same man, Anne substantially revises the *tabula rasa* quality of most heroines of the novel of courtship, including

Austen's own, for whom love and courtship are new sensations. (Fanny Burney's youthful and innocent Camilla, to take an example, not only doesn't seem to know what she is doing, but she seems not to remember very much from one moment to the next. Her courtship consists of blind repetitions of embarrassing moments.) The nature of Anne's and Wentworth's courtship is the result of its taking place within a context heavy with memory and repetition. Anne is always "resuming an agitation" (60), experiencing a "revival of former pain" (30).

The temporal structure of the plot, its concern with the reunion of lovers whose actions and feelings are always in reference to an earlier courtship, fundamentally shapes both Anne's ways of knowing and the novel's understanding of the origins of feelings. It is the existence of this past desire—and past submission to prohibition—that makes Anne a "romantic" person today: "How eloquent could Anne Elliot have been,—how eloquent, at least, were her wishes on the side of early warm attachment, and a cheerful confidence in futurity, against that over-anxious caution which seems to insult exertion and distrust Providence!—She had been forced into prudence in her youth, she learned romance as she grew older—the natural sequel of an unnatural beginning" (30). "Romance" in this context would seem to mean, roughly speaking, "feelings first," as well as all the other things we mean by "romance." But in this novel romance does not mean spontaneous, innocent feeling: Anne and Wentworth's early involvement is discussed rather perfunctorily: "He had nothing to do, and she had hardly any body to love" (26). Romance comes late, is about belatedness: Austen's narrative stresses that feelings may have "unnatural" origins which defy our conventional expectations of the effects of maturation and chronological time.

In *Persuasion*, the realm of feelings is the realm of repetitions, of things happening within a strong context of memory. Revising the plot of the origin of romance, Austen's novel also revises an empiricist account of the experience of sensation. The sensational quality of Anne's and Wentworth's encounters arises not from the newness of stimuli but rather from stimuli that work on a consciousness already prepared by memories of earlier sensations. Anne's conscious recollection seems to function the way Walter Benjamin, following Freud, describes the function of consciousness: formed for the protection against stimuli rather than the reception of stimuli, consciousness serves as a protective shield that puts its energies against energies from the outside world. In *Beyond the Pleasure Principle*, Freud models the origins of consciousness on that of a primitive organism whose exterior develops into a "crust" "baked through" by stimulation. Consciousness, continues Benjamin (quoting Freud), is "located in a part of the cortex which is 'so blown out by the effect of the stimulus' that it offers the most favorable situation for the reception of stimuli."[17] The job of consciousness is to register energies from the outside world as shocks; the more readily it does so, the less likely they are to have a traumatic effect. This account of consciousness and sensation consists of paradoxes: what allows one to resist stimuli from the outside world is precisely the condition of having been traumatized by them before; at the same time, what allows one to go on registering outside stimuli is the condition that makes one resistant to them.

We can perhaps sharpen our sense of the ways in which the impressions Wentworth makes on Anne are conditioned by repetition and recollection by comparing them to Wentworth's effects on Mrs. Musgrove. For Wentworth is a blast from the past not only for Anne but for the Musgrove family as well. He activates a sense of loss for their deceased and troublesome son, when Mrs. Musgrove remembers that Wentworth was the very name of the captain her son had spoken of in the only letters he'd ever written:

In each letter he had spoken well of his captain; but yet, so little were they in the habit of attending to such matters, so unobservant and incurious were they as to the names of men or ships, that it had made scarcely any impression at the time; and that Mrs. Musgrove should have been suddenly struck, this very day, with a recollection of the name of Wentworth, as connected with her son, seemed one of those extraordinary bursts of mind which do sometimes occur. (51)

This "burst of mind" spurred by the name "Wentworth" throws Mrs. Musgrove "into greater grief" for Richard "than she had known on first hearing of his death" (51). Austen's interest in memory and feeling is stressed here by the experimental attitude she takes toward Mrs. Musgrove's recollection. She puts it into the category of "bursts of mind," a curiosity of science or philosophy. The narrative point of view here is neither that of an authoritative narrator nor that of any particular character. It is rather that of a speculative observer: Mrs. Musgrove's flash of recollection "*seemed* one of those extraordinary bursts." Anne, of course, has also to cope with sensations arising from hearing the name of Wentworth repeated so often (52). However, Mrs. Musgrove's burst of mind is a moment of *mémoire involuntaire*, a random, unforeseeable moment when something that barely entered consciousness the first time around pops into consciousness, bringing with it an emotional force that belongs not to itself but to its associations. As for Mrs. Musgrove here, for Anne impressions typically take the form of repetitions. But Anne's memory is the opposite of Mrs. Musgrove's; she practices sustained and conscious recollection. Of the memory of pain she says, "when pain is over, the remembrance of it often becomes a pleasure" (184). Of all of her experiences it might be said, as it is said of her stay at Uppercross, "she left it all behind her; all but the recollection that such things had been" (123). Anne leaves very little behind her.

Indeed, Anne is often so occupied with her own rumination and recollection that impressions from the outside seem to have a hard time finding their way in. This is not to say that Anne seems self-absorbed; rather, the way Austen frequently represents Anne's consciousness is *as absorption*. While many readers have stressed Anne's acute perceptions of the outside world, I'm interested in the way in which Austen's representation of Anne's innerness takes the form of an *inward*ness that oddly seems only penetrated from the outside with difficulty. A locution that Austen uses frequently when Anne is addressed by the outside world is "Anne found herself": in the carriage on the way home from Lyme, Anne "found herself" being addressed by Wentworth (117). At Uppercross she "found herself" having the child removed from her back (80). This phrase has a way of suggesting that what precedes these moments of contact is a state somewhat like unconsciousness: it is an absorption within. The phrase has consequences for our sense of Anne as a knower: she appears as someone who does not want to know anything but what she already knows. At the concert hall, for example: "These were thoughts, with their attendant visions, which occupied and flurried her too much to leave her any power of observation; and she passed along the room without having a glimpse of him, without even trying to discern him" (186). In the climactic scene at the White Hart hotel, Anne, absorbed in her thoughts, becomes "gradually sensible" that Captain Harville is addressing her (231). Sensations from the outside are often surprises, like physical shocks, as when she is "electrified" by Mrs. Croft's suddenly saying something of interest (49). It is above all, as many of these examples suggest, contacts with Wentworth that take these sensory, sensational forms. Their renewed courtship takes place through moments of physical contact—as when Anne finds herself handed into the carriage—which are both erotic and strangely intrusive, described as impingements from the outside world. It seems fitting that their whole re-courtship is framed by the fact that Wentworth's family—and Wentworth himself—have taken over Anne's house.

This combination of eroticism, claustrophobia, and sensation can be found above all in the scene in chapter 9 in which Wentworth removes the child from Anne's back. Maria Edgeworth singled out this passage in a letter, drawing attention to its surprising tactility: "The love and lover admirably well-drawn: don't you see Captain Wentworth, or rather *don't you in her place feel him* taking the boistrous child off her back as she kneels by the sick boy on the sofa?" (my emphasis).[18] This scene constitutes a pivotal moment. It seems on the one hand a moment where Wentworth asserts his potentially liberating role in Anne's life, by freeing her from the claustrophobia of family duties, actually removing a burden from her back. But the agitation it produces in the "nervous," "overcome" Anne ("such a confusion of varying, but very painful agitation, as she could not recover from" [80, 81]) seems to come not only from Anne's confusion over Wentworth's motives—his coming to her aid, his attempts to avoid her thanks—but also from the sheer physicality of this moment of contact. Wentworth removes a physical pressure from her back, but also creates a physical sensation there, at a part of the body where we are most vulnerable. In our semiotics of knowledge, we associate knowledge of others conceptually with vision, with facing forward toward the object of apprehension: to have this moment of contact at the back stresses how removed Anne's experience of Wentworth is from an everyday knowledge of another's presence.

Organized around moments such as these, the structure of Anne and Wentworth's relationship produces many of the aspects of the text we evaluate as "lyric." Austen's depiction of their courtship stresses sensory experience, touch, sound; Anne's knowledge of the beloved is organized into heightened moments of "shock." Anne and Wentworth's courtship allows Austen to conduct a typically lyric investigation of the claims and resistances to the outside world. The text's organization of experience into heightened moments of shock might recall for us Benjamin's discussion of the experience of "shock" as the condition of possibility for the production of nineteenth-century lyric poetry in his essay on Baudelaire. For Benjamin, the modern world—and he is specifically writing in this essay about the experience of being surrounded by the urban crowd—is fundamentally unassimilable for "poetic experience" unless consciousness meets it as discrete shock-like encounters. We tend to think of the romantic and postromantic lyric as a mode that involves the repression or exclusion of the social; for Benjamin, lyric is a mode of registering the social. It is this lyric mode, this way of parrying the shocks of social experience, that the Austen novel and its contemporary, the romantic lyric, might share.

Because of the way in which Austen represents Anne's consciousness, the presence of her lover is apprehended as invasive, much as the presence of others is. This may seem surprising, since to some extent *Persuasion* conceives of Wentworth, and the realm of romantic love he represents, as an alternative to the pressures of other people. We could, perhaps, see this as a strategy that attempts to reconcile or resolve a conflict in the novel between Anne's submission to duty in refusing Wentworth in the past (which Anne, at least, maintains to the end of the novel was the right thing to do), and her fulfillment of her own desires in the present by marrying him.[19] Indeed, Austen seems to break down the distinction between persuasions from without and internal states and desires by, for example, frequently using the word "persuasion" to signify either external forces or inner feelings. Anne, for example, feels the "persuasion" of having pleased the despondent Captain Benwick with her conversation about poetry (100). And later, Austen reveals the "internal persuasions" that lead Elizabeth to decide not to invite her relatives to dinner (219). And Austen renders Anne's experience of Wentworth in such a way that suggests that love itself is a form of persuasion. At the end of the novel, Wentworth acknowledges Anne's influence over him in terms of "the perfect, unrivalled hold" her mind "possessed over his own" (242).

But if Austen's lyric mode helps to resolve the conflict between pressures from without and internal desires, it does so only by simultaneously highlighting how thoroughly consciousness is conditioned by the presence of others, *and* representing a kind of consciousness that is constituted *as* resistance to outside influence—much like Freud's "baked crust," or the glossy hazelnut that Wentworth ironically holds out to Louisa Musgrove as an illustration of firmness of mind (88).

There are moments in *Persuasion* that reveal the proximity of Benjamin's "shock" to another romantic aesthetic of trauma, the sublime. Anne's crucial encounters with Wentworth are accompanied by overwhelming moments of access to the outside world. These moments often seem claustrophobic, moments when she is crowded in by or at least surrounded by her awareness of her environment. At Anne's first meeting with Wentworth, as "a thousand feelings" rush in on her, she has the impression that "the room seemed full—full of persons and voices" (59). Anne experiences Wentworth's sudden presence as something that ushers in acute awareness not only of him but of the presence of all around her. This "all" loses its normal perceptual form—individual persons who speak particular utterances—and turns into bloated abstractions. "Persons" are separated from "voices."

As the novel progresses, Anne's moments of shock and inundation increasingly take a typically sublime turn: a trauma from without is parried and inverted to become part of a power within. What before seemed to bring an inundation by the outside world now becomes part of her resistance to it. In the Octagon Room at the concert hall in Bath, a wash of noise signals her subjectivity's dominion over the outside world: "in spite of the agitated voice in which [Wentworth's speech] had been uttered, and in spite of all the various noises of the room, the almost ceaseless slam of the door, and ceaseless buzz of persons walking through, [Anne] had distinguished every word" (183). Here too, heightened awareness of Wentworth's presence ushers in as well a heightened awareness of all that is not Wentworth, a room full of persons and voices. As is often the case in *Persuasion*, sensory experience is rendered primarily in terms of aural interference. But here, the narrator impresses these noises upon us in order to assert that Anne can subordinate them. The sounds of the room are reduced to ceaseless (the word is repeated), abstract, continuous sound, affirming the capacity of mind, even as it has been traumatized by the rushing in of sensations, to reduce the external world to a blur. These moments of shock suggest that the more Anne appears resistant to the outside world, the more she knows: these moments are crucial to her reunion with Wentworth. The outside world, however, never goes entirely away. When, reunited at last, Anne and Wentworth retire to the gravel walk, it might seem that the outside world intrudes into the text only to affirm the characters' absorption in each other:

And there, as they slowly paced the gradual ascent, heedless of every group around them, seeing neither sauntering politicians, bustling housekeepers, flirting girls, nor nursery maids and children, could they indulge in those retrospections and acknowledgements . . . which were so poignant and so ceaseless in interest. (241)

Anne and Wentworth are no longer in a crowded concert room but rather in a more expansive public space: the outside world gets bigger and more populous even as they become more enclosed in each other. The list of urban characters here is reminiscent of Austen's earlier urban pastoral of the sounds of Bath (135). The listing serves to stress that a sense of the presence of other people does not go away: it maintains, as in the earlier "sounds of Bath" passage, its continuous, one-thing-after-another form. The progress that organizes the list—from politicians to housekeepers to flirting girls to infants—might seem to follow a descending scale of political importance, though from an early nineteenth-century woman's perspective, this list may not be descending in its claims to attention. The appearance here, however, of the word "ceaseless," previously linked to the "white noise" of the world, signals the inversion that has occurred. Here, what is "ceaseless" are not the noises of the outside world but the absorptions of love.

༄

I'd like to return now to the question of the value of the literary in *Persuasion* that I raised at the beginning of this chapter. If we read *Persuasion* in part for its lyric pleasures, what do the characters in the novel read for? How are reading's pleasures allied—in Sir Walter Scott's terms—to the pleasures of their "social habits"? Austen's Sir Walter is not the only reader in the Elliots' world. Even Mary Musgrove seems to read: she enjoys her stay at Lyme in part because she gets so many books at the library, "and changed them so often" (130). Elizabeth Elliot's rejection of the books Lady Russell lends her is surely a sign of her complete apostasy (215). But Austen herself sometimes appears to reject the notion that a taste for reading accompanies a higher moral sense, a deeper emotional sensitivity. Captain Wentworth seems to think that because Captain Benwick is "a reading man" (182), he must be subject to deep mental sufferings and long-lived feelings: "He considered his disposition as of the sort which must suffer heavily, uniting strong feelings with quiet, serious, and retiring manners, and a decided taste for reading" (97). Captain Wentworth is of course wrong about Benwick, who quickly overcomes the loss of Fanny Harville to fall in love with Louisa Musgrove. Books do not prepare or extend the psyche's receptivity to pain; they do not supplement or aid memory. Nor, as Anne Elliot discovers, does literature always provide consolation. On the walk to Winthrop in chapter 10, Anne mediates her enjoyment of the autumn day, "repeating to herself some few of the thousand poetical descriptions extant of autumn, that season of peculiar and inexhaustible influence on the mind of taste and tenderness, that season which has drawn from every poet, worthy of being read, some attempt at description, or some lines of feeling. She occupied her mind as much as possible in such like musings and quotations" (84). When she overhears a disturbing conversation between Wentworth and Louisa, however, "Anne could not immediately fall into a quotation again" (85).

But Austen's most condemning and grotesque suggestions about the literary concern Louisa Musgrove, whose conversion to literature seems the effect of a fall not into quotation but onto her head: "The idea of Louisa Musgrove turned into a person of literary taste . . . was amusing, but she had no doubt of its being so. The day at Lyme, the fall from the Cobb, might influence her health, her nerves, her courage, her character, to the end of her life" (167). Louisa, recovered, is later described as a kind of semivegetable, responsive only to violent sensory stimuli—and poetry: "She is altered: there is no running or jumping about, no laughing or dancing; it is quite different. If one happens only to shut the door a little hard, she starts and wriggles like a young dab chick in the water; and Benwick sits at her elbow, reading verses, or whispering to her, all day long" (218). Here, in the figure of Louisa Musgrove, the novel's meditations on consciousness, sensation, and literature begin to come together. Louisa is now the opposite of the hazelnut that Wentworth held up to her as an image of firmness of mind. She has no "baked crust" of consciousness to parry sensations from the outside world. The "slam of the door" that Anne was able to subordinate in the Octagon Room works on Louisa as a physical trauma. Louisa falls into literature because it is all she can take.

The only people in *Persuasion* who have satisfying relations to books are men. Both Sir Walter Elliot and Captain Wentworth find pleasure and consolation in reading books that mark their own place in national history, Sir Walter in the Baronetage, and Wentworth in the Navy List, a "precious volume" he cradles in his hands (66). While men can find their past in books of public chronicle, women, like Anne Elliot, can turn only to personal memory, for which there is no book. Not only Baronetages and Navy Lists exclude women from finding consolation in books. In the climactic debate between Anne Elliot and Captain Harville about the comparative strengths and duration of the feelings of both sexes, Harville appeals to books as his witnesses: "If I had such a memory as Benwick, I could bring you fifty quotations in a moment on my side of the argument, and I do not think I ever opened a book in my life which had not something to say upon woman's inconstancy" (234). Harville's last phrase suggests that to read at all is to read about women's fickleness. But Anne Elliot, who has a memory full of quotations, claims that quotation is no good: "If you please, no reference to examples in books. Men have had every advantage of us in telling their own story . . . the pen has been in their hands" (234).

It seems, then, that the gap between mind and books that emerges in *Persuasion* is in part an indictment of a masculine literary tradition. But the issue is more complicated than this. As Daniel Cottom has pointed out, Anne and Harville's debate is in a way quotation itself—from one of the *Spectator* papers. In *Spectator* 11, "Arietta" is arguing with a gentleman about women's inconstancy: when he refers to "Quotations out of Plays and Songs," she, like Anne Elliot, claims that male authors have maligned the whole sex.[20] And one thing that had happened over the course of the eighteenth century, between the date of the *Spectator* and Austen's "quotation," was that literature, penned by both men and women, had become full not of inconstant and unfeeling women but of abandoned and perpetually feeling women.

Austen also calls our attention to herself as a writer, and as a woman writer, here. Shortly before Anne protests that literature is no good record of women's feelings because "the pen has been in [men's] hands," Anne and Harville hear a noise, coming from where Wentworth has been sitting and writing:

A slight noise called their attention to Captain Wentworth's hitherto perfectly quiet division of the room. It was nothing more than that his pen had fallen down, but Anne was startled at finding him nearer than she had supposed, and half inclined to suspect that the pen had only fallen, because he had been occupied by them, striving to catch sounds, which yet she did not think he could have caught. (233-34)

In a novel in which noises frequently are the means by which other presences make themselves felt, it seems appropriate that in this climactic scene Anne is once again "startled" aurally into an awareness of Wentworth's presence. But this noise is also an interruption of writing, a pen "which has been in their hands" falling down. This noise, I would suggest, also calls our attention to the fact the pen is now in Austen's hands. Using a metaphor that seems appropriate to *Persuasion*'s poetics of noise and absorption, William Gass has said about reading, "It seems incredible, the ease with which we sink through books quite out of sight, pass clamorous pages into soundless dreams."[21] This moment serves to startle us from our soundless absorption in the text, into self-consciousness about the "noise" of its production. The well-known image from James Austen-Leigh's *Memoir* of his aunt, of Austen's own mode of production, suggests that the woman writer's scene of writing—like her heroine's consciousness—was surrounded by a domestic "white noise." He described her working "in the general sitting-room, subject to all kinds of casual interruptions." The "ceaseless slams" and shuttings of doors that punctuate Anne's awareness would have their analogue, in the nephew's account, in the creaking of the door that alerted Austen to the presence of others: "There was, between the front door and the offices, a swing door which creaked when it was opened; but she objected to having this little inconvenience remedied, because it gave her notice when anyone was coming."[22]

The notion that there may be some doubling at the end of *Persuasion* between the characters' experiences in the text and our experiences *of* the text—that there is a foregrounding of authorial rustlings and of our sensations as readers and that we, like Anne, are being startled out of a certain kind of absorption—is confirmed as well through the device of the letter that Wentworth has been writing.[23] When letters are set into a novel there is, of course, always a sense in which reader and character find themselves in the same place, as both are supposedly reading the same words at the same time. For a number of reasons this effect seems especially strong here. The effect of this letter upon Anne is overwhelming:

Such a letter was not to be soon recovered from. Half an hour's solitude and reflection might have tranquillized her, but the ten minutes only, which now passed before she was interrupted, with all the restraints of her situation, could do nothing towards tranquillity. Every moment rather brought fresh agitation. It was an overpowering happiness. (238)[24]

And the reader? Certainly, if I may draw on my own adolescent experience, the crowning glory of rereading *Persuasion* (which I did often—reading, perhaps, like Sir Walter, to escape from "unwelcome sensations, arising from domestic affairs" [3]) was getting to read Wentworth's letter: indeed, I remember on occasion opening the book just to read the letter alone. My point is not simply that some readers may still be learning feelings from books, convincing themselves that their pleasures are, as Scott felt, "ordinary." That Anne and the reader may be aligned here tempts me to point out the way in which the temporal structure of Anne's story—the repetition between the first courtship and the second courtship—produces an isomorphism between the doubling of first courtship and second courtship, *and* the doubling of Anne's experience and a reader's experience. Critics sometimes point out that *Persuasion* seems to begin where the "typical" Austen novel ends—that it seems not unlike a "second novel" that begins where a "first novel" has gone wrong.[25] The text itself suggested earlier that Anne's romance is the belated effect of "unnatural" origins—from being "forced" to follow a conventional story of first love and family prohibition; Anne's early experience is like a text that she is now repeating with renewed feeling.

However, if there is something literary in the temporal *structure* of the novel, there are also aspects of Anne's experience that seem to liken it to that of a reader. Frequently figured, as I've argued, as absorbed in a consciousness that registers other persons as sensations, Anne's state seems not unlike the kind of absorption Gass refers to. The novel presents us with several images of readerly absorption. Anne is so "engrossed" in Mary's letter from Uppercross that she cannot hear what her father is saying to her (162). Admiral Croft is the very image of absorption when Anne finds him in such "earnest contemplation" of a print in a shop window that she is "obliged to touch as well as address him before she could catch his notice" (169). And Mary exclaims of Captain Benwick (after Charles says "Give him a book, and he will read all day long"): "Yes, that he will! . . . He will sit poring over his book, and not know when a person speaks to him, or when one drops one's scissors, or any thing that happens" (132). Readers—or people in readinglike states of absorbed contemplation—appear to attain the kind of imperviousness to the outside world that is how the novel often figures autonomy of mind.

But do books merely function as a kind of persuasion that simply shields us from other influences and presences? I'd like to return to the walk to Winthrop, where Anne could not fall into quotation, where literature failed to protect her from unwelcome sensations from the outside world. It is here above all that Austen's critique of the limits of literature as consolation is accompanied by a pervasive intimation of literature's inevitability. Here also we can begin to understand how *Persuasion* construes the connection between women as readers and women as knowers of feeling. This chapter is notable both for its seeming satire on the idea of mediating one's relation to both nature and one's own feelings with literature, and for its own heightened literariness. Somewhat like the trip to Sotherton in *Mansfield Park*, the walk to Winthrop on a lovely November day seems to take characters into a heightened literary atmosphere. It is in part the scene's autumnal tones, in such evident harmony with Anne's predicament, tones which, as Austen points out, had become by this point synonymous in English literature with the poetical itself. Repeating poetry to herself, Anne clearly has done the kind of reading that would furnish her with what late eighteenth-century conduct book writers and anthologists advised for women, a "mind . . . stored with a lasting treasure of sentiments and ideas."[26] In her disquisition on female reading in chapter 5 of *Northanger Abbey*, Austen satirized anthologies, noting that while the novelist is unjustly maligned, "the man who collects and publishes in a volume some dozen lines of Milton, Pope, and Prior, with a paper from the Spectator and a chapter from Sterne" is "eulogized by a thousand pens." But like Catherine Morland in Austen's earlier novel, Anne has clearly "read all such works" that women must read in order to "supply their memories with those quotations which are so serviceable and so soothing in the vicissitudes of their eventful lives."[27] Austen pokes fun at the conduct books' functionalist attitudes toward women's reading, but she nevertheless supplies the memories of her heroines with "such like musings and quotations." And while Anne may not be able to "fall" into a quotation readily after this interference, the text insists on supplying her with one in any case: "Anne could not immediately fall into a quotation again. The sweet scenes of autumn were for a while put by—unless some tender sonnet, fraught with the apt analogy of the declining year, with declining happiness, and the images of youth and hope, and spring, all gone together, blessed her memory" (85). The description might remind us of the sonnets of Charlotte Smith, which remained popular—and widely imitated—through the first decades of the nineteenth century. In the words of Leigh Hunt, "No young lady, fond of books and flowers, would be without Charlotte Smith's poems, if once acquainted with them."[28] This autumn walk, moreover, is most thoroughly bookish even at the moments when real life is said to push literature aside. This is especially true in the passage where, pursuing their walk, "after another half mile of gradual ascent through large enclosures, where the ploughs at work, and the fresh-made path spoke the farmer, counteracting the sweets of poetical despondence, and meaning to have spring again, they gained the summit of the most considerable hill" (85). The structure of this sentence seems itself to enclose more poetical images rather than expelling them, while the diction here animates the scene with pathetic fallacy. This is poetical agriculture, the georgic, which extends the poetical rather than counteracting it.

Thus, while the walk to Winthrop stresses the limits of literature as consolation, it simultaneously suggests that it is hard to fall out of literature.[29] If one of the things people read for is the kind of absorption that resembles the way Austen frequently figures consciousness, reading also conditions people's reception of the outside world, not only of melancholy landscapes but of overheard voices and of other people. Austen is ironical here at the expense of women's reading, or perhaps rather of the uses to which it is put. But these passages suggest, as much as *Northanger Abbey* or Charlotte Smith's *Elegiac Sonnets* do, that women have learned to feel and to recognize feeling from literature. The notion that "the pen has always been in their hands," that the true nature of women's feelings falls outside of literature, can only be one moment in what this book has to say on this subject: Austen's ambivalence may have to do as well with its opposite—with a sense that literature has been too much with women.

In *Persuasion*, Austen painstakingly evokes the claustrophobia of the social world of the novel of manners, but she is skeptical of offering up consciousness as a realm of freedom impervious to others. The novel warns that mental space is always impinged upon. Anne and Wentworth's history of love, far from freeing Anne from the pressures of others, structures the representation of her consciousness in a way that heightens their effects. Austen represents consciousness as a form of resistance only by showing how it is paved over with recollections and repetitions of sensations. Autonomy of mind often appears as an extreme form of absorption which renders one simply incapable of attending to the outside world. I suggested earlier that threats to the mind's autonomy may be represented by the novel's repeated references to bumps on the head. Louisa Musgrove might have to fall on her head to start reading, but for Anne Elliot, it may be that reading is what has already knocked her over the head. Literature, that is, may be another thing that both produces consciousness as a form of resistance to unwanted pressures and constricts mental space as a realm of freedom or autonomy. At the end of the novel, Mrs. Musgrove worries that Anne's disordered condition after reading Wentworth's letter might be the result of her having "slipped down, and got a blow to her head," and she will not rest until she is sure of Anne's "having had no fall" (238). But it is only love, or reading. I noted earlier that there is something "literary" about the temporal structure of *Persuasion*: that Anne's experience resembles a reader's, that the first courtship is to the second courtship as a book is to a reader. For Anne, we could say, the repetition of romance renders her early experience as one she is now quoting. For Anne Elliot, there is no falling out of quotation.

Coda

Quotation and the Circulation of Feeling in Early Nineteenth-Century England

> Ruin hath taught me thus to ruminate
> That Time will come and take my love away.
> This thought is as a death, which cannot choose
> But weep to have that which it fears to lose.
>
> Shakespeare, Sonnet 64

This book has suggested that literary and philosophical obsession with extravagant emotion may be inseparable from an ambivalence about locating feelings' origins in experience. Contemporary speculation on emotion—both as it concerns the period on which I have been focusing and as it concerns the present—has often addressed the ethics and politics of untoward feeling, asking questions about when and whether such feelings are good or bad, and with whom they are affiliated. The point here has been to demonstrate how thoroughly such evaluative judgments are enmeshed in—often determined by—theories of how we know feelings and their causes. In particular, I have explored how the passions both extend and demarcate the limits of empiricism. An allegiance to empiricist explanation of feeling can take one down strange and circuitous paths. My book has discovered, in a variety of genres, stories of feelings' histories and origins: these stories have often opened up gaps between feelings and their causes, tensions between ways of explaining them, and impasses over their etiologies—in life or literature, for example. The epistemological preoccupation of the works I've studied has often taken the form, thematically, of an interest in feelings that appear to be impersonal and transsubjective. If feelings at times seem to be their own evidence and proof, and to belong infallibly to the self, they often seem at times impossible to know or to claim as one's own: a fascination with knowing feelings is closely coupled with a sense of their difficulty. These narratives, however, have not demonstrated the emotions' inherent ineffability; rather, they have charted out the paths along which it *becomes* productive to see feelings as difficult to measure. To refuse or defer knowing how or where feeling fits may be as aesthetically, personally, and socially generative as is claiming them for one's own. In the following coda I seek to stress more broadly the relevance of this constellation of ideas to our thinking about the literature and culture of the romantic period.

༄

I begin by pondering the phrase with which my discussion of *Persuasion* ended, and I end with a dead princess. If Austen's heroine is in some sense incapable of falling *out* of quotation, falling *into* quotation—as Anne Elliot tries to do on her troubling country walk—was something that romantic writers did impulsively, when the matter at hand was feelings. Just as Captain Harville wishes "fifty quotations" to be his witnesses in *Persuasion*'s debate about the comparative strength and duration of men's and women's feelings, many of the authors who appear in the present study fall into quotation when accounting for their own feelings, other people's, the knowability of feelings, their origins and their movements. Lord Kames, for example, whose quotation of *Othello* I discussed at the beginning of this study, frequently turned to the quotation of Shakespeare and other authors to ratify his points about literary feeling. Discussions of feelings became occasions for quotation: his predilection for quoting Shakespeare in particular was thought to be one of the chief attractions of his work. Dr. John Gregory wrote to James Beattie that "what has made Lord Kames' 'Elements of Criticism' so popular in England is his numerous illustrations and quotations from Shakespeare. If his book had wanted these illustrations . . . it would not have been so generally read in England."[1] In this opinion, Kames's illustrations outrun his argument, and the attractions of his book are those of a "quotation book": it is a place to find dramatic and affecting passages from Shakespeare, rather than a theory of the influence of the passions. Kames's practice of quotation encourages the notion that feelings have a certain knowability and self-evidence about them, that we need only to quote to know what feelings we are talking about.

Quotation, moreover, has emerged—in between Kames and Austen—as a crucial topic in this study. In Charlotte Smith's poetry, the quoted phrase or line lies at the heart of the dilemmas her poems raise. The expression of woe ensconced in quotation marks troubles the sonnets, suggesting both that the feelings Smith expresses come from elsewhere and that quotation itself is a kind of emotional perturbation. In my chapters on both Smith and Wordsworth, quotations in poems raise questions about what belongs to women and what belongs to men. Quoting, in the literature described by this book, is not only something poems do, but also something people do. The people in Ann Radcliffe's novels quote poetry to themselves all the time, and *Udolpho*'s wandering book of Petrarch poems—with its underlined phrases marking passages quoted out loud—can stand as a figure for the vagaries of quoted sentiments. In Austen, the image of the mind full of quotation served to represent the novelist's ambivalence about literary emotions that can disappoint by being either too effective or not effective enough. Quotations, in other words, can be the topographical features of the space of the mind as well as of the space of a sonnet. Locating feelings elsewhere, shifting between textual practice and a mental or social practice, quotation can serve as a name for the problems of this book as a whole: the tendency of affective life to get located among rather than within people, or in the interstices between different explanations and stories of their origins, arising as much from rhetorical or fictional situations as from the mind's own motions.

Dr. Gregory's remark on Kames's popularity should remind us that late eighteenth- and early nineteenth-century discussions of emotion took place in a literary culture in which popular quotation flourished. A number of quotation books—books that promised readers what Kames's *Elements of Criticism* seems inadvertently to have provided—that is, collections of literary passages for contemplation, consolation, and use—appeared in the first decades of the nineteenth century.[2] The practice of quoting when talking of one's own feelings was considered both a common habit and a common error. Guides to letter writing, which advised writers of the familiar letter to follow a natural, easy, and frank style of expression, felt it necessary to caution that while "a quotation or happy phrase judiciously introduced is certainly an elegance in style," their too-frequent use was "an unpardonable affectation."[3] In Jane Austen's late satire of Regency fashion, *Sanditon*, Charlotte is convinced of the handsome Sir Edward Denham's being a true sentimental "man of feeling" because he begins to "stagger her with the number of his quotations." Collecting quotations on one's own was a popular entertainment. Among Austen's characters we find evidence for this not only in Anne Elliot's reciting poetry to herself and Catherine Morland's learning the lines all heroines need to know but also in Harriet Smith's collecting "enigmas," sentimental charades, and conundrums for her commonplace book: "In this age of literature," Austen declares, "such collections on a very grand scale are not uncommon." Emma glosses the nonexistent courtship between Harriet and Mr. Elton that the commonplace book has invented with a quotation presumably from her own collection: "The course of true love never did run smooth—."[4]

Jonathan Bate has argued that the prevalence of casual quotation of Shakespeare during the last decade of the eighteenth century and the first decades of the nineteenth is inseparable from the emergence of romanticism.[5] My goal in the first section of this final chapter is to speculate on the conjunction of feeling and quotation, as a way of exploring further its implications for the study of romantic feeling. My ambition here is not to classify quotation as a particular kind of literary reference, or to ponder the connections between romanticism and intertextuality, or to claim that an interest in quotation itself was something new in English letters. Rather, by looking at two brief examples from Wordsworth and De Quincey, I will explore how the practice of quotation might help us understand the epistemological and ontological status of romantic feeling, as well as its social currency.[6]

If the first half of this chapter asks what happens when romanticism's expressions of emotion are situated in a culture of quotation, the second half leaves literature behind to affirm that in early nineteenth-century England, a fascination with the traveling of feelings itself traveled beyond the romantic poem, the romantic autobiography, the novel of manners, and the quotation book, and into the heart of national life. My texts here will be a wide range of writings reporting the spread of public feeling in response to the death in 1817 of Princess Charlotte, heir to the British throne. In ending here I do not wish to suggest that a fascination with the passing of public feeling passes out of public or literary life after 1817, though I would argue that Victorian culture transformed the contagion of extravagant feeling into something much more suspicious, something to be studied by doctors and students of the crowd.[7] However, the stories of public mourning and private passion put into circulation by the princess's death speak in an idiom distinctly derived from the eighteenth century, in its fascination with feelings' origins. The two sections of the chapter thus approach the topics of this book through different kinds of writing and from two different directions, one literary, one political. Both the social and literary practice of quoting feelings and the phenomenon of the public feeling occasioned by the death of the princess allow us to study this culture's interest in the mobility of feelings: the former in the minutiae of two writers' accounts of their habits of quotation, the latter in wider public spectacle.

༄

Wordsworth's quotation book is his "book of books," book 5 of *The Prelude*. The poet admits that quotation was a sociable habit in his youth, something to be done—as Anne Elliot knew—on country walks. Speaking of a schoolboyish friendship bonded by books, he describes himself and his companion:

>   for the better part
> Of two delightful hours we strolled along
> By the still borders of the misty lake
> Repeating favorite verses with one voice.[8]

Thus it is not surprising that the book of books is bookish, particularly given to echo, allusion, and quotation. More surprising perhaps are the strange feelings Wordsworth expresses toward books. As book 5 opens, the poet is grieving over the frailties of books, which he terms earthly "garments" for our souls:

>   Tremblings of the heart
> It gives, to think that the immortal being
> No more shall need such garments; and yet man,
> As long as he shall be the child of earth,
> Might almost *"weep to have"* what he may lose—
> Nor be himself extinguished, but survive
> Abject, depressed, forlorn, disconsolate (5.21–27; my emphasis)

As awe-inspiring as is the thought that after death we will no longer need books (the "garments"), the thought that all books might perish and leave man "abject, depressed, forlorn, disconsolate" without them is more melancholy. Wordsworth proceeds to imagine ("A thought is with me sometimes," he confesses) an apocalypse after which life itself could be rekindled, but in which books would be destroyed:

> Where would they be? Oh, why hath not the mind
> Some element to stamp her image on
> In nature somewhat nearer to her own?
> Why, gifted with such powers to send abroad
> Her spirit, must it lodge in shrines so frail? (5.44–48)

Thinking about books seems inherently sad for Wordsworth; to think of them is to think of their inadequacy. Books elicit a thought which, in the words of the Shakespeare sonnet he quotes, "is as a death which cannot choose / But weep to have that which it fears to lose."

Rejecting the notion that consoles us for the brevity of life with the immortality of art, Wordsworth's line of thought here seems somewhat perverse and out of the way; it seems intended to make him sad, as he acknowledges himself when he admits " 'Twas going far to seek disquietude" (5.52). The emotional posturing of this elegy for books seems uncharacteristically forced, as when, for example, speaking of books once loved that now seem empty, he insists, "I am sad . . . Even unto tears I sometimes could be sad" (5.568–70). The oddness of tone here matches the proleptic, anticipatory elegiac mode of the Shakespearean phrase, "weep to have," that he quotes. The phrase suggests that the objects of our affections cause us sorrow even in their presence; the mind's wayward motions lead us indiscriminately forward to their loss. Once you start "weeping to have," there's no end to weeping. This odd kind of having which is also a not-having also redounds onto the status of the quotation itself. On the one hand, quoting Shakespeare's sonnets (a book that we know Wordsworth himself owned) to say that we should "weep to have" books reminds us that we, in fact, have books to quote. On the other hand, on what terms does Wordsworth "have" this sentiment? Quoted from Shakespeare, he has this thought from afar (" 'Twas going far to seek inquietude . . . "), on borrowed time, on loan. The mere presence of a quotation here satisfies mixed emotions. It is both a perturbation—something cut out and pasted in from afar—and a consolation. Hovering between being something that one has and something that belongs elsewhere, the quoted phrase functions somewhat like a Freudian fetish, a materialized remainder that simultaneously covers over and admits an absence. The Shakespearean phrase "weep to have" ensconced in quotation marks is like a badge or emblem. It declares Wordsworth's allegiance to a logic in which borrowed feelings of the highest extravagance may be more consoling than one's own.[9]

We could situate the odd status of the quoted feeling by pondering the changing meanings that a quotation of Shakespeare might have: this was, as the characters in *Mansfield Park* point out, a period where one was meeting with his thoughts and feelings almost everywhere ("His celebrated passages are quoted by everybody; they are in half the books we open.... His thoughts and beauties are so spread abroad that one touches them everywhere"). The late eighteenth-century personalization of the sonnet, which we noted in connection with Charlotte Smith, was particularly influential in the case of Shakespeare's sonnets. Romantic readers viewed them as "personal" poems in which Shakespeare "seemingly profess[es] to describe [his] own sentiments," as Charles Brown, a romantic reader of the sonnets, put it. In the "Essay, Supplementary to the Preface" of 1815, Wordsworth affirmed that in the sonnets "Shakspeare expresses his own feelings in his own person" and listed sonnet 64 as one of those exemplifying the sonnets' merits.[10] In this romantic reading, the feelings of sonnet 64 are those of Shakespeare the melancholy lover. Studying the changing reception of Shakespeare's sonnets in the early nineteenth century, Margreta de Grazia sees a connection between the view of sonnets as Shakespeare's private feelings, and the practices of anthologies and concordances of Shakespearean "beauties" which helped to put into circulation the writer's words as "citations belonging to Shakespeare." Quotation books attributed to Shakespeare a first-person voice that quotes himself on various sentiments. De Grazia connects this change to changes in the meaning of quotation itself. Until the eighteenth century, quotation marks set off *sententiae* or common phrases, rather than individuals' own words; and "to quote" could mean "to mark" or "to observe" rather than "to cite": "Quotations were distinguished from the rest of discourse ... not because they originally belonged somewhere else, but rather because they belonged everywhere."[11] Only by the late eighteenth century did it become an ethical offense to forget to put quotation marks around someone else's words: quotation became individuated.

But if romantic readers of Shakespearean sonnets would have understood the tears of sonnet 64 as Shakespeare's own tears—the habit of quotation having personalized his words—the period's addiction to quotation had also made Shakespeare's words and feelings everybody's—the property of all Englishmen, as Henry Crawford declares in *Mansfield Park*. In Wordsworth's quotation of sonnet 64 we have an example of how quotation might deindividualize as much as it individualizes expressions of feeling. First we must notice the strange place of emotion in the sonnet itself. The question raised by Wordsworth's quotation—to whom does this sentiment belong? Wordsworth? Shakespeare?—is compounded by the way Shakespeare's line passes ownership of these tears along to "thought" itself. The "thought" here is that "Time will come and take my love away," which is said in turn to be "as a death, which cannot choose / But weep." A modern annotator, Stephen Booth, puzzles over the final couplet: "the antecedent [of 'which' in line 13] is vague: *death*, the nearest potential antecedent, cannot choose, but it cannot weep or fear either; *thought* makes better sense, but it is the thinker who does the weeping and fearing."[12] Shakespeare's sonnet attenuates the question of whose weeping this is; these are tears that belong to no one but a figurative death. Once quoted, this "weeping to have" takes on a life of its own. The quotation marks are a kind of visa that allows feeling to travel incognito. The odd feelings that Wordsworth expresses toward books are neither his feelings nor Shakespeare's, nor are they generally inclusive: they are somewhere in between. Wordsworth's use of quotation here exemplifies a characteristic of Wordsworthian emotion: its ability to be simultaneously subjective and impersonal, at once perverse and idiosyncratic, and utterly authoritative.[13]

❧

Like Anne Elliot, Thomas De Quincey seems hardly ever to have fallen out of quotation. His writings often seem to radiate out from a particular quotation—often from Wordsworth, among others—like ripples from a pebble. His tale "The Household Wreck," for example, constitutes a sustained, mournful gloss on the very Shakespeare passage that Wordsworth also quotes—on what it means to "weep to have." "The Household Wreck" lingers on a presentiment of loss; it is an exercise in emotional extravagance. The narrator admits, of his overanxious concern for his too-perfect, too-happy wife: "If in anything I ran into excess, it was in this very point of anxiety as to all that regarded my wife's security." He then misquotes: "To sum up the whole in a most weighty line of Shakspere":

"I wept to have [absolutely, by anticipation, shed tears in possessing] what I so feared to lose" (insert De Quincey's).

De Quincey's narrator misquotes the line, apportioning the tears of the sonnet to Shakespeare in order to appropriate them for himself. "I lived," he glosses,

under the constant presence of a feeling which only that great observer of human nature (so far as I am aware) has ever noticed; viz. that merely the excess of my happiness made me jealous of its ability to last, and in that extent less capable of enjoying it; that, in fact, the prelibation of my tears, as a homage to its fragility, was drawn forth by my very sense that my felicity was too exquisite.[14]

In this account of emotional excess, happiness steals from itself. The narrative spins out from this feeling: it is a story of a love that is synonymous with the presentiment of loss; of a Hungarian fortune-teller who tells the narrator to begin weeping for sorrows that will happen later; and of an innocent woman—the narrator's wife—accused of shoplifting. Agnes is caught with a piece of lace that belongs to the shopkeeper, Mr. Barratt, in her muff. Thus the story that glosses the borrowed Shakespearean line is itself about questions of lifting and borrowing, possession and theft. Agnes ultimately vindicates herself before her husband (though not before the court, which sentences her to hard labor): Mr. Barratt put the lace in her muff himself, to blackmail her into sex. But in a sense Agnes, whose name marks her as an innocent victim but who is glossed not only with Shakespeare but also as Milton's Eve, is always guilty. Woman is what one "weeps to have," and the literary man's musings over borrowed emotions, and emotions that steal from themselves, devolve onto her.

Quotation for De Quincey is a kind of currency. It is a coin that circulates like the ancient Roman coin depicting Judea veiling her head and "sitting under her palm-tree to weep" that he advises fellow-sufferers to imitate when memorializing great grief: "Therefore now . . . do you veil your head like Judea in memory of that transcendent woe, and in testimony that, indeed, it surpassed all utterance of words."[15] In De Quincey's autobiographical writings, the coin of quotation passes among De Quincey's past and present selves, and between himself and his readers, making them rich not only in an exterior language but also in the inner experiences of emotional trouble. Quotation is both exotic—often dressed up in De Quincey's orientalist and antiquarian fantasies—and too close to home. For example, he associates the feelings of dread occasioned by a debt to a bookseller he cannot pay with a passage from an *Arabian Nights* story ("Oh, Mr. Magician . . . I never had money enough to buy so beautiful a set of ropes!") that he used to ventriloquize to his sister: "Should I have ventriloquized, would my sister have laughed, had either of us but guessed the possibility that I myself, and within one twelve months . . . *should repeat within my own inner experience the shadowy panic of the young Bagdat intruder* . . . ?" (135; my emphasis). Quoting the fictive figure's words, De Quincey's *Arabian Nights* story implies, does not defer one's own suffering but rather hastens another's entry into one's own "inner experience."

De Quincey also describes quotation as a particular kind of social currency, a token of circulation much more contemporary than the ancient coin: a lady's seal. In his gloomy love affair with grief, *Suspiria de Profundis*, he footnotes a word borrowed from Wordsworth:

"Glimmering."—As I have never allowed myself to covet any man's ox nor his ass, nor any thing that is his, still less would it become a philosopher to covet other people's images, or metaphors. Here, therefore, I restore to Mr Wordsworth this fine image. . . . I borrowed it for one moment in order to point my own sentence. . . . On the same principle I often borrow their seals from young ladies—when closing my letters. Because there is sure to be some tender sentiment upon them about "memory," or "hope," or "roses," or "reunion:" and my correspondent must be a sad brute who is not touched by the eloquence of the seal, even if his taste is so bad that he remains deaf to mine. (147)

The young lady's seal with a "tender sentiment" on it that De Quincey borrows is a bit like the coin with the weeping Judea on it: they are both freely circulating tokens of feeling that can be pressed—into someone's palm, perhaps, or onto a letter—affecting the recipient with its traveling sentiment. However, the lady's seal does not belong to the arcane realm of De Quincey, the classically educated, self-styled "philosopher" and man of letters, but to a sentimental middle-brow culture. Here, one romantic writer's borrowing of another is delivered under the cover of an early nineteenth-century woman's world of exchanging sentiments, quotation books, and commonplace books. It places De Quincey's habit—his addiction to quotation—in the context of a world sealed up by generic feminine sentiments.

If De Quincey has trouble falling out of quotation, this is especially true, as these examples might suggest, in his autobiographical writings. *Confessions of an English Opium-Eater* and *Suspiria de Profundis* struggle to tell the stories of the origins of both the literary man's feelings and his addictions. His accounts of feeling must be more complex than the simple eloquence of the sentiments on ladies' seals: like Wordsworth, De Quincey often goes far to seek disquietude. His autobiographical writings therefore are veritable quotation books in which he constantly requotes his early experiences; for De Quincey, accounting for himself and quoting seem to be one and the same thing. He testifies to the strength of his memory by describing his insomniac mind as a kind of automatic manufacturer of quotation books:

Hence it happens that passages in Latin or English poets which I never could have read but once, (and *that* thirty years ago,) often begin to blossom anew when I am lying awake, unable to sleep. I become a distinguished compositor in the darkness; and, with my aerial composing-stick, sometimes I "set up" half a page of verses. . . . Said but once, said but softly, not marked at all, words revive before me in darkness and solitude; and they arrange themselves gradually into sentences, but through an effort sometimes of a distressing kind, to which I am in a manner forced to become a party. (116–17)

Memory here plays the role of a bossy shop-steward at the printing house; in a manner "forced" to set up verses in his mind, he finds quotation a troubling, involuntary visitation. The youthful De Quincey's skill at quotation rivals, sometimes eclipses, his much boasted powers of classical translation: on one occasion, at the beginning of his classical career, he is asked to translate extemporaneously from a Latin Bible "the great chapter of St. Paul on the grave and resurrection," and "read[s] it off" with rapture not from the Latin but from memory of the English (132). De Quincey describes autobiographical writing as a sympathetic encounter between the adult self and the childhood self: the writer "feels the differences between his two selves as the main quickeners of his sympathy" (92). Autobiographical writing in his case involves both a fall into sympathy with a former self and a fall into quotation. Quotation *is* childhood: the stuff within quotation marks occupies a kind of preserve granted not only chronological priority but also innocence and emotional intensity. Quotation serves as a figure for the transitivity of feelings in autobiography, as De Quincey explores whether the feelings of which he writes belong to the child or to the adult who writes (113).

If the relation between past and present is one of quotation for De Quincey, it is one particular "passage" (he puts it in quotes, 92) in childhood that circulates and repeats through his later life: the death of his sister Elizabeth. Elizabeth's life and death are ringed round with quotation; it is on account of her death that he can quote St. Paul on the grave and resurrection so feelingly. De Quincey names Elizabeth's premature death as the "origin" (92) of his emotional susceptibility in later life. His mourning for her moves throughout his texts, his grief "revived," "restored," and "kept alive" (129, 131) by the way his memory bonds his grief for her with books.[16]

In an action that he describes, retrospectively, as motivated by "sentimental" feeling, De Quincey surreptitiously enters his dead sister's room to pay a final visit to her corpse. He describes the room as echoless ("no echo ran along the silent walls" [103]), but in fact he brings to the chamber of death many echoes. In his account of her death, De Quincey's text is pieced together with quoted passages from Goethe, Milton, Wordsworth, Coleridge, Virgil, and passages from the Gospels. In the room of the dead girl itself—the transgressive room which "swells" with light and sound and puts De Quincey into a sublime "trance" (105)—are echoes of Sir Thomas Browne's *Urne-Buriall*.[17] If the young De Quincey trespasses in the chamber of death to find what's there, what he finds are quotations.

De Quincey's experience of entering Elizabeth's forbidden room and finding it full of quotations has an analogy in what happens the very next day, when the doctors open up Elizabeth's *head* to see what is in it (108). After the doctors examine the contents of the head and close it up, the room in which she lies is shut: "The door was now locked—the key was taken away—and I was shut out for ever" (108). What is in the eight-year-old Elizabeth's head is either water or an expanded intellect—or both. Elizabeth died of hydrocephalus, or water on the brain; yet her head was also, De Quincey boasts, "for its superb developments . . . the astonishment of science": an eminent authority "pronounced her head to be the finest in its structure and development of any that he had ever seen" (99). De Quincey suggests that there is some connection between the expansion of Elizabeth's intellect and its susceptibility to water:

Meantime, as I would be loth that any trait of what might seem vanity should creep into this record, I will candidly admit that she died of hydrocephalus; and it has often been supposed that the premature expansion of the intellect in cases of that class, is altogether morbid—forced on, in fact, by the mere stimulation of the disease. I would, however, suggest, as a possibility, the very inverse order of the relation between the disease and the intellectual manifestations. Not the disease may always have caused the preternatural growth of the intellect, but, on the contrary, this growth coming on spontaneously, and outrunning the capacities of the physical structure, may have caused the disease. (99)[18]

Did water on the brain cause Elizabeth's head to swell with intellect? Or did she die from an inundation caused by having, like her brother, a precocious head full of stuff? Has Elizabeth died in a flood of quotation? De Quincey himself repeatedly links his own head with water; that there is something intellectual about the watery contents of Elizabeth's head confirms that the infant sister's head—and the examination of its contents—is an image of his own. Her astonishing, watery head, moreover, is akin to that of another of the writer's female relatives: that of his mother who falls in a brook as a child and almost drowns. While under water, "a mighty theatre expanded within her brain," expanding like Elizabeth's swollen head or the swelling chamber in which she lies (145). Elizabeth's head swells with the fluid in De Quincey's own. The fluid on her brain is the golden tincture of laudanum which makes his early experiences—and his early readings—sweep in upon the brain (137).

De Quincey admonishes elsewhere: "Of this let everyone be assured—that he owes to the impassioned books which he has read, many a thousand more of emotions than he can consciously trace back to them. Dim by their origination, these emotions yet arise in him, and mould him through life like forgotten incidents of his childhood."[19] The quotation-filled place of the dead sister Elizabeth suggests that it is difficult to separate books and the incidents of childhood; accounting for the origins of feelings in De Quincey constructs a Piranesian architecture that leads everywhere and nowhere.[20] De Quincey's quotation-addicted narratives confirm that romantic emotion is perhaps not a spontaneous overflow of feeling but rather a slowly rising tide—something like the sea of papers that sometimes rose up and "snowed up" De Quincey's chambers—that comes from an often distant shore.[21]

In his *Confessions*, De Quincey prefaces an account of how opium altered his dreams by noting a change that occurred in his visual powers of hallucination, sometime during the year 1817: "In the middle of 1817, I think it was . . . this faculty became positively distressing to me; at night, when I lay awake in bed, vast processions passed along in mournful pomp; friezes of never-ending stories, that to my feelings were as sad and solemn as if they were stories drawn from times before Oedipus or Priam—before Tyre—before Memphis" (67). This vast procession wending its way before De Quincey's eyes "in mournful pomp" may have been drawn not from times before Tyre and Memphis but from an image from the year 1817 itself, in November of which all Britain was reverberating with the image of a royal funeral procession, the funeral of the prince regent's popular daughter Princess Charlotte, who died in childbirth.

The funeral of Princess Charlotte was described to the English public in detail—in newspapers across the country, in sermons, in popular prints, in commemorative volumes. Readers learned about the slow, stately procession of Charlotte's remains and those of her stillborn infant on a silent moonlit night, from the royal residence at Claremont to Windsor, preceded by thirty horsemen in mourning and a party of the Tenth Dragoons; about how the procession was silent except for "the deep sighs of afflicted spectators" and the bells that tolled in every town as the procession passed through; about how, upon their arrival at Windsor, the moon was suddenly covered with clouds, causing a sudden darkness that "visibly affected thousands of spectators" and filled them with sorrow. Prints and testimonials depicted the details of the funeral procession the following night from the lodge where the bodies lay in state to the chapel, describing the order of the mourners and the appearance of Charlotte's husband, Prince Leopold of Saxe-Coburg, in his long black cloak with train.[22] The death of the princess was, in the words of one clergyman, "an occasion which furnishes more real matter to excite the sensibilities of our nature—more real cause of regret—more present and more permanent calamity and woe, than any other event in the history of this or perhaps any other civilized nation."[23] Because Charlotte was the direct heir to the throne, her death caused a crisis of succession and a fear that the crown might fall into foreign hands at a time when the popularity of the House of Hanover was low. This melancholy and important event, which may

have left its mysterious impression on De Quincey's nocturnal mind—
much like quotations from Latin poetry, or from the *Arabian Nights*—
allows us to trace the transmission and quotation of feelings in a less
private arena. It is an event which suggests that in early nineteenth-
century England, a perception of emotion as fascinating, transsubjective, and difficult to know was as crucial to national as to poetic
identity.

This book began by evoking the ways in which late eighteenth-
century observers expressed both fascination and alarm about feelings'
tendency to travel. The crisis in English culture over the French Revolution is often taken to have exacerbated people's suspicion about
whether extravagant sensibility could be a positive social force. However, the popular response to the death of Princess Charlotte reveals
that the forms and idioms of late eighteenth-century emotional extravagance were very much alive in the national life of Regency England. In her book, *Bearing the Dead: The British Culture of Mourning
from the Enlightenment to Victoria*, Esther Schor persuasively argues that
the rhetorics of public emotion surrounding Princess Charlotte are evidence of the continuity of eighteenth-century sentimental politics in
the crisis-ridden years of the Regency, the writings documenting her
death often echoing the emotional rhetoric of the political debates of
the 1790's. As Schor demonstrates, the mourning for Princess Charlotte
appeared as an expression of royalist adulation and national consensus
that transcended political difference, while simultaneously serving as a
vehicle for dissent. The mourning for the popular princess, seen during her lifetime as more sympathetic than her father toward political reform and religious dissent, gave voice both to antimonarchist sentiment directed at the unpopular prince regent and to appeals for reform and religious toleration. Further, Schor argues that Charlotte's
death intersects crucially with early nineteenth-century ideologies of
gender: while her death prompted conservative, Burkean representations of the nation as a family all mourning a lost sister or daughter, it
also challenged the division of social life into private feminine and
public masculine spheres by making it possible to imagine an authoritative female public virtue.[24]

I will focus in the pages that follow on how the meanings of the
emotions occasioned by Charlotte's death were both made possible and
complicated by some of the assumptions about how we know feelings,
the effects of which I have traced in this book. Charlotte's death pro-

voked a widespread fascination with feelings' tendency to travel, and a desire to document the empirical evidence of their spread. But at the same time, mourning for her provoked a worry about the authority of emotion that seemed merely contagious. The public emotions occasioned by her death, moreover, depended on an epistemology that posited private, secret feelings as necessary fictions. And finally, her story reveals how the public's claims to know—or not know—the extravagance or insufficiency of a person's passions were bound up with assumptions about gender.

༄

A fascination with feelings' ability to travel becomes literal in accounts of public sentiment on Charlotte's death, as the spread of mourning maps out England and English influence abroad. One massive account, Robert Huish's *Memoirs of the Princess Charlotte of Saxe Coburg*, takes a tour of the country, recounting reports of the spread of the tragic news and of the sadness in every town. The courier, the mail coachman, and the messenger are the crucial figures in his narrative. In Bristol, for example, the mail coachman announces to the crowd waiting for news of Charlotte and the newborn heir to the throne, "Both are dead!": "'Both are dead!' was reverberated by the crowd, and the flash spread like lightning. Dejection marked every countenance, and I think it is not too much to say, that 'tears gushed into every eye'" (*M*, 631–32). The writer's last phrase reminds us that Charlotte's death was an eminent occasion for quotation, as shared feelings seemed to elicit shared and well-worn words. Huish's particular concern with the spread of the public's feelings, rather than simply with "the progress of this disastrous information," is especially evident when he describes the spread of mourning to English people abroad. When he follows the progress of Mr. Kerr, a messenger, to the European courts, the spread of feelings becomes an enactment of England's dominion over its rivals. Only two years after the end of the Napoleonic Wars, Charlotte's death allowed an English public at peace to represent their victory over the French as accomplished by feelings, rather than on the battlefield:

Never was the national character of the country so proudly and eminently displayed, as on the occasion of the decease of the Princess Charlotte. It shewed the extent of British feelings, when waked by a national loss; and, in the estimation of foreigners, it has added more to the fame and honour of the country, than the noblest victory which was ever gained by her warriors. Mr. Kerr, the messenger, no sooner arrived at Brussels with dispatches . . . announcing the deplorable calamity, which we all lament, than the English, resident in that city, immediately . . . appeared overwhelmed with that acute grief, which he would have felt upon the loss of a dear and valued friend. (*M*, 659–60)

"This simultaneous action on the part of the English," continues Huish, led French newspaper editors to laud English feelings: "It must be highly pleasing to the British nation, to see itself represented by those who, but a short time ago, were its most inveterate foes." Charlotte's death allowed the English public to reimagine foreign relations as conquest by tears, and to take pleasure in being represented to the rest of the world as a nation based on the bonds of feeling rather than on borders. In the words of one sermon: "Britain has offered to surrounding countries, a sight rarely beheld. A great nation dissolved in the sorrows of an unfeigned condolence, voluntarily paying a tribute of loyalty and affection to their departed Princess, and bound to each other, by the ties, not of political concord and of civil interest, so much as by the bonds of a generous and all-pervading sympathy."[25]

However, while this emphasis on the spread of English feelings abroad rendered the nation knowable, the English communities on the Continent, in their very isolation from the nation, also served as a kind of laboratory for the study of how feelings travel. They provided proof that the grief for Charlotte was not simply the effect of contagion but a spontaneous response to a just cause. Of the English at Hamburg, who were "deeply affected by the melancholy tidings," he notes:

Indeed, it may be said, that one and all acted from a spontaneous sentiment of admiration and affection for the virtues of the Princess, *without waiting to know what had been done by their countrymen elsewhere*; for true feeling waits not the authority of precedent to teach it how to weep, and is as remote from the affectation, as it is regardless of the forms of sorrow. (*M*, 664; my emphasis)

At stake in Huish's account of the spread of mourning is an attempt to sort out where exactly the mass feelings for Charlotte were coming from. Were they the mere effect of contagion or mass agitation—something like the "electric touch" Mrs. Barbauld described, or the "flash of lightning" that "spreads through all," as Huish's Bristol correspondent suggests? Were people's feelings fundamentally imitative of others' feelings, as when the crowd at Bristol repeats the mail coachman's announcement, "Both are dead"? Or were each person's feelings for Charlotte—as Huish seeks to demonstrate in the case of the English at Hamburg—a spontaneous response to the death of a virtuous princess?[26] Huish's insistence on the latter in this passage suggests a paradox embedded in his—and other commentators'—fascination with the traveling of feelings: such a fascination can make these feelings seem like the effects merely of an infectious transmission, undermining the very moral identity they are supposed to represent. In a period of mass agitation over prices and wages, contagious emotion could seem as likely to fragment the fiction of national unity as to heal it—as the wave of anti-king sentiment at the trial of Charlotte's mother, Queen Caroline, would prove three years later. Thus the important lesson at Hamburg is that "true feeling waits not the authority of precedent to teach it how to weep": the authority of feelings must rest in their own immediacy and isolation.

The death of Charlotte, then, raised questions about what causes feelings to travel, and about the relationship between feelings and authority: what authorizes feelings? What is authorized by them? The question of the relations between feeling and authority in this case was often posed quite literally. Thomas Laqueur and Esther Schor have both demonstrated that radicals and dissenters were militantly skeptical of the purported spontaneity of the public emotions elicited by the event. They charged that the government had actively encouraged and even staged the widespread display of mourning. The government-affiliated daily paper *The Courier* had indeed dropped explicit hints about what was going "spontaneously" to happen, announcing several days before the funeral: "There is no doubt that on Wednesday next, the day of the funeral, all business will be suspended; and that the empire will afford the awful and appropriate spectacle of a whole people spontaneously engaged in religious exercise and devotion." The politics of feeling thus took the form of competing claims about what caused them. In the radical journal *The Black Dwarf*, T. J. Wooler called the mourning of Charlotte a "State Theatrical."[27]

While there was dissent on the matter of how feelings spread, the written accounts of the nation's feelings for Charlotte—the countless poems, prints, and "true accounts"—played a constitutive role in producing themselves the appearance of the unanimous emotional response they sought to document. The immediate outpouring of written material—the detailed accounts of the universality of grief—was itself remarkable, and remarked upon.[28] A striking aspect of the commentary on Princess Charlotte's death is how little went without saying. As the skeptical voices of radicals suggested, the memoirists and chroniclers like Huish, the clergymen who preached funeral-day sermons from their pulpits, and "all the poetical talent of the country" who "daily sent their lucubrations to the diurnal prints" (M, 647), testifying to the widespread public melancholy and lamentation, were not simply reporting on emotions that were already there but spreading feelings they claimed already existed. In this respect, it is Huish and other writers who act as the messengers, the mail coachmen they write about. That so much needed to be said on the occasion of Charlotte's death testifies to the political importance of the event—its effect on the question of succession, its ability to mobilize popular discontent; it also testifies to some of the paradoxes in the epistemology of feeling that we have traced throughout this book. On the one hand, these many testimonials of public sentiment operate according to an assumption about the self-evidence of feelings: if you say feelings exist, they do. On the other hand, as Huish's account of the Hamburg episode suggests, these writers desired to find evidence of "true feeling" and to account for its causes in moments that existed outside of the circulation of representations. The mourning of Charlotte testified to an abiding fascination with the circulation of feelings; but it also came up against questions about who controlled that circulation. Accounting for the circulation of feeling was both dangerously easy and almost impossibly difficult.

Like the practice of quotation, the responses to Charlotte's death both individualized and deindividualized feeling: reports of the melancholy event pondered how the public might know whose feelings properly belonged to whom. The people were said over and over to be feeling what they would feel if their own daughters, sisters, or wives had died. Henry Brougham noted later, "It is scarcely possible to exaggerate . . . how universal and how genuine those feelings [of sorrow on Charlotte's death] were. It really was as if every household throughout Great Britain had lost a favourite child." A minister testified that "'*one dead*' in every family could not have excited more general consternation." The *Ladies' Monthly Museum* noted that on the day of the funeral, "houses [were] actually shut up as if a death had happened in every family." Felicia Hemans's "Stanzas on the Late National Calamity, the Death of the Princess Charlotte," describes the horror struck into the heart of the onlookers of the funeral procession:

> Silent the throngs that fill the darkened street,
> Silent the slumbering Thames, the lonely mart;
> And all is still, where countless thousands meet,
> Save the full throbbing of the awe-struck heart!
> All deeply, strangely, fearfully serene,
> As in each ravaged home th'avenging one had been.[29]

If the English people felt as if they were mourning a daughter or sister, it was because, the rhetoric suggested, they were experiencing the feelings of the bereft royal family. "Royalty," in the words of one poem, "hath felt / A wound, that every bosom feels its own" (*M*, 645). The public became members of the royal family, their own familial sentiments extending to include those mourning at Windsor. Some observers did object to this rhetoric, seeing these claims as a form of falseness. The reiterated claims in public responses to royal deaths, that individuals were feeling the personal feelings of the royal family, "infuriated" William Cobbett. After the death of George III in 1820 elicited a rhetoric of mourning similar to that which poured out for Charlotte, he queried, "Is it not in us, impertinence as well as affectation, to pretend that we are overcome by those feelings, which, in the case of the parents, children, wives . . . lead men to express their sorrow?" The very rhetoric of unfeigned sorrow places people in the position of experiencing feelings that seemed to exist uneasily between real and fictive feelings. This may explain the recurrence, in a number of written accounts, of an anecdote about the first night's performance at Drury Lane theater after the princess's death. Huish and others quote the monody by Thomas Campbell recited from the stage by the actress Mrs. Bartley, which contrasts the players' usual job—"to show / The scenes and passions of fictitious woe"—with that of which the monody speaks: "These were not rites of inexpressive show, / But hallowed as the types of real woe."[30] If these accounts invested the public arena with feelings derived from the private, familial realms of life, they also described individuals as participating in a collective fiction, a large "as if."

However, Charlotte's demise also teaches some interesting lessons about sympathy, as the public's feelings often intersected with and construed the feelings of the principal players in this drama in complex, contradictory ways. While the public was seen as feeling the royal family's feelings, they were also seen as making up for the royal family's *lack* of feeling. Charlotte was cast in death as in her life as a neglected child, a mere pawn in her incompatible parents' warring relationship. George, Prince of Wales, and his consort, Princess Caroline of Brunswick, separated shortly after Charlotte's birth, and her relationships with both were always tense. In the initial response to her death, many writers expressed shock that no relatives—and particularly no female relatives—attended Charlotte in her accouchement and that she consequently died abandoned by her family.[31] The *Ladies' Monthly Museum* explicitly contrasted the family's evident lack of feeling to the responsiveness of the public: "No deficiency of feeling however can be charged against the people."[32] Burdened with a boorish father and an erratic mother, the princess was particularly interesting in both her life and death because she was herself "cradled . . . in sorrow, and nursed in the school of grief" (*M*, iii–iv). In this respect, the public discourse surrounding Charlotte is oddly reminiscent of the public's response to another Charlotte, the poet Charlotte Smith: for both the celebrated writer and the dead princess, public response took the form of imagining and sympathizing with *their own feelings*. Tears for Charlotte somehow got mixed up with Charlotte's tears: mourning her involved animating her as weeping.

This emphasis on Charlotte's own emotional susceptibility reminded Charlotte's mourners that in mourning her they were in part voicing criticism of the rule of the prince regent, for his lack of both domestic affection and affection for his people. Before and after her death Charlotte's own tears had political power, as she was seen as more sympathetic to both parliamentary opposition and religious dissenters than her increasingly unpopular father. Byron's "Lines to a Lady Weeping" reveals the powers of Charlotte's own sympathetic distresses. Appearing anonymously in 1812, Byron's poem responded to a report that Charlotte had burst into tears when the prince regent openly denounced the Whigs in a toast at a dinner party on her own birthday:

> Weep, daughter of a royal line,
> A Sire's disgrace, a realm's decay:
> Ah, happy! if each tear of thine
> Could wash a father's fault away!
>
> Weep—for thy tears are Virtue's tears—
> Auspicious to these suffering isles;
> And be each drop in future years
> Repaid thee by thy people's smiles![33]

In the history of this poem, the histories of national feeling and romantic emotion come together. Peter Manning has demonstrated that Charlotte's tears played a crucial role both in defining Byron's political profile and in circulating Byronic emotion: the appearance of "To a Lady Weeping" in the early editions of *The Corsair* boosted sales dramatically. Referring later to the verses on Charlotte as "The Weepers," Byron confided, "I wish to give them all possible circulation."[34] In any case, the people repaid Charlotte's tears not with smiles, but in kind, with tears of mourning. Very much in the idiom of Wordsworth's "On Seeing Miss Helen Maria Williams Weep at a Tale of Distress," the poem suggests that a woman's tears can be politically as well as poetically generative.

Three years after her death, Charlotte's tears still had their political uses. Mourning Charlotte, as I will discuss below, was revived at the time of the Queen Caroline affair. In his chapbook poem *Claremont* published at the height of popular support for Caroline, the radical shoemaker and journalist Allen Davenport addresses the *dead* Charlotte weeping for her mother's plight:

> But oh! thou had'st a Mother long exiled
> From thou her Daughter and her only child.
> And, O, what pleasure arises in one thought,
> That thou has practis'd what thy Mother taught!
> One cloud hung o'er thy mind, —Thy Mother's fate
> From which distilled (Felicity's alloy)
> A tear, that oft obscured a beam of joy.[35]

The dead Charlotte was imagined weeping not only for her mother but for her stillborn child. The author of "The Last Pious Aspirations of the Idolized Princess Charlotte" gives us access to Charlotte—"the mother of a moment"—in the hours before her own death weeping over her infant:

> Must I weep for thee, Babe? Nor shall my *single sorrow*
> In fast falling currents thy obsequies lave?
> For o'er thy hapless fate, ere the night of *to-morrow,*
> The sorrows of *millions* shall stream o'er thy grave!

As Esther Schor notes, this poem suggests that Charlotte's tears "are also the basis for the "sorrows of *millions* that are to follow hers. . . . Princess Charlotte is shown implicitly to instruct the entire nation in the moral affections of mourning."[36]

As these poems suggest, the meanings of the spread of feelings occasioned by Princess Charlotte's death depended in part on writers' and readers' claims to know and to represent the truth about other people's—including Charlotte's—own feelings. Rumors went back and forth about the true state of the regent's feelings: he was claimed to be either prostrate with sorrow or woefully indifferent. Many poems, such as those collected in *A Cypress Wreath*, focused on the private grief of Charlotte's husband, Prince Leopold, who was apotheosized as a paragon of masculine domestic virtue. Meanwhile, Anna Laetitia Barbauld's "On the Death of Princess Charlotte" turns from the people's woes to enter into the secret, mysterious response of the isolated monarch, Charlotte's grandfather, George III:

> ———Yet one there is
> Who midst this general burst of grief remains
> In strange tranquillity; whom not the stir
> And long-drawn murmurs of the gathering crowd,
> That by his very windows trail the pomp
> Of hearse, and blazoned arms, and long array
> Of sad funereal rites, nor the loud groans
> And deep-felt anguish of a husband's heart,
> Can move to mingle with this flood one tear:
> In careless apathy, perhaps in mirth,
> He wears the day.[37]

Barbauld turns to the mad, passive king in order to evoke the paralysis of the nation: the mourning for the princess, her poem suggests, should be a mourning for the country. But her poem also confirms that amidst the rhetoric of public, shared, visible emotion, a crucial place was made for concealed emotions, even emotional absences: public response was constructed *through* claims to represent emotional states concealed from the public eye.

In order to explore this idea, I will conclude by discussing how reflections on the meaning and status of emotion were embodied in the public's understanding of the feelings of two crucial figures: Sir Richard Croft, Charlotte's physician and principal accoucheur, and Charlotte's mother, Princess Caroline. In both cases, writers had particular investments in pinning down and claiming to know what appeared to be excessive or insufficient responses to Charlotte's death. At stake in the public's negotiations over the extravagance of their emotions and epistemological claims on their behalf were public differences over the relationships between class and gender. The story of the doctor who seemed to feel too much and the complicated narrative of Caroline's maternal sentiment reveal how charges of extravagance depended on changing assumptions about professional men and maternal women. Their stories confirm that narratives about feeling's origins and effects are social stories. My discussions of these two figures, then, are brief sketches, designed to suggest what their stories might tell us about the public construction of private passion in Regency England.

The truly melodramatic figure in Charlotte's story was that of her doctor, Sir Richard Croft. Croft attended Charlotte throughout her pregnancy and confinement, and he oversaw the delivery of the stillborn child. After Charlotte's death, Croft was criticized in the press, subject to allegations that his practices had brought about the tragedy at Claremont. The royal family sincerely absolved the doctor of any wrongdoing, but Croft apparently fell into a deep melancholy from which he never recovered: while attending the delivery of another socially prominent lady three months later, he shot himself.[38] Croft had been at the height of his professional career: having married the daughter of the preeminent aristocratic accoucheur of the day, he had gradually taken over his father-in-law's practice and was in demand among England's aristocratic ladies. In Charlotte's death, however, this socially ambitious professional man was transformed into a man of feeling. Huish attributed Croft's suicide to "an excess of delicate feeling, a susceptibility to painful regret, an extreme overanxiousness in respect to the proper discharge of professional duty" (*M*, 685). At the inquest following Croft's death, the surgeon George Hollings testified to his recent melancholy and his tendency to "sigh very much." When asked if the "death of the Princess had been the exciting cause of his temporary derangement of intellect," Hollings reported "that he had no doubt whatever of the insanity of the deceased having been caused by the unfortunate events at Claremont." One detail revealed at the inquest was that Croft appeared to have been reading Shakespeare's plays right before he pulled the trigger. Of the trajectory of Croft's feelings from despondency to suicide, the *New Monthly Magazine* commented, "when such sentiments as these grow too painful for the wounded spirit to bear, and rise into momentary madness, it is difficult to conceive a case more strongly appealing to our sympathy and sorrow."[39]

These accounts describe Croft as Charlotte's sincerest mourner, his death the final chapter in her story. The *Times*, for example, began its story on his death, "It is with feelings of uncommon pain that we find ourselves obliged to wind up the melancholy catastrophe at Claremont by relating the violent death of Sir Richard Croft."[40] Their story becomes a sentimental romance, Croft a young Werther committing suicide over a Charlotte. Amid the rhetoric of extreme sympathy and grief, the story of Charlotte's mourning contains its own caution about the dark side of feelings that go too far. The doctor's susceptibility to a typically late-eighteenth-century narrative about the man of feeling was, I would argue, symptomatic of his ambiguous status, his position at the crossroads of early nineteenth-century assumptions about gender, class, and professionalism. In early nineteenth-century England, the aristocratic accoucheur lived and worked on the borders of social respectability and of the medical establishment itself. A man doing the job traditionally done by female midwives, the accoucheur was met with hostility by the medical establishment; an intimate in the aristocratic household whose business involved the bodily details of its female inmates that only their female servants knew, the accoucheur could nevertheless claim the status of a gentleman. As Judith Schneid Lewis argues in her study of early nineteenth-century childbirth, the accoucheurs' role was strangely undefined and flexible, their relations with their patients and patients' families ambiguous and susceptible to speculation. For example, Croft's death caused certain "romantic" rumors to resurface, concerning his involvement in an alleged baby-swapping scandal twenty years earlier. Noting his death, the *Ladies' Monthly Museum* commented, "of private occurrences, none has occasioned more surmise and conjecture."[41] Croft's role in the "national calamity" of Charlotte's death—was he an irresponsible doctor? a faithful retainer? an accomplice to scandal or a man of honour?—made it expedient that the melancholy narrative of a man of feelings should fill the gap that he occupied, between eighteenth-century royal servant and nineteenth-century professional man. His fatal fit of passion seemed to have solved an ambiguity about where a man such as Croft would fit into such a story.[42]

But the public's feelings about Charlotte most crucially turned on one woman's feelings: Princess—then Queen—Caroline, whose own true feelings on the loss of her daughter were, until and even after her own death in 1821, a subject of intense debate and frequent revision. The history of representations of Caroline's grief constitutes a crucial chapter in the public use made of the emotions inspired by Charlotte's death; they made the story of her death part of the histories of maternal sentiment, middle-class values, and popular radicalism in early nineteenth-century England. At the time of Charlotte's death, Caroline's absence from Charlotte's side contributed to rumors of her want of maternal sentiment. Always somewhat careless of her reputation and permanently estranged from her husband, Caroline had obtained permission to leave England in 1814 and had been living on the Continent in an extravagant style that disturbed even her supporters. Evidence of Caroline's erratic response to the news of her only child's death filtered back from Italy: though she was reported to have passed out cold on first hearing the news, she surprised her guests the following day by resuming an ordinary cheerfulness and grumbling about having to wear mourning. One lady visitor from England was shocked both by Caroline's complaints and by her refusal to wear conventional mourning; and her replies to expressions of condolence on the occasion were said to be odd. Lady Charlotte Campbell confided that the letter she got from Caroline in response to her own note of condolence seemed "unfeeling and light-minded": "Truly, did I not know the Princess of Wales, I should be tempted to believe the letter was a *forgery*. It is such a strange manner of writing immediately after her poor daughter's decease."[43]

However, both at the time of Charlotte's death and three years afterward at the time of the queen's trial for adultery, Caroline's supporters made claims for her maternal grief central to agitation on her behalf. As a number of historians have argued, public responses to George IV's unsuccessful attempt to divorce Queen Caroline in 1820 galvanized and transformed the political consciousness of different constituencies of Britons. In Hazlitt's opinion, the queen's affair "was the only question I have ever known that excited a thorough popular feeling."[44] Her story has recently become a test case of sorts for cultural historians wishing to understand the meanings of class, gender, public opinion, and politics itself in early nineteenth-century England. Leonore Davidoff and Catherine Hall have analyzed the public's transformation of the scandalous queen into a sympathetic figure of wronged female virtue as evidence of the triumph of middle-class views of marriage, sexuality, and domesticity. Other historians have seen the Queen Caroline affair as a demonstration of the power of working-class radicalism to mobilize public opinion and to make alliances with liberal reformers. Thomas Laqueur has used the popular response to the queen to demonstrate the weakness of a popular radicalism that depended on ultimately conservative, melodramatic representations of a wronged and helpless queen; and most recently Anna Clark and Iain McCalman have suggested that popular support for the queen revealed, alternatively, precisely the subversive potential of melodramatic imagery—in particular its power to voice the concerns of working-class women.[45]

A central issue that these accounts do not fully explore is *how* exactly Caroline—an unlikely and even "bizarre" (Laqueur's word) candidate for canonization for virtue—was transformed into an object of people's feelings. Part of the answer lies in the way representations of Caroline made claims about her own feelings for Charlotte. Radical journals, ballad sheets, and chapbooks both before and during the trial portrayed Caroline as a wronged and grieving mother. So did fashionable magazines: there, Caroline became part of a cult of glamorous, wronged mothers whose sad stories reinforced the sanctity of the maternal bond.[46] Caroline's maternal sentiment, such representations asserted, guaranteed her virtue. Caroline turns out to be a quotation of Charlotte herself: "A London minister argued that the 'unrivaled purity and excellence' of her late daughter was evidence of Caroline's great virtue and of her right to be venerated as 'our civil mother.'"[47] The centrality of the image of the mourning Caroline to her trial for adultery and the dissemination of this image among different constituencies suggest a lesson about the complex political meanings that feelings can have. To middle-class, provincial women, Caroline's tears could serve as proof of the importance of *their* values: the sentimental, domestic virtues. To working-class women, those tears may have expressed *their* anxieties about family instability, their control over their children, and state intervention into the family.⁴⁸ In spite of—or indeed because of—the different meanings these tears could have, Caroline's maternal sentiment could temporarily unify men and women of different interests into an ocean of public feeling.

Most relevant to the interests of this book, finally, is the way in which the power of Caroline's feelings—or what were purported to be Caroline's feelings—depended on the ways in which the strange epistemic space that feelings were thought to occupy could be maneuvered. Caroline was an exile. Though her exile on the Continent during the last years of her daughter's life was largely self-willed, to the English people she appeared banished from the funeral, isolated and alone with her feelings. At least one poem written on Charlotte's decease ends by imagining Caroline's private feelings:

> But, alas! who can tell
> What she feels for a Daughter she ever loved well,
> While an exile she pines on a foreign strand,
> Far away from her friends and her native land?

"Oh! those only can tell, for those only can know," the poem continues, who have known what it is like to lose a child.⁴⁹ Like the miseries of the exiles in Hume's *Treatise*, who became more sympathetic the more that they fled, Caroline's feelings could be made up, sympathized with, made meaningful precisely because they were located in the space of exile. Feelings, this episode could teach us, become most public when they appear to be most private.⁵⁰

Caroline's exile rendered her emotions residents of a space at once hidden from view and open to speculation. One pro-Caroline clergyman evoked sympathy for the queen by exhorting his congregation to imagine this space: "In solitude . . . she hears the funeral knell announcing her daughter's unexpected dissolution; imagine the mother's anguish—describe it I cannot."⁵¹ The clergyman's plea—that we imagine someone having feelings, so we can have feelings about them ourselves—demonstrates that there can be political consequences to a speculative gesture we've seen throughout this book, in poetry, philosophy, and aesthetic theory. Political as well as aesthetic matters could turn on a claim to know a woman's feelings. I'd like to pause for a moment, however, on the second half of the clergyman's phrase: "imagine the mother's anguish—describe it I cannot." It designates feelings themselves as belonging to a space of exile, a place that can be imagined but not described. Coming in an era in which feelings were endlessly described, scrutinized, attributed, given life and origins, the clergyman's phrase should alert us that people make claims about feelings' unrepresentability when it is productive or convenient to do so. A reading of eighteenth- and early nineteenth-century epistemologies of feelings should teach us that feelings are not inherently impossible to know; they only become so. These histories of the claims to know feelings suggest that feelings may be most powerful, however, when they are where they are not supposed to be.

Reference Matter

Notes

Introduction

1. Hume, *Treatise of Human Nature*, 605, 317.
2. Tickell, 3, iii.
3. Chapone, 2: 41–42.
4. More, "Essay"; Wollstonecraft, *Rights of Woman*, 60–61.
5. For different accounts of antisentimental politics, see, for example, Butler; Todd; Barker-Benfield; Conger, ed.; and C. L. Johnson, *Equivocal Beings*.
6. Kames, 1:120.
7. Baillie, 11.
8. Hume, *Treatise of Human Nature*, 576.
9. Kames, 1:488, 471, 481. Subsequent references to this text will be in parentheses.
10. For an interesting discussion of the gendering of the epistemological dramas of Shakespeare's play in the context of seventeenth-century skepticism, see Scheman, 57–74.
11. On feeling in eighteenth-century social and political thought see Pocock; Hirschman; Eagleton; and Mullan. Two studies that focus on the social and political contexts for eighteenth-century sentiment are C. L. Johnson, *Equivocal Beings*; and Schor. For a view of a "long era of sensibility" that includes romanticism, see Ellison, "The Politics of Fancy," and also "Race and Sensibility" on colonialism and sensibility on both sides of the Atlantic. Barker-Benfield covers some aspects of the connections between sentiment, gender, and consumerism, as does Campbell.
12. S. Johnson, "Preface to Shakespeare," cited by Fox, 1. The arguments my study makes about the centrality of epistemological speculation

to eighteenth- and early nineteenth-century views of feeling could be complemented and confirmed by the study of other kinds of texts: medical writing, theories of theater and of acting, and religious and political writing. On medicine and feeling, see, for example, Mullan, 201–40; on relations between theater and feeling, I have benefited enormously from Marshall, *The Surprising Effects of Sympathy*; "Adam Smith" in *The Figure of Theater*, 167–92; and "True Acting."

13. The trend away from romantic feeling continues in postdeconstructive romantic studies: Ferguson's *Solitude and the Sublime* sees romanticism (primarily in the form of Kantian idealism) as a displacement of the role of affect in eighteenth-century aesthetics by questions about the nature of objects.

14. Recent book-length studies include Ross; Jacobus; Ellison, *Delicate Subjects*; and Mellor.

15. Two excellent recent studies that explore the relationships among gender, emotion, and power are Cvetkovich and Schiesari. Much of the recent literary-critical debate about women and feeling has centered on sentimentality in nineteenth-century American literature. The most unequivocal view of the damaging effects of feminine sentimentality is Douglas's *Feminization of American Culture*. The rehabilitation of sentimentality takes place in Tompkins, *Sensational Designs*. More complex accounts can be found in G. Brown; Sanchez-Eppler; and Samuels, ed.

16. Code, 11. For a brilliant approach to emotion that sees emotion—particularly sentimentality—at the junctures among gender, sexuality, and epistemology in modern culture, see Sedgwick, *Epistemology of the Closet*.

17. For more on the place of rhetoric in histories of emotion, see Pinch, "Emotion and History."

18. See, for example, Macpherson; Pocock; Luhmann; and Izenberg.

19. I must distinguish, however, the premise of this book from that of A. T. McKenzie's *Certain, Lively Episodes: The Articulation of Passion in Eighteenth-Century Prose*. For McKenzie, eighteenth-century discussions of the passions run *counter* to the individualism unleashed by empiricism: "The passions offered writers an invaluable element in this discourse, a set of terms consistent, traditional, exchangeable, and individually verifiable. They could, because of their uniformity, do a lot . . . to circumvent 'wayward individuality'" (20). In this view, passions represent no epistemological problems but are distinguished by their neoclassical generality and clarity.

20. Cited by Oxenhandler, 117.

21. Historical and sociological arguments for the role of the late eigh-

teenth century in the rise of the private, affective individual include Stone; Sennett; and Zaretsky. For important recent work on the construction of the subject in the eighteenth century, see de Bolla; F. Nussbaum; and Armstrong. The burden of much new historicist work on romantic literature is to demonstrate that the (masculine) romantic egotist is not as self-creating as he thinks; see, for example, Ross. There is another group of critics who see the eighteenth century and romantic periods not as consolidating but rather as experiencing a crisis about the status of the self. Variants of this position include Bogel; M. Brown; and Rzepka. For a study of the origins and tensions among different models of identity in the romantic period, see A. Henderson's *Romantic Identities*.

22. See Maus, 29–31.

23. Regarding the compatibility of skepticism and conservatism in Hume, I am indebted to Christensen, *Practicing Enlightenment*; David Miller; and Whelan.

24. Post-Lacanian psychoanalysis has been especially concerned with reexamining the place of affect. See, for example, Borch-Jacobsen; and Green, *Le Discours vivant*, and "Conceptions of Affect" in *On Private Madness*, 174–213. See also Brennan, who argues that the "mystery" of femininity can be accounted for precisely by seeing Freud's work as a theory of how emotions traverse the boundaries between persons.

25. Wordsworth, note to "The Thorn," *Lyrical Ballads*, 289.

26. Kames, 1:41. For a philological discussion of eighteenth-century emotion words, see, for example, Erametsa.

Chapter 1

1. For the "transcendence" view, see, for example, Abrams; and Davies. For the "continuities" view, see Tuveson; and Aarsleff. On this subject see also Law on the persistence of empiricist rhetoric in nineteenth-century aesthetics; Caruth, who argues that empiricism and claims to transcend it are always bound together and may be found within both "empiricist" and romantic texts; Knapp, who argues that romantic gestures toward idealism are a development of eighteenth-century ambivalence toward belief; and Christensen, *Coleridge's Blessed Machine of Language*, on Coleridge's continued and complicated indebtedness to Hartley's associationism.

2. For an account of eighteenth-century representations of feeling that stresses the neoclassical, see A. T. McKenzie.

3. Brissenden, 24. For an account of the relationship between em-

piricism and romanticism which construes individual feeling as a direct link between them, see W. J. Bate, 94.

4. Hume, *A Treatise of Human Nature*, 317. Subsequent page references will be in parentheses, noted *T*.

5. See Hirschman. For a general survey, see *Feeling and Emotion* by Gardiner, Metcalf, and Beebe-Center.

6. See Locke, 249–50.

7. Hume, *An Enquiry Concerning Human Understanding*, 1–2. Subsequent page references will be in parentheses, noted *E*.

8. *History of the Works of the Learned* 2 (Nov. 1739): 357.

9. The phrase comes from Box's description of the conclusion (101).

10. See, for example, N. K. Smith.

11. Rorty, 160–61. See also McIntyre; and Baier, esp. 129–45. For a related view of individuation as an effect of the practice of affect, see Deleuze, 17, 85–121.

12. Locke, 395.

13. Baier, 29.

14. See Kay, 131–41. Other recent discussions of the social dimensions of Hume's sympathy include Mullan; Eagleton; and Christensen, *Practicing Enlightenment*.

15. The last phrase is from Hume's autobiographical essay, "My Own Life," in *Essays, Moral, Political, and Literary*, 2. For Christensen's discussion of the autobiographical resonances of this example, see *Practicing Enlightenment*, 84.

16. On Hume's name change, see Christensen, *Practicing Enlightenment*, 57 n. 14.

17. While Hume used the notion of sympathy to think about theater, his is not a theatrical conception of sympathy. On this point I differ from Christensen, who suggests that sympathy enlists Hume's "theatrical" model of mind: "the mind is a kind of theatre, where several perceptions successively make their appearance; pass, re-pass, glide away, and mingle in an infinite variety of postures and situations" (*T*, 253). Here is Christensen: "The theater, like sympathy at large, works as an implicit guarantor of property rights because appropriation conventionalized is not the theft of property but its transfer. Post-Cartesian representation of the passions contributed both to the stability of their possession and to the facility of their transfer in an exchange with another passion owner" (72). Hume never, however, discusses sympathy in terms of theater. The theatrical metaphor in book 1—which is used primarily to indicate the constant flux of the mind—is not central to Hume's notion of how perception works, in the

way that, say, Locke's metaphor of the mind's "presence-room" is. For excellent discussions—from which I have learned much—of the theatricality of sympathy in other eighteenth-century writers such as Adam Smith, see Marshall, *The Figure of Theatre* and *The Surprising Effects of Sympathy*.

18. Christensen, *Practicing Enlightenment*, 71.

19. There is a relationship between the structure of sympathy that is revealed here, and the aesthetics of absorption in mid-eighteenth-century French art that Fried identifies in his influential book, *Absorption and Theatricality: Painting and Beholder in the Age of Diderot*. Fried charts the emergence, as an aesthetic desideratum, of the painting that behaves as if the beholder did not exist. This created a special interest in paintings of figures who seem absorbed in their own activities or consciousnesses, who turn away from the viewer; the image of a person asleep is for Fried a paradigm of the aesthetics of absorption.

20. *History of the Works of the Learned* 2 (Dec. 1739): 402.

21. Christensen, *Practicing Enlightenment*, 68. Christensen may reify "system" in Hume prematurely.

22. See the editor's footnote to the *Enquiry Concerning Human Understanding*, 10.

23. The association between affect and force is a persistent one; see Derrida; and Green's discussion of Freud's early tendency to quantify affect, *On Private Madness*, 174–213. I say "most passions" here because Hume does sometimes treat passions in antithetical ways—as instinct, for example.

24. In the appendix to the *Treatise*, Hume rejects the notion that one could actually *know* what force is in any essential way by consulting either the energies of our own minds or our projection of those energies into the world of matter: "No internal impression has an apparent energy, more than external objects have. Since, therefore, matter is confess'd by philosophers to operate by an unknown force, we shou'd in vain hope to attain an idea of force by consulting our own minds" (*T*, 633). For a related approach to empiricism, eighteenth-century philosophy's relation to Newton, and in particular to the notion of force (in Kant), see Caruth, 1–43, 58–71.

25. Reid, 19, 18. For the view of the *Treatise* as "uncouth and gloomy," and of Hume as an evil fanatic, see Beattie, *Essay on the Nature and Immutability of Truth*, 516. See also Beattie's allegory, unpublished in his lifetime, "The Castle of Scepticism," which features Hume as the lord of a gloomy, gothic castle.

26. See Box, 104–10.

27. See Richetti, 217, 228; Baier, 1–27; Williams, "David Hume," 123–45.

28. Compare the questioning of the passage above to that in a Puritan diary cited by Starr: "I was advised by my father to put these three questions to myself, for my help in preparation, and to examine myself upon them. What am I? What have I done? and what do I want? And by these three questions I did search and try myself, according to my weak ability, and what was amiss therein I humbly beg of God to pardon" (30).

29. Box, 104.

30. Hume himself raises the possibility of the presence of egotism and the violation of modesty in his own writing at the end of the conclusion; but interestingly, the forms that seem most immodest to Hume are not those that use "I" but rather those that are most *im*personal. He apologizes for seeming to have forgotten his modesty in being too positive about the obviousness of some points, in having overused "such terms as these, *'tis evident, 'tis certain, 'tis undeniable*; which a due deference to the public ought, perhaps, to prevent" (*T*, 274). He apologizes for not saying "I." Hume's truly autobiographical writings are "My Own Life" (in *Essays*), and the long letter to Dr. Arbuthnot, written at the age of eighteen, in which he describes his victory over the "Disease of the Learned," nervousness and hypochondria. For discussions of these texts, see Mossner; Williams, "David Hume"; Christensen, *Practicing Enlightenment*, 45–53.

31. See Marshall, *The Surprising Effects of Sympathy*.

32. The "sensationalist" view can be found in Burke; for the "associationist" view see Gerard. For a survey of late eighteenth-century affective aesthetics, see G. McKenzie, esp. chap. 5. Chapters 3 and 4 of this book will return to some of these issues.

33. Seward to Miss Weston, July 20, 1786, 1:164.

34. Bronson, 174.

35. Richard Stack, "An Essay on Sublimity of Writing," *Transactions of the Royal Irish Academy* 1 (1787); cited by Wasserman, 442.

36. Beattie, *Essays: on Poetry and Music*, 251.

37. Joseph Priestley, *A Course of Lectures on Oratory and Criticism* (1777); cited by Wasserman, 442.

38. Donaldson, 48.

39. The rule that personification is especially suited to the representation of passions themselves, or at least that personifications must be impassioned figures, is suggested as well by Kames's vehement disapproval of Pope's Dullness in *The Dunciad*, a figure of the absence of passion (2:251). On the relationship between personification, fanaticism, and questions of agency, see Knapp.

40. In this context I find suggestive B. Johnson's remark that "per-

sonification is a trope available for occupancy by either subjects or linguistic entities" (45).

41. Ferguson, *Language as Counter-Spirit*, 27–28.
42. Donaldson, lxiv.
43. Wordsworth, Preface to *Lyrical Ballads*, in *Prose Works*, 1:131, 135.
44. Kames, 2:235.

Chapter 2

1. "Of the Delicacy of Taste and Passion," *Essays, Moral, Political, and Literary*, 1:91. Subsequent references will be in parentheses.
2. Hatfield, 15. The general late eighteenth-century trend toward seeing women as custodians of a range of cultural values has been studied by Poovey, *The Proper Lady*; Armstrong; Davidoff and Hall; and Barker-Benfield.
3. See Scott, 777–97; see also K. B. Jones, 186–235; for a study that explores the ways in which nineteenth-century women writers confront the tensions between experience and language, see Homans.
4. On the role of emotion in feminism, see, for example, Cvetkovich; Jaggar, 145–71; and Scheman, 22–35.
5. In an influential essay, Kaplan demonstrates the long-lasting effects of Wollstonecraft's emphasis on subjectivity and sexuality; see 31–56.
6. Wollstonecraft, *Rights of Woman*, 60, 61, 62.
7. On the history of eighteenth-century feminism, and contexts for Wollstonecraft, see Sapiro; Cott; Rodgers; Staves; Kelly; Conger; and Poovey, *The Proper Lady*. On sensibility and feminism generally, see also Poovey, "Ideology and *The Mysteries of Udolpho*"; and C. L. Johnson, "A 'Sweet Face.'"
8. Barker-Benfield, xviii; see also 287–350. For a study that persuasively challenges this point of view, see C. L. Johnson's *Equivocal Beings*, which argues that sensibility in late eighteenth-century England was a masculine prerogative: "woman's presence in a sentimental public sphere is not to be confused with her empowerment there" (14).
9. Mayo, 487; on copyright law, see Collins. The phrase "prodigiously multiplied" appears in the *Monthly Review* 80 (Apr. 1789): 368. On late eighteenth-century reading, see de Bolla; on poetry anthologies, see Benedict.
10. Knox, preface to *Elegant Extracts*. Wordsworth and his brothers and sister grew up reading from *Elegant Extracts*; see Fink.
11. *The Female Aegis*, 78.

12. Goldsmith, preface to *Poems for Young Ladies* (1767), 9:226.
13. "Introductory Address," *The Lady's Poetical Magazine*, 1–2.
14. Quoted in Poovey, *The Proper Lady*, 37. For an overview of the position of the woman poet in late eighteenth-century literary culture, see Ross, 187–231.
15. *The European Magazine* 10 (Aug. 1786): 91.
16. For a related reading of Smith's sonnets along with those of William Bowles and Gray's influential "Sonnet on the Death of Dr. Richard West," see Schor, *Bearing the Dead*, 60–69. Schor places Smith's work in the context of the expanding meaning of the elegiac in eighteenth-century poetry. She also focuses on the reflexivity and allusiveness of Smith's sonnets, though her reading of the tension between "natural and fabricated feeling" in Smith's and Bowles's sonnets is different from mine.
17. See Coleridge, preface to *Poems*; Wordsworth, note to "Stanzas Suggested in a Steamboat Off St. Bees' Heads," *Poetical Works* 4:403.
18. *Gentleman's Magazine* 52 (1786): 334; see also *Monthly Review* 71 (Nov. 1784): 368.
19. Polwhele, 22–23.
20. From *Elegiac Sonnets*, 5th ed., in *The Poems of Charlotte Smith*. Subsequent references to Smith's poetry will be to this edition. See Curran's discussion of this poem in "Romantic Poetry: The I Altered."
21. Seward, letter to Theophilus Swift, July 9, 1789, 2:287. An obituary notice in the *European Magazine* distinguished Smith from poets lacking originality (*European Magazine* 50 [Nov. 1806]: 339–40).
22. "Preface to Third and Fourth Editions," Smith, 4.
23. Cowper to Charlotte Smith, Oct. 26, 1793, *Letters*, 4:418. For a fascinating approach to another poet, Keats, whose poetry also self-consciously advertises "its own fine phrases" and its appropriations of the canon, see Levinson. Levinson reads the excesses and appropriations of Keats's style—and the scandal they created—in terms of the poet's relation to structural tensions within early nineteenth-century middle-class social aspirations.
24. Smith was not likely to have known the sonnets of Renaissance writers such as Elizabeth I and Lady Mary Wroth. On gender and genre in women's sonnets, see A. R. Jones; N. J. Miller; Feinberg; Fried; and Mermin.
25. Smith's seventh sonnet also links hearing to quotation. Compare this to Collins's "Ode Occasioned by the Death of Mr. Thomson" (also a river poem), in which Collins imagines Thomson's aeolian harp from *The Castle of Indolence* absorbed into the reeds of the Thames:

Then maids and youths shall linger here,
And, while its sounds at distance swell,
Shall sadly seem in Pity's ear
To hear the woodland pilgrim's knell. (9–12)

26. Smith's literary miseries are of course not completely without reference to nonliterary matters. A later sonnet, "To Dependence," clearly refers to the miseries of economic uncertainties that Smith knew well (*Poems*, 51).

27. *European Magazine* 10 (Aug. 1786): 125; *Gentleman's Magazine* 56, part 1 (Apr. 1786): 333; *Gentleman's Magazine* 56, part 2 (Sept. 1786): 791.

28. Smith, *Poems*, 5.

29. Cowper to William Hayley, Jan. 29, 1793, *Letters*, 4:281. The fullest account of Smith's life is that of Hilbish; see also Turner.

30. Smith to Mrs. Rose, Jan. 16, 1804. Permission to quote granted by the Henry W. and Albert A. Berg Collection, The New York Public Library, Astor, Lenox, and Tilden Foundations.

31. Smith to Reverend J. Warton [1791?], British Museum Add. MS.42561.

32. Smith, *Poems*, 6.

33. Lamb, 1:19; quoted by MacLean, 458. On romantic uses of the sonnet, see Curran, 29–55.

34. I owe this formulation to Paul Fry.

35. Berlant, 243–44.

Chapter 3

1. Seward, 6:367, quoted in Hartman, 4; Lucy Aikin in *Annual Review*, quoted in Ross, 50; *Le Beau Monde, or, Literary and Fashionable Magazine*, quoted ibid., 51–52; Coleridge, *Biographia*, 2:109.

2. See, for example, Sperry; Ferry; see also Rzepka.

3. Hartman, 3, 6.

4. Preface to *Lyrical Ballads* (1802), *Prose Works*, 1:128. Subsequent references to this edition will be included in the text.

5. "Strange Fits of Passion I Have Known," ll. 25–26, in *Lyrical Ballads*, ed. Brett and Jones.

6. Wordsworth to Alexander Dyce, Dec. 4, 1833, *Letters*, 2:664; see also 4, 157, 236–39, 260, 604. Dyce's *Specimens of British Poetesses* (1827) was the first anthology of women's poetry after *Poems by Eminent Ladies* (1755), which was reprinted several times during the latter half of the eighteenth century. On Wordsworth's early attachment to women poets, see Moorman, 54.

7. Wordsworth's manuscript album for Lady Lowther has been published as *Poems and Extracts Chosen by William Wordsworth for an Album Presented to Lady Mary Lowther*; the extract from Laetitia Pilkington's "Sorrow" is on pages 74–75. Throughout Pilkington's career, her activities as a writer were often confused with her sexual activities; see her *Memoirs*, 90, 133–34, 137–39.

8. See, for example, Averill. While Averill claims that "even in his mature work, Wordsworth draws more from the sentimental movement than does any other major English Romantic poet" (10), his project is Wordsworth's purification of sentimental convention, the infusion of "humanized" moral value into representations of suffering. Averill's understanding of sentimentality, moreover, depends on the one hand on assimilating its ideas to eighteenth-century aesthetic theory and, on the other, on dismissing its popular literary manifestations as debased, feminine, mass culture. Recent approaches to the romantics' relationships to popular literary genres have challenged this view: I am especially indebted to the essays of Swann. See also Bewell, who suggests that Wordsworth's interest in marginal, often feminine, social figures in the "experimental" poems was in part a legacy of empiricism, Enlightenment anthropology, and moral philosophy; and Simpson, *Wordsworth's Historical Imagination*.

9. See Wolfson's "*Lyrical Ballads* and the Language of (Men) Feeling," which argues that possession by feminine feeling and feminine voice are central to Wordsworth's poetics in the *Lyrical Ballads*. Relevant also is J. Page, *Wordsworth and the Cultivation of Women*, which appeared too recently to be incorporated here.

10. *The European Magazine* 11 (Mar. 1787): 202; reprinted in *Poetical Works*, 1:269. Wordsworth's only acknowledgment of the poem occurs in a note written in a copy of *An Evening Walk* that he presented to his son William, Mar. 16, 1846: "Previous to the appearance of these two attempts [*An Evening Walk* and *Descriptive Sketches*] I had not published anything, except a sonnet printed in the European Magazine about June or July 1786 when I was a School-Boy. The sonnet was signe[d] Axiologus." Wordsworth misremembered the date; the sonnet to Williams is signed "Axiologus." See Reed, 71. For an excellent reading of this poem see Schor, 69–72.

11. See M. Tanner.

12. See Averill, 38.

13. "To Miss Helen Maria Williams: On her Poem of *Peru*," signed "Eliza, Woolwich June 25," *Gentleman's Magazine* 54, 2 (July 1784): 532; "Sonnet to Mrs. Smith, on Reading her Sonnets Lately Published," signed

"'D,' Chichester May 8, 1786," *The European Magazine* 9 (May 1786): 366; "To the Muse, on Reading Miss Smith's Sonnets," "by a Lady of Fifteen," *Gentleman's Magazine* 55, 2 (Dec. 1785): 991; "Sonnet to Mrs. Smith," *The European Magazine* 10 (Aug. 1786): 125.

14. Steele, *Tatler* 181 (1710), cited in A. Richardson, 15.

15. For a recent approach to Wordsworth's account of the origins of feelings in *The Prelude*, see Miall. While Miall recognizes feeling as a problem, his approach affirms the notion that feelings are fundamentally prelinguistic, unsayable entities that reveal the inadequacies of the discourses that represent them.

16. Wordsworth, Note to "The Thorn," *Lyrical Ballads*, 289.

17. Locke, 399, 397. Caruth similarly sees Locke, Wordsworth, and Freud as belonging to a tradition of inquiry in which empirical arguments and the need to transcend or displace them are always intertwined.

18. Freud, *Standard Edition*, 17:180; further references to this edition, abbreviated *SE*, will be included in the text.

19. Bewell compares Wordsworth's early interest in hysterical women to Freud's (142–83), and provides as well important historical context for Wordsworth's poetic investigations of socially marginal women in extreme mental states.

20. Hazlitt, "My First Acquaintance with Poets," *Selected Writings*, 57.

21. See, for example, Brooks; and Averill. For alternatives, see, in addition to the critics cited in notes 8 and 9, Christensen's discussion of "The Thorn," which proposes that the persons in Wordsworth's lyrics of suffering are not dramatic characters properly speaking, but rather figures in the improper circulation of language and affect ("Wordsworth's Misery").

22. See, for example, De Quincey's definition of sympathy: "the act of reproducing in our minds the feelings of another" ("On the Knocking at the Gate in Macbeth," *Confessions*, 83).

23. Editors Owen and Smyser are baffled by the apparent literalness with which real bodies appear to surface in this passage: "The force of this application of the principle escapes us," they comment flatly, "unless it refers merely to the perception that the male and female bodies are at once like and unlike" (*Prose Works*, 1:184). This contribution to the theory of sexuality reappears, at a moment of bathetic violence, in James Hogg's parody of Wordsworth: "for on similitude, / In dissimilitude man's sole delight, / And all the sexual intercou[r]se of things / Do most supremely hang" ("The Stranger," in *The Poetic Mirror*, 142).

24. For a discussion of the often circular logic in the Preface con-

cerning passion and its relationship to meter, see Wolfson, "Romanticism and the Measures of Meter."

25. In her "Prospectus" for the *Cheap Repository of Publications on Religious and Moral Subjects* (1795), Hannah More both deplores the spread of "poison" through "the channel of vulgar and licentious publications" which have "a mischevious popularity among the lower ranks," and proposes her plan to manipulate popular forms and mass distribution to didactic, socially conservative purposes. On middle-class anxieties about popular literature, mass literacy, and the spread of revolutionary ideas, see Webb. Wordsworth's audience during this period was of course not the broadside- and chapbook-reading masses. Casting his claim about the effects of form in reformist rhetoric, Wordsworth displaces his concerns about middle-class reading culture's taste for popular forms (see Preface, 43–44) onto a real "mass" audience.

26. "Goody Blake and Harry Gill," ll. 17, 18, 20, 42, 51, 56, in *Lyrical Ballads*; all references to the poem will be by line number to this edition.

27. Hartley, 1:143.

28. Laplanche, 88, 97.

29. Ibid., 91.

30. Bersani, 9.

31. The efficacy of a "feminine" chatter for producing poetry is suggested by Wordsworth's characterization of the narrator of "The Thorn"— a narrator not unlike that of "Goody Blake"—as a chatterer, a man who has "become credulous and talkative from indolence" (Note to "The Thorn," *Lyrical Ballads*, 288).

32. *The Vale of Esthwaite*, ll. 53–58, *Poetical Works*, 1:271. On the connection between sadism and voice, see also Barthes, 143–44. The subject of romantic ventriloquism, whether romantic poets speak in voices not their own, has been admirably studied by Parker, Eilenberg, and others.

33. Darwin, 2:359; Southey, review of *Lyrical Ballads*, in *Critical Review*, 2d ser., 24 (Oct. 1798): 200, reprinted in Reiman, ed., *The Romantics Reviewed*, part A, 1:308.

34. Coleridge, *Biographia*, 2:6.

35. Wordsworth's claim to have disseminated the story to "many hundreds" was not unfounded. It was one of the most popular poems of the first edition of the *Lyrical Ballads*, often singled out in reviews. In 1798 and 1799 it was reprinted in full by the *Analytical Review*, the *Edinburgh Magazine*, the *New Annual Register for 1798*, the *Ipswich Magazine*, and the *Universal Magazine*, as well as by a magazine in New Hampshire. It was

one of the few poems from the *Lyrical Ballads* to find a place in turn-of-the-century anthologies such as Sidney Melmoth's *Beauties of English Poetry* (1801) and C. Earnshaw's *The Wreath* (1802)—see Mayo, 519; Bateson, 17; Bauer, 37–45. It was not the poem's "impressive metre" that insured its popular transmission but the conditions of a literary marketplace which permitted without restraint the mechanical repetition of poems through widely circulating periodicals, a literary market that was buoyed in part by increasing numbers of popular women writers and women readers.

36. Sedgwick, "A Poem Is Being Written," 115.

37. Cottle, 260, footnote.

38. "Poor Susan," ll. 11–12, in *Lyrical Ballads*; all references to the poem will be by line number to this edition.

39. See Manning, "Placing Poor Susan: Wordsworth and the New Historicism," in *Reading Romantics*, 300–319. There are many points of agreement between Manning's discussion of this poem and my own.

40. Glen, 103; Averill, 212.

41. *Lyrical Ballads*, 302.

42. J. and Z. Boyd point out rightly that the effect of the present perfect at the beginning of the poem suggests continuity and repetition, but they fail to grasp how the tense changes, particularly in the last line. The last line of stanza four should be compared to the appearance of this tense in the "Intimations" ode: "That there hath passed away a glory from this earth" (l. 18).

43. Lamb, *Letters*, 2:158.

44. Quoted by Manning, *Reading Romantics*, 363.

45. Simpson, "What Bothered Charles Lamb," 597, 595–96.

46. On the conditions of working women, see Pinchbeck.

47. Simpson, "What Bothered Charles Lamb," 604. For a reading of why Wordsworth himself may connect prostitution, theater, and representation, see Jacobus, "'Splitting the Race of Man in Twain': Prostitution, Personification, and *The Prelude*," in *Romanticism, Writing, and Sexual Difference*, 206–36.

48. Mayo, 495.

49. See Klancher's analysis of the Preface, 140. For a study of how the figure of the prostitute in nineteenth-century literature represented questions about social determination and agency, see Anderson; for a related argument about how prostitution haunts another Wordsworth ballad, see Goodwin, 163–67.

50. Hazlitt, 57.

51. The word "mismatch" is from Hartman's account in his "Retro-

spect 1971" in *Wordsworth's Poetry*, xix; for other accounts of the poem's mismatches see Ferguson, *Language As Counter-Spirit*; and Caraher, 103–15.

52. "Strange Fits of Passion," *Lyrical Ballads*, ll. 16–17. All references to the poem are to this edition, except where noted.

53. The concordance yields two instances of "slide" in the *Lyrical Ballads*, both of which confirm its tactile, surreptitious qualities: "And I could run and slide," from "We Are Seven"; and "Old Daniel his hand to the treasure will slide," from "The Two Thieves."

54. Wolfson, "*Lyrical Ballads* and the Language of (Men) Feeling," 35, 40.

55. *Poetical Works*, 2:29.

Chapter 4

1. Burke, *Reflections on the Revolution*, 175; for other accounts of radicals' emotional insensitivity see *The Anti-Jacobin; Or, Weekly Examiner* (Nov. 20, 1797): 7; (Dec. 4, 1797): 28, 31; Wollstonecraft, *Rights of Men*, 2, 5, 6, 10, 27. Most accounts of the relationship between the gothic novel and the French Revolution focus on the genre's themes and iconography; see, for example, Paulson, 215–47. For a discussion of the political connotations of "enthusiasm," see Tucker, 93–106; for a study of the language of the Revolution debates, see Boulton.

2. Austen, *Northanger Abbey*, *Novels*, 5:41.

3. Radcliffe, *Mysteries of Udolpho*, 248–49. Subsequent page references to this text will be in parentheses.

4. Burke, *Philosophical Enquiry*, 131, 50–51, 248.

5. Sedgwick argues in "The Character in the Veil" that what lies behind veils in gothic fiction may be little different from the veils themselves. We could propose an associationist explanation of Emily's terror in which the cause would not be what's behind the veil but rather a chain of associations surrounding the veil itself (which strikes Emily with fear before she lifts it). This is neither the first black veil Emily sees nor the last. The first belongs to a nun who leads Emily to her father's tomb: "Emily paused a moment at the door; a sudden fear came over her, and she returned to the foot of the stair-case, where, as she heard the steps of the nun ascending, and, while she held up the lamp, saw her black veil waving over the spiral balusters, she was tempted to call her back" (90–91).

6. Hume, *Treatise*, 630–31; Hume, "Of Tragedy," in *Essays*, 1:261. For a survey of associationist views, see G. McKenzie.

7. Burke, *Treatise*, 47.

8. Ibid., 49–50. For an account of the Burkean sublime which sees as central Burke's tendency to render objects and images indistinguishable, see Ferguson, *Solitude and the Sublime*.

9. Ibid., 47–48.

10. Kames, 1:92.

11. Castle's essay "The Spectralization of the Other" is one of the few sustained approaches to the pre- and post-*Udolpho* sections of the novel. I find Castle's phenomenological description of the novel's representations of others excellent.

12. Kiely, 65. Kiely's phrase seems a more apt description of Radcliffe's prose than Castle's assessment of her language as "vulgar": she speaks of the need "to restore to view the powerful current of feeling in her work, however awkwardly or crudely this feeling is expressed" (307, n. 3). If Radcliffe's prose is crude or vulgar, it is precisely because it so dramatically attaches feeling to itself, not because "genuine feeling" is hidden under it.

13. I am indebted here to the anthropologist K. Stewart's eloquent essay, "Nostalgia—A Polemic." For a view of the historical displacements of eighteenth-century gothic fiction, see Punter. *Udolpho*'s meditations on time may be seen as meditations on its own length and status as a time occupier (or waster) in a context in which increased leisure time for middle-class women was accompanied by prohibitions against wasting time; see Davidoff and Hall, 225–28. The author of the "Memoirs of the Life and Writings of Mrs. Radcliffe" (published with Radcliffe's posthumous *Gaston de Blondeville*) makes much of her predicament as the wife of a busy newspaperman (William Radcliffe owned and edited *The English Chronicle*); he claims that she wrote in order to fill up her evenings in her husband's absence (1:6).

14. S. Stewart, "Notes on Distressed Genres," 67, 73, 74. Stewart means by "distressed" what the fashion industry means when it refers to "distressed leather"—manipulated to look old.

15. On Radcliffe and travel literature, see Batten; Railo; and Wright. For a related discussion of the relationship of aesthetic dilemmas of Radcliffe's fiction to her *Journey*, see Cottom. In *The British Abroad*, Black documents how the journeys of English travelers were thwarted not only by the French Revolution but by military and political conflict throughout the century.

16. Radcliffe, *Journey*: on Dutch towns, 18; on the Lake District, 419; on the decorum of detail, 103 (Radcliffe is citing Samuel Johnson).

17. It is instructive to compare Radcliffe's *Journey* with Dorothy

Wordsworth's "Journal of a Visit to Hamburgh, and of Journey from Hamburgh to Goslar" (1798).
  18. Radcliffe, *Journey*, 136.
  19. Ibid., 411.
  20. Sedgwick, "The Character in the Veil," 264.
  21. The author of the "Memoirs of the Life and Writing of Mrs. Radcliffe" alludes to the possibility that Radcliffe's own prestige and glamour at a certain point in her life were inseparable from the rumors that she was herself dead (in *Gaston de Blondeville* 1:3–83).
  22. Another example would be the opening sections of *The Romance of the Forest*, which follow La Motte's self-conscious explorations of the very literary forest into which he has wandered. For an interesting interpretation of the gothic novel's high degree of reference to its own formalism, see A. Henderson, "An Embarrassing Subject." Henderson argues that the novels' formalism of characterization expresses a fear that identity itself may be purely formal and relational; she persuasively links both the formalism and the fears about it to a contemporary perception of the nonnatural, machinelike dimensions of the late eighteenth-century middle classes' emergent position.
  23. In *Solitude and the Sublime*, Ferguson argues that the Gothic novel specializes in staging a conflict between the claims of experience and the claims of a systematic or formal world view; see 97–98.
  24. Kiely, 79.
  25. In her essay on the relationship between the heroic epistle and the gothic romance, Beer argues that it is the gothic's indebtedness to some of the characteristics of a very old form that allowed women writers to express certain kinds of emotions.
  26. Compare Castle: "Whoever he is, wherever he is, the lover is always a *revenant*" (236). While I find her descriptions of the haunting behavior of other people brilliant, we differ in our explanations of this effect. For Castle, *Udolpho* documents the emergence of the romantic individual, who reduces others to specters (see 237). My reading finds no romantic individuals in the novel, and finds it stressing how oppressively, invasively present—rather than spectralized—other people are.
  27. Psychoanalytic approaches to *Udolpho* tend to focus on either the father or the mother. Kahane's Chodorowian discussion of the gothic treats the missing mother as the center of the novel, a figure who is fantasized as both self and other and whose projections onto the various female characters in the novel, as well as onto the body of the castle itself, chart Emily's explorations of femininity. Such a focus on the mother provides a

useful corrective to oedipal, gothic-as-the-law-of-the-father approaches. It could be argued, however, that the novel scrambles the critic's temptation to choose between the oedipal and the pre-oedipal by strangely confusing maternity with paternity. While the figure of the potentially transgressive father is an entirely familiar plot device, this novel questions not St. Aubert's paternity but Mme St. Aubert's maternity. When the Lady Laurentini asserts that Emily is the daughter of the Marchioness de Villeroi, Emily responds that she is, rather, the daughter of M. St. Aubert (647), thus begging the question. The book seems to forget, that is, that maternity and paternity operate differently, and in some respects treats *St. Aubert père* as the mother. For essays that make related arguments, see Kowaleski-Wallace and Yeager, eds., *Refiguring the Father*.

28. This argument belongs to Fawcett's *"Udolpho's* Primal Mystery," 487, 488.

29. See, for example, P. Brooks, "The Fictions of the Wolf Man," in *Reading for the Plot*; Laplanche and Pontalis, "Fantasy and the Origins of Sexuality."

30. Abraham, 291. For a literary critical use of Abraham and Torok's notion of the phantom, see Rashkin.

31. Abraham and Torok, 8.

32. Ibid., 15.

33. Abraham, 292.

34. Ibid., 291.

35. The literature on gothicism and psychoanalysis includes Day; Masse; and Morris.

36. My point is not unrelated to the sense of many readers, from Walter Scott onward, that Radcliffe subordinates character to feeling. Compare Kelly: "It is the emotions themselves which Radcliffe is interested in, not their embodiment in character" ("A Constant Vicissitude," 50).

37. S. Stewart, *On Longing*, 20, 24, 23.

38. In "Anger and the Politics of Naming," Scheman takes the example of women learning to recognize anger in 1970's consciousness-raising groups as an instance of the way politics can shape epistemologies of feeling.

39. Coward, 7.

40. Ibid., 7–8.

Chapter 5

1. Radcliffe, *Mysteries of Udolpho*, 6; *Female Aegis*, 78.
2. For an interesting account of the range of issues, social and aes-

thetic, that reading raised for the late eighteenth century and of the diversity of writings about reading during this period, see de Bolla, "Of the Transportation of the Reader: the Reading Subject," in *Discourse of the Sublime*, 230–80. On the class politics of reading in the late eighteenth and early nineteenth centuries, see Webb.

3. Austen, *Persuasion*, *Novels*, 5:3. Subsequent page references to the novel will be in parentheses. Tanner (208–9) has also noticed the self-referential nature of the novel's opening paragraph.

4. See Moler, 187–223; see also C. L. Johnson, *Jane Austen*, 149–50. It should perhaps be stressed that while the forces that cause Lady Russell to pressure Anne into refusing Wentworth are in part specifically those of a landed gentry for whom alliances of rank and fortune were crucial, the general pressures that sought to make propriety, family, and "a sense of duty" (232) essential to woman's nature stem from an ideological matrix that was shared by that class *and* the bourgeois and professional classes. Thus it would be incorrect to say that it is strictly an aristocratic class system that is responsible for Anne's predicament; but it would also be wrong to feel, as critics sometimes have, that in thoroughly discrediting the Elliots, *Persuasion* is opening up a liberating new world for female autonomy. For differing views on politics and class in Austen's fiction and in *Persuasion* in particular, see Williams, *The Country and the City*, 108–19, as well as Butler; Spring; Evans; and M. Stewart.

5. Scott, review of *Emma*, *Quarterly Review* (Mar. 1816), in Southam, ed., *Critical Heritage*, 59, 61, 62, 63, 68.

6. Ibid., 68, 69.

7. Austen, *Sense and Sensibility*, *Novels*, 1:360.

8. Austen, *Emma*, *Novels*, 4:408.

9. Ibid., 4:407.

10. Nussbaum, "Love's Knowledge," 263–72.

11. Morgan, 7.

12. Austen, *Novels*, 4:412.

13. Inchbald, 225.

14. On Austen and Wordsworth, see Tave; Litz; Ruoff; and Siskin, 125–47. Auerbach alludes to Shelley and Keats. The most comprehensive treatments of the lyric and romantic nature of the novel are those of Thomas and of Favret, 165–75. For comparisons to Woolf, see N. Page, 48, 107.

15. Austen, *Mansfield Park*, *Novels*, 3:392.

16. Cf. D. A. Miller (60–64) on Austen's frustration with this body's resistance to meaning.

17. Freud, *Beyond the Pleasure Principle*, Standard Edition, 18:26; W. Benjamin, "On Some Motifs in Baudelaire," *Illuminations*, 162.
18. Maria Edgeworth, Feb. 21, 1818, quoted in Southam, 17.
19. See Poovey, *The Proper Lady*, 224–40.
20. Cottom, 122; Steele, 463. Gilbert and Gubar (11) have taken Anne and Harville's debate as part of their accumulation of evidence that women have lacked authority over their own images in literature.
21. Gass, "The Medium of Fiction," cited in Nell, 1.
22. Austen-Leigh, 102.
23. Another moment at the end of the novel where authorial rustlings can be heard is in the odd allusion to Scheherazade's head at the very beginning of chapter 11: Anne wishes to tell Lady Russell the revelations about Mr. Elliot's character, but she must "defer her explanatory visit" because she is engaged with the Musgroves: "Her faith was plighted, and Mr. Elliot's character, like the Sultaness Scheherazade's head, must live another day" (229). The allusion reminds us, just as the story is winding down, that the events in Anne's life are events in a story, both deferring and bringing about an ending. This seems especially true since we know that Austen in fact had difficulty writing the ending of *Persuasion*. Dissatisfied with her original ending, she wrote two new chapters—and this allusion appears right at the beginning of the second new chapter. Revision involved adding an extra chapter, deferring both the revelation of Elliot's reputation and the conclusion of the book.
24. For an excellent discussion of how Wentworth's letter disrupts and realigns relations within the novel and between the novel and its reader, see Favret, 165–75. On the temporal coincidence of the fictional recipient's reading and the reader's reading of a fictional letter, see Michel Butor, *Inventory*, 20–21, cited in S. Stewart, *On Longing*, 9.
25. See Tanner, 211–12.
26. *The Female Aegis*, 78.
27. Austen, *Northanger Abbey*, Novels, 5:37, 15.
28. Hunt, *Men, Women and Books*, 2:140.
29. Cottom's discussion of the walk to Winthrop has yielded similar insights. He conceives of Austen's characters as existing in an "environment of quotation" (119) in order to stress Austen's apperception of the rigorously social and cultural contents of her heroines' psyches. Cf. his assessment of the love plot of *Persuasion*: "The passage of time intervenes here to characterize the nature of love as the repetition or 'quotation' of an earlier experience that is not personal and immediate but cultural and historical, and embodied in literature as in the institutions of society" (120).

Coda

1. Sir William Forbes, *An Account of the Life and Writings of James Beattie* (1806), cited in J. Bate, 17.

2. Reprinted frequently in the last decade of the eighteenth and first decades of the nineteenth century were D. E. MacDonnel, *A Dictionary of Quotations, in Most Frequent Use*; in 1823–25 appeared William Kingdom's three-volume *Dictionary of Quotations from the British Poets*. See Bohn, v–vi, for a Victorian quotation-collector's history of quotation books.

3. *The Complete Letter Writer*, vi; see also *The Epistolary Guide*, 2. I am indebted for these references to the research of Jennifer Richardson, unpublished bibliography, University of Michigan, 1994.

4. Austen, *Sanditon*, in *Lady Susan / The Watsons / Sanditon*, 184; *Emma*, *Novels*, 4:69, 75. On commonplace books and the use of quotations in diaries among the provincial middle classes, see Davidoff and Hall, 157–62.

5. J. Bate, 6.

6. A true genealogy of quotation would have to include, for example, Montaigne's *Essays*, Burton's *Anatomy of Melancholy*, or Emerson's essay, "Quotation and Originality." Three studies of quotation to which I am indebted are Compagnon; Flesch; and Balfour.

7. Beginning in the romantic period itself and intensifying throughout the nineteenth century is a view of contagious emotion—including certain kinds of literary affects—as "sensation," as a debased experience belonging to mass culture and urban crowds. On high culture's ambivalence toward the transmission of sensation, see Swann's work on Coleridge ("'Christabel,'" "Lovely Ladies and Literary Gentlemen"); and Cvetkovich. While emotion attracted the attention of eighteenth-century medical science, as Mullan and others have discussed, emotional contagion became further medicalized, in the Victorian period, as a social *disease*: see Vrettos.

8. Wordsworth, *Prelude* (1805), 5.585–89.

9. On the quotation as a kind of wound, transitional object, or fetish, see Compagnon, 15–45.

10. C. Brown, 3; Wordsworth, "Essay, Supplementary to the Preface" (1815) in *Prose Works*, 3:69. Shaver reports a copy of the sonnets in the poet's collection. Sonnets 64 and 73 were the only Shakespeare sonnets in George Henderson's 1803 sonnet anthology, *Petrarcha: A Selection of Sonnets*. On romantic views of the sonnet, see Curran, *Poetic Form*, 29–55.

11. De Grazia, 215.

12. Booth, 246.

13. For a phenomenology of quotation that sees quotations working not as fragments of other texts but as texts with lives of their own—like "an organ removed and put in reserve"—see Compagnon, 18. For a discussion of the impersonality of Wordsworthian affect to which I am deeply indebted, see Hertz, 21–39.

14. De Quincey, "The Household Wreck," *Collected Works*, 12:176.

15. De Quincey, *Suspiria de Profundis* in *Confessions*, 156. Subsequent references to this volume will be in parentheses.

16. Excellent discussions of the role of Elizabeth's death in De Quincey's writings can be found in J. H. Miller, 17–23, 73–80; Jacobus, 130–36; Barrell; and Hubbard.

17. On the echoes of Browne, and for a different discussion of De Quincey's "poetics of quotation," see Jacobus, 134–36.

18. On Elizabeth's hydrocephalus and De Quincey's fears about his susceptibility to that malady, see Barrell, 25–36.

19. De Quincey, "The Poetry of Pope," *Collected Writings*.

20. See De Quincey, *Confessions*, 70.

21. De Quincey in later life would "rent a room to live in, and then gradually fill it up with books and papers . . . until it was literally impossible to walk from the door to the desk. Then he would say the room was 'snowed up,' lock the door, and move to other lodgings" (J. H. Miller, 41, n.9).

22. Robert Huish, *Memoirs of the Princess Charlotte of Saxe Coburg*, 571–77. All subsequent page references to this text will be in parentheses, noted *M*.

23. Sermon by Richard Frizell in Carlow Church, in Huish, ed., *A Sacred Memorial*, 14.

24. Schor, 196–229. For more typical views of the revolutionary period as ringing the death knell for sensibility, see Barker-Benfield; and Butler.

25. Huish, *A Sacred Memorial*, 63.

26. "As with electric touch": Barbauld, "On the Death of the Princess Charlotte," *Works*, 281, l. 1. Byron's stanzas on Charlotte's death in canto 4 of *Childe Harold's Pilgrimage* also use the figure of electricity: he describes an "electric chain of . . . despair" linking monarch and subjects (*Complete Poetical Works* 2:179, l. 1546).

See the attempts of the editor of *A Cypress Wreath* to name what exactly the public's tears were responding to: "the offering was not made to the Princess, but to the lovely and accomplished woman; not to the daughter of our kings, but to a young female who was a pattern of filial piety," and so on (77–78).

27. *Courier* cited in Colley, 114; Wooler cited in Laqueur, 440. Some radicals found a different meaning altogether in Charlotte's death, seeing it as a divine judgment for three deaths the state in fact had authorized—the unjust executions of three laborers for treason—and viewed Charlotte's funeral as an occasion for demonstrations, not mourning; see McCalman, 146. See also Schor's discussions of Presbyterian ministers in Scotland who refused to preach on the funeral day, and of Percy Bysshe Shelley's linking of Charlotte's funeral to the Pentridge uprising, 212–18, 200–207.

28. See, for example, *Gentleman's Magazine*, supplement to vol. 88, pt. 1 (1818): 614–15.

29. Brougham quoted in Hibbert, 2:102; sermon by the Rev. Robert Philip, Liverpool, in Huish, *A Sacred Memorial*, 116; *Ladies' Monthly Museum* (Dec. 1817): 312; Hemans, 296.

30. Cobbett cited in Colley, 125, n. 100; monody cited in Huish, *Memoir*, 644, 645. See also Coote, 75–77.

31. For biographical background, see Holme; and Plowden; for observations on Charlotte's isolation in her final days, see remarks quoted in J. Richardson, 168; Lewis, 172; and Schor, 227.

32. *Ladies' Monthly Museum* (Dec. 1817): 312.

33. Byron, 3:10.

34. Quoted in Manning, *Reading Romantics*, 204.

35. Quoted in McCalman, 166.

36. "Mother of a moment" is from *Childe Harold's Pilgrimage*, 4.1509 (*Poetical Works*, 2:180); "The Last Pious Aspirations of the Idolized Princess Charlotte," Coote, 92, ll. 5–8; Schor, 224–25.

37. For rumors about the regent's response, see Bury, 2:147, 149; for poems focusing on Leopold, see "The Funeral; Or, Elegiac Stanzas on Contemplating the Obsequies of Her Royal Highness the Princess Charlotte Augusta, at Windsor," by John Gwilliam, in Coote, 67; "The Blighted Hope," 124–27, in Coote; and Barbauld, "On the Death of Princess Charlotte," *Works*, 281, ll. 9–19.

38. For biographical background on Croft, see Lewis, 97–119; and Crainz.

39. *The New Monthly Magazine* (Mar. 1818): 170–71; see also *Ladies Monthly Museum* (Mar. 1818): 164–65. The account of the inquest is from *The Annual Register* (Feb. 1818): 22–24: "On a chair by the side of the bedstead on which the deceased lay were several of Shakspeare's plays. The room was very small, and it appeared as if the deceased had been reading." The accounts of Croft's suicide conform completely to the reimag-

ining of suicide as an affective (and very literary) rather than a moral or legal matter in the late eighteenth century; see MacDonald and Murphy.

40. *Times*, Feb. 16, 1818, 2.

41. Lewis, 85–121; on the rumors, see the *Times*, Feb. 16, 1818, 2–3; *The Ladies' Monthly Museum* (Mar. 1818): 164.

42. Croft was certainly no stranger to stories of eighteenth-century men of feeling and fatal fits of passion: his older brother was Herbert Croft, publisher of Chatterton's letters and author of *Love and Madness* (1780), the popular fictionalized account of the sensational murder of Martha Ray by her lover James Hackman.

43. Bury, 2:153, 155–56. For Caroline's letter to Lady Charlotte Campbell see L. Benjamin, 2:366–67.

44. Hazlitt quoted in Davidoff and Hall, 150.

45. See Davidoff and Hall, 150–55; Laqueur; McCalman, 162–77; Clark, 47–68.

46. See Gelpi's discussion of the cult of aristocratic motherhood, 62–72.

47. Laqueur, 443.

48. See Clark, 58–63.

49. "Ah Then! Art Thou Gone to the Heavens Above," Coote, 116, ll. 25–28.

50. Interestingly, this paradox—that feelings become more public when they appear most private—attracted the attention, at roughly this time, of critics attempting to understand the phenomenon of Byronic emotion. See Manning's discussion of John Wilson's explanation of the paradox of *Childe Harold's Pilgrimage* in 1818 ("Childe Harold," 185–86).

51. Cited in Laqueur, 443.

Works Cited

Aarsleff, Hans. *From Locke to Saussure: Essays on the Study of Language and Intellectual History.* Minneapolis: University of Minnesota Press, 1982.
Abraham, Nicolas. "Notes on the Phantom: A Complement to Freud's Metapsychology." *Critical Inquiry* 13 (1987): 287–92.
Abraham, Nicolas, and Maria Torok. "A Poetics of Psychoanalysis: The Lost Object-Me." *SubStance* 43 (1984): 3–18.
Abrams, M. H. *The Mirror and the Lamp.* New York: Oxford University Press, 1953.
Anderson, Amanda. *Tainted Souls and Painted Faces: The Rhetoric of Fallenness in Victorian Culture.* Ithaca, N.Y.: Cornell University Press, 1993.
The Annual Register, 1817–18.
The Anti-Jacobin; Or Weekly Examiner, London, 1797–98.
Armstrong, Nancy. *Desire and Domestic Fiction: A Political History of the Novel.* Oxford: Oxford University Press, 1987.
Auerbach, Nina. "O Brave New World: Evolution and Revolution in *Persuasion.*" *ELH* 39 (1972): 112–28.
Austen, Jane. *Lady Susan/The Watsons/Sanditon.* Ed. Margaret Drabble. Harmondsworth: Penguin, 1974.
———. *The Novels of Jane Austen.* Ed. R. W. Chapman. 3d ed. 5 vols. Oxford: Oxford University Press, 1933.
Austen-Leigh, James. *A Memoir of Jane Austen.* London: Century, 1987 [1871].
Averill, James H. *Wordsworth and the Poetry of Human Suffering.* Ithaca, N.Y.: Cornell University Press, 1980.
Baier, Annette C. *A Progress of Sentiments: Reflections on Hume's Treatise.* Cambridge, Mass.: Harvard University Press, 1991.

Baillie, Joanna. *A Series of Plays: In Which It Is Attempted to Delineate the Stronger Passions of the Mind.* London, 1798.
Balfour, Ian. "Reversal, Quotation (Benjamin's History)." *Modern Language Notes* 106 (1991): 622–47.
Barbauld, Anna Laetitia. *The Works of Anna Laetitia Barbauld.* 2 vols. London, 1825.
Barker-Benfield, G. J. *The Culture of Sensibility: Sex and Society in Eighteenth-Century England.* Chicago: University of Chicago Press, 1992.
Barrell, John. *The Infection of Thomas De Quincey: A Psychopathology of Imperialism.* New Haven: Yale University Press, 1991.
Barthes, Roland. *Sade/Fourier/Loyola.* Trans. Richard Miller. New York: Hill and Wang, 1976.
Bate, Jonathan. *Shakespeare and the English Romantic Imagination.* Oxford: Oxford University Press, 1986.
Bate, Walter Jackson. *From Classic to Romantic: Premises of Taste in Eighteenth-Century England.* New York: Harper and Row, 1961.
Bateson, F. W. *Wordsworth: A Re-interpretation.* London: Longman, Green, 1954.
Batten, Charles. *Pleasurable Instruction: Form and Convention in Eighteenth-Century Travel Literature.* Berkeley: University of California Press, 1978.
Bauer, N. Stephen. "Wordsworth and the Early Anthologies." *The Library*, 5th ser., 27 (1972): 37–45.
Beattie, James. *An Essay on the Nature and Immutability of Truth, in Opposition to Sophistry and Scepticism.* 2d ed. Edinburgh, 1771.
———. *Essays: On Poetry and Music, as They Affect the Mind.* London, 1776.
Beer, Gillian. "Our Unnatural No-Voice: The Heroic Epistle, Pope, and Women's Gothic." *Yearbook of English Studies* 12 (1982): 125–51.
Benedict, Barbara M. "Literary Miscellanies: The Cultural Mediation of Fragmented Feeling." *ELH* 57 (1990): 407–30.
Benjamin, Lewis. *An Injured Queen: Caroline of Brunswick.* London: Hutchinson, 1912.
Benjamin, Walter. "On Some Motifs in Baudelaire." In Hannah Arendt, ed., *Illuminations.* New York: Schocken, 1969.
Berlant, Lauren. "The Female Complaint." *Social Text* 19/20 (1988): 237–59.
Bersani, Leo. "Representation and Its Discontents." *Raritan* 1 (1981): 3–17.
Bewell, Alan J. *Wordsworth and the Enlightenment: Nature, Man, and Society in the Experimental Poetry.* New Haven: Yale University Press, 1989.

Black, Jeremy. *The British Abroad: The Grand Tour in the Eighteenth Century*. New York: St. Martin's, 1992.
Bogel, Fredric V. *Literature and Insubstantiality in Later Eighteenth-Century England*. Princeton: Princeton University Press, 1984.
Bohn, Henry George. *A Dictionary of Quotations from the English Poets*. London, 1867.
Borch-Jacobsen, Mikkel. *The Emotional Tie: Psychoanalysis, Mimesis, and Affect*. Stanford, Calif.: Stanford University Press, 1993.
Boulton, James T. *The Language of Politics in the Age of Wilkes and Burke*. London: Routledge and Kegan Paul, 1963.
Box, M. A. *The Suasive Art of David Hume*. Princeton: Princeton University Press, 1990.
Boyd, Julian, and Zelda Boyd. "The Perfect of Experience." *Studies in Romanticism* 16 (1977): 3–13.
Brennan, Teresa. *The Interpretation of the Flesh: Freud and Femininity*. New York: Routledge, 1992.
Brissenden, R. F. *Virtue in Distress: Studies in the Novel of Sentiment from Richardson to Sade*. New York: Macmillan, 1976.
Bronson, Bertrand H. "Personification Reconsidered." *ELH* 14 (1947): 163–77.
Brooks, Cleanth. "Wordsworth and Human Suffering: Notes on Two Early Poems." In Frederick W. Hilles and Harold Bloom, eds., *From Sensibility to Romanticism: Essays Presented to Frederick A. Pottle*. New York: Oxford University Press, 1965.
Brooks, Peter. *Reading for the Plot: Design and Intention in Narrative*. New York: Knopf, 1984.
Brown, Charles. *Shakespeare's Autobiographical Poems, Being His Sonnets Clearly Developed with His Character Drawn Chiefly From His Works*. London, 1838.
Brown, Gillian. *Domestic Individualism: Imagining Self in Nineteenth-Century America*. Berkeley: University of California Press, 1990.
Brown, Marshall. *Preromanticism*. Stanford, Calif.: Stanford University Press, 1991.
Burke, Edmund. *A Philosophical Enquiry into the Origin of Our Ideas of the Sublime and Beautiful*. Ed. James T. Boulton. Notre Dame: University of Notre Dame Press, 1958.
———. *Reflections on the Revolution in France*. Ed. Conor Cruise O'Brien. Harmondsworth: Penguin, 1968.
Bury, Lady Charlotte Campbell. *Diary of a Lady-In-Waiting*. 2 vols. London: Lane, 1908.

Butler, Marilyn. *Jane Austen and the War of Ideas*. Oxford: Oxford University Press, 1975.
Byron, George Gordon, Lord. *The Complete Poetical Works*. Ed. Jerome J. McGann. 7 vols. Oxford: Clarendon Press, 1980–86.
Campbell, Colin. *The Romantic Ethic and the Spirit of Modern Consumerism*. Oxford: Basil Blackwell, 1987.
Caraher, Brian G. *Wordsworth's 'Slumber' and the Problematics of Reading*. University Park: Pennsylvania State University Press, 1991.
Caruth, Cathy. *Empirical Truths and Critical Fictions: Locke, Wordsworth, Kant, Freud*. Baltimore: Johns Hopkins University Press, 1991.
Castle, Terry. "The Spectralization of the Other in *The Mysteries of Udolpho*." In Laura Brown and Felicity Nussbaum, eds., *The New Eighteenth Century: Theory, Politics, English Literature*. New York: Methuen, 1987.
Chapone, Hester. "On Enthusiasm and Indifference in Religion" [1777]. In *The Works of Mrs. Chapone*. 4 vols. London, 1807.
Christensen, Jerome. *Coleridge's Blessed Machine of Language*. Ithaca, N.Y.: Cornell University Press, 1981.
——. *Practicing Enlightenment: Hume and the Formation of a Literary Career*. Madison: University of Wisconsin Press, 1987.
——. "Wordsworth's Misery, Coleridge's Woe: Reading 'The Thorn.'" *Papers on Language and Literature* 16 (1980): 268–86.
Clark, Anna. "Queen Caroline and the Sexual Politics of Popular Culture in London, 1820." *Representations* 31 (1990): 47–65.
Code, Lorraine. "Responsibility and Rhetoric." *Hypatia* 9 (1994): 1–20.
Coleridge, S. T. *Biographia Literaria*. Ed. J. Shawcross. 2 vols. Oxford: Oxford University Press, 1907.
——. *Poems*. 2d ed. Bristol, 1797.
Colley, Linda. "The Apotheosis of George III: Loyalty, Royalty, and the British Nation 1760–1820." *Past and Present* 102 (1984): 94–129.
Collins, A. S. "The Growth of the Reading Public, 1780–1800." *The Nineteenth Century and After* 101 (1927): 749–58.
Compagnon, Antoine. *La Seconde main; ou, le travail de la citation*. Paris: Editions du Seuil, 1979.
The Complete Letter Writer, or, the Art of Correspondence. New York, 1815.
Conger, Syndy McMillen, ed. *Sensibility in Transformation: Creative Resistance to Sentiment from the Augustans to the Romantics*. Rutherford, N.J.: Fairleigh Dickinson University Press, 1990.
Coote, J., ed. *A Cypress Wreath, for the Tomb of Her Late Royal Highness the Princess Charlotte of Wales*. London, 1817.

Cott, Nancy. *The Grounding of Modern Feminism.* New Haven: Yale University Press, 1987.
Cottle, Joseph. *Reminiscences of Samuel Taylor Coleridge and Robert Southey.* London, 1847.
Cottom, Daniel. *The Civilized Imagination: A Study of Ann Radcliffe, Jane Austen, and Sir Walter Scott.* Cambridge: Cambridge University Press, 1985.
Coward, Rosalind. *Patriarchal Precedents: Sexuality and Social Relations.* London: Routledge and Kegan Paul, 1983.
Cowper, William. *The Letters and Prose Writings of William Cowper.* Ed. James King and Charles Ryskamp. 5 vols. Oxford: Oxford University Press, 1980.
———. *The Poems of William Cowper.* Ed. John D. Baird and Charles Ryskamp. 2 vols. Oxford: Oxford University Press, 1980.
Crainz, Franco. *An Obstetric Tragedy: The Case of Her Royal Highness the Princess Charlotte Augusta.* London: Heinemann, 1977.
Curran, Stuart. *Poetic Form and British Romanticism.* New York: Oxford University Press, 1986.
———. "Romantic Poetry: The I Altered." In Anne K. Mellor, ed., *Romanticism and Feminism.* Bloomington: Indiana University Press, 1988.
Cvetkovich, Ann. *Mixed Feelings: Feminism, Mass Culture, and Victorian Sensationalism.* New Brunswick, N.J.: Rutgers University Press, 1992.
Darwin, Erasmus. *Zoonomia, or the Laws of Organic Life.* 2 vols. London, 1796.
Davidoff, Leonore, and Catherine Hall. *Family Fortunes: Men and Women of the English Middle Class, 1780–1850.* Chicago: University of Chicago Press, 1987.
Davies, Hugh Sykes. "Wordsworth and the Empirical Philosophers." In Hugh Davies and George Watson, eds., *The English Mind.* Cambridge: Cambridge University Press, 1964.
Day, William Patrick. *In the Circles of Fear and Desire: A Study of Gothic Fantasy.* Chicago: University of Chicago Press, 1985.
de Bolla, Peter. *The Discourse of the Sublime: Readings in History, Aesthetics, and the Subject.* Oxford: Basil Blackwell, 1989.
de Grazia, Margreta. *Shakespeare Verbatim: The Reproduction of Authenticity and the 1790 Apparatus.* Oxford: Oxford University Press, 1991.
Deleuze, Gilles. *Empiricism and Subjectivity: An Essay on Hume's Theory of Human Nature.* New York: Columbia University Press, 1991.
De Quincey, Thomas. *The Collected Writings of Thomas De Quincey.* Ed. David Masson. 14 vols. Edinburgh, 1889–90.

———. *Confessions of an English Opium-Eater and Other Writings.* Ed. Grevel Lindop. Oxford: Oxford University Press, 1985.
Derrida, Jacques. "Force and Signification." In *Writing and Difference.* Trans. Alan Bass. Chicago: University of Chicago Press, 1978.
Donaldson, John. *The Elements of Beauty.* Edinburgh, 1780.
Douglas, Ann. *The Feminization of American Culture.* New York: Knopf, 1977.
Dyce, Alexander. *Specimens of British Poetesses.* London, 1827.
Eagleton, Terry. *The Ideology of the Aesthetic.* Oxford: Basil Blackwell, 1990.
Eilenberg, Susan. *Strange Power of Speech: Wordsworth, Coleridge, and Literary Possession.* New York: Oxford University Press, 1992.
Ellison, Julie. *Delicate Subjects: Romanticism, Gender, and the Ethics of Understanding.* Ithaca, N.Y.: Cornell University Press, 1990.
———. "The Politics of Fancy in the Age of Sensibility." In Carol Shiner Wilson and Joel Haefner, eds., *Re-Visioning Romanticism: British Women Writers 1776–1837.* Philadelphia: University of Pennsylvania Press, 1994.
———. "Race and Sensibility in the Early Republic: Anne Eliza Bleecker and Sarah Wentworth." *American Literature* 65 (1993): 445–74.
Erametsa, Erik. "A Study of the Word 'Sentimental' and of other Linguistic Characteristics of Eighteenth-Century Sentimentalism." *Annales Academia Scientiarum Fennicae,* ser. B, 74. Helsinki, 1951.
The European Magazine, 1786–1806.
Evans, Mary. *Jane Austen and the State.* London: Tavistock, 1987.
Favret, Mary A. *Romantic Correspondence: Women, Politics, and the Fiction of Letters.* Cambridge: Cambridge University Press, 1993.
Fawcett, Mary Laughlin. "Udolpho's Primal Mystery." *Studies in English Literature* 23 (1983): 481–94.
Feinberg, Nona. "Wroth and the Invention of Female Poetic Subjectivity." In Naomi J. Miller and Gary Waller, eds., *Reading Mary Wroth.* Knoxville: University of Tennessee Press, 1991.
The Female Aegis; or, The Duties of Women From Childhood to Old Age. London, 1798.
Ferguson, Frances. *Solitude and the Sublime: Romanticism and the Aesthetics of Individuation.* New York: Routledge, 1992.
———. *Wordsworth: Language as Counter-Spirit.* New Haven: Yale University Press, 1977.
Ferry, David. *The Limits of Mortality.* Middletown, Conn.: Wesleyan University Press, 1959.
Fink, Z. S. *The Early Wordsworthian Milieu.* Oxford: Oxford University Press, 1958.

Flesch, William. "Quoting Poetry." *Critical Inquiry* 18 (1991): 42–63.
Fox, Christopher. *Psychology and Literature in the Eighteenth Century.* New York: AMS Press, 1987.
Freud, Sigmund. *The Standard Edition of the Complete Psychological Writings of Sigmund Freud.* Ed. and trans. James Strachey. 24 vols. London: Hogarth Press, 1953–64.
Fried, Debra. "Andromeda Unbound: Adroit Designs in Millay's Sonnets." *Twentieth-Century Literature* 32 (1986): 1–22.
Fried, Michael. *Absorption and Theatricality: Painting and Beholder in the Age of Diderot.* Chicago: University of Chicago Press, 1980.
Gardiner, H. M., Ruth Clark Metcalf, and John G. Beebe-Center. *Feeling and Emotion: A History of Theories.* New York: Greenwood, 1970.
Gelpi, Barbara Charlesworth. *Shelley's Goddess: Maternity, Language, Subjectivity.* New York: Oxford University Press, 1992.
Gentleman's Magazine, 1784–86.
Gerard, Alexander. *An Essay on Taste.* London, 1759.
Gilbert, Sandra M., and Susan Gubar. *The Madwoman in the Attic: The Woman Writer and the Nineteenth-Century Literary Imagination.* New Haven: Yale University Press, 1979.
Glen, Heather. *Vision and Disenchantment: Blake's Songs and Wordsworth's Lyrical Ballads.* Cambridge: Cambridge University Press, 1983.
Goldsmith, Oliver. *The Works of Oliver Goldsmith.* Ed. Peter Cunningham. 10 vols. New York, 1908.
Goodwin, Sarah Webster. "Romanticism and the Ghost of Prostitution." In Goodwin and Elizabeth Bronfen, eds., *Death and Representation.* Baltimore: Johns Hopkins University Press, 1993.
Green, André. *Le Discours vivant: la conception psychanalytique de l'affect.* Paris: Presses Universitaires de France, 1973.
———. *On Private Madness.* Madison, Conn.: International Universities Press, 1986.
Hardie, James. *The Epistolary Guide.* New York, 1817.
Hartley, David. *Observations on Man.* 2 vols. London, 1749.
Hartman, Geoffrey. *Wordsworth's Poetry 1787-1814.* Cambridge, Mass: Harvard University Press, 1987 [1964].
Hatfield, Miss S. *Letters on the Importance of the Female Sex.* London, 1803.
Hazlitt, William. *Selected Writings.* Ed. Ronald Blythe. Harmondsworth: Penguin, 1970.
Hemans, Felicia. *The Poetical Works of Mrs. Felicia Hemans.* Philadelphia, 1855.
Henderson, Andrea. "An Embarrassing Subject: Use Value and Exchange

Value in Early Gothic Characterization." In Mary A. Favret and Nicola J. Watson, eds., *At the Limits of Romanticism*. Bloomington: Indiana University Press, 1994.

———. *Romantic Identities*. Cambridge: Cambridge University Press, 1996.

Henderson, George. *Petrarcha: A Selection of Sonnets*. London, 1803.

Hertz, Neil. *The End of the Line: Essays on Psychoanalysis and the Sublime*. New York: Columbia University Press, 1985.

Hibbert, Christopher. *George IV: Regent and King, 1811–1850*. London: Allen Lane, 1973.

Hilbish, Florence. *Charlotte Smith, Poet and Novelist (1749–1806)*. Philadelphia: University of Pennsylvania Press, 1941.

Hirschman, Albert O. *The Passions and the Interests: Political Arguments for Capitalism Before Its Triumph*. Princeton: Princeton University Press, 1977.

History of the Works of the Learned, 1739.

Hogg, James. *The Poetic Mirror*. London, 1816.

Holme, Thea. *Prinny's Daughter*. London: Hamish Hamilton, 1976.

Homans, Margaret. *Bearing the Word: Language and Female Experience in Nineteenth-Century Women's Writing*. Chicago: University of Chicago Press, 1986.

Hubbard, Stacy Carson. "Telling Accounts: De Quincey at the Booksellers." In Bill Readings and Bennet Schaber, eds., *Postmodernism Across the Ages*. Syracuse, N.Y.: Syracuse University Press, 1993.

Huish, Robert. *Memoirs of the Princess Charlotte of Saxe Coburg*. London, 1817.

———., ed. *A Sacred Memorial of Her Late Royal Highness Charlotte Augusta, Princess of Wales . . . Being Extracts from Upwards of One Hundred and Twenty Sermons*. London, 1818.

Hume, David. *An Enquiry Concerning Human Understanding*. Ed. Eric Steinberg. Indianapolis: Hackett, 1977.

———. *Essays, Moral, Political, and Literary*. Ed. T. H. Green and T. H. Grose. 2 vols. London, 1882.

———. *A Treatise of Human Nature*. Ed. L. A. Selby-Bigge. 2d ed., ed. P. H. Nidditch. Oxford: Oxford University Press, 1978.

Hunt, Leigh. *Men, Women, and Books*. 2 vols. London, 1847.

Inchbald, Elizabeth. *A Simple Story*. Oxford: Oxford University Press, 1988.

Izenberg, Gerald N. *Impossible Individuality: Romanticism, Revolution, and the Origins of Modern Selfhood, 1787–1802*. Princeton: Princeton University Press, 1992.

Jacobus, Mary. *Romanticism, Writing, and Sexual Difference: Essays on The Prelude*. Oxford: Oxford University Press, 1989.

Jaggar, Alison M. "Love and Knowledge: Emotion in Feminist Epistemology." In Alison Jaggar and Susan M. Bordo, eds., *Gender/Body/Knowledge: Feminist Reconstructions of Being and Knowing*. New Brunswick, N.J.: Rutgers University Press, 1989.

Johnson, Barbara. *A World of Difference*. Baltimore: Johns Hopkins University Press, 1987.

Johnson, Claudia L. *Equivocal Beings: Politics, Gender, and Sentimentality in the 1790's*. Chicago: University of Chicago Press, 1994.

———. *Jane Austen: Women, Politics, and the Novel*. Chicago: University of Chicago Press, 1988.

———. "A 'Sweet Face as White as Death': Jane Austen and the Politics of a Female Sensibility." *Novel* 22 (1989): 159–74.

Jones, Ann Rosalind. *The Currency of Eros: Women's Love Lyrics in Europe 1540–1620*. Bloomington: Indiana University Press, 1990.

Jones, Kathleen B. *Compassionate Authority: Democracy and the Representation of Women*. London: Routledge, 1993.

Kahane, Claire. "The Gothic Mirror." In Shirley Nelson Garner, Claire Kahane, and Madelon Sprengnether, eds., *The M(O)ther Tongue*. Ithaca, N.Y.: Cornell University Press, 1985.

Kames, Henry Home, Lord. *Elements of Criticism*. 7th ed. 2 vols. Edinburgh, 1788.

Kaplan, Cora. "Wild Nights: Pleasure/Sexuality/Feminism." In *Sea Changes: Culture and Feminism*. London: Verso, 1986.

Kay, Carol. *Political Constructions: Defoe, Richardson, and Sterne in Relation to Hobbes, Hume, and Burke*. Ithaca, N.Y.: Cornell University Press, 1988.

Kelly, Gary. "A Constant Vicissitude of Interesting Passions: Ann Radcliffe's Perplexed Narratives." *Ariel* 10 (1979): 45–64.

———. *Revolutionary Feminism*. New York: St. Martin's, 1992.

Kiely, Robert. *The Romantic Novel in England*. Cambridge, Mass.: Harvard University Press, 1972.

Kingdom, William. *Dictionary of Quotations from the British Poets*. 3 vols. London, 1823–25.

Klancher, Jon P. *The Making of English Reading Audiences, 1790–1832*. Madison: University of Wisconsin Press, 1987.

Knapp, Steven. *Personification and the Sublime: Milton to Coleridge*. Cambridge, Mass.: Harvard University Press, 1985.

Knox, Vicesimus, ed. *Elegant Extracts; or Useful and Entertaining Pieces of Poetry Selected for the Improvement of Youth.* London, 1805.
Kowaleski-Wallace, Beth, and Patricia Yeager. *Refiguring the Father.* Carbondale: Southern Illinois University Press, 1990.
Ladies' Monthly Museum, 1817–18.
Lady's Poetical Magazine, or Beauties of English Poetry. James Harrison, ed. 4 vols. London, 1781–82.
Lamb, Charles. *The Letters of Charles Lamb: To Which Are Added Those of His Sister, Mary Lamb.* Ed. E. V. Lucas. 3 vols. London, 1935.
Laplanche, Jean. *Life and Death in Psychoanalysis.* Trans. Jeffrey Mehlman. Baltimore: Johns Hopkins University Press, 1976.
Laplanche, Jean, and J. B. Pontalis. "Fantasy and the Origins of Sexuality." *International Journal of Psycho-analysis* 49 (1968): 1–18.
Laqueur, Thomas. "The Queen Caroline Affair: Politics as Art in the Reign of George IV." *Journal of Modern History* 54 (1982): 417–66.
Law, Jules David. *The Rhetoric of Empiricism: Language and Perception from Locke to I. A. Richards.* Ithaca, N.Y.: Cornell University Press, 1993.
Levinson, Marjorie. *Keats's Life of Allegory: The Origins of a Style.* Oxford: Basil Blackwell, 1988.
Lewis, Judith Schneid. *In the Family Way: Childbearing in the British Aristocracy, 1760–1860.* New Brunswick, N.J.: Rutgers University Press, 1986.
Litz, A. Walton. "Persuasion: Forms of Estrangement." In John Halperin, ed., *Jane Austen: Bicentenary Essays.* Cambridge: Cambridge University Press, 1975.
Locke, John. *An Essay Concerning Human Understanding.* Ed. P. H. Nidditch. Oxford: Oxford University Press, 1977.
Luhmann, Niklas. "The Individuality of the Individual: Historical Meanings and Contemporary Problems." In Thomas C. Heller, Martin Sosna, and David E. Welbery, eds., *Reconstructing Individualism.* Stanford, Calif.: Stanford University Press, 1986.
McCalman, Iain. *Radical Underworld: Prophets, Revolutionaries, and Pornographers in London, 1795–1840.* Oxford: Oxford University Press, 1993 [1988].
MacDonald, Michael, and Terence R. Murphy. *Sleepless Souls: Suicide in Early Modern England.* Oxford: Oxford University Press, 1990.
MacDonnel, D. E. *A Dictionary of Quotations, in Most Frequent Use.* 3d ed. London, 1799.
McIntyre, Jane L. "Personal Identity and the Passions." *Journal of the History of Philosophy* 27 (1989): 545–57.

McKenzie, Alan T. *Certain, Lively Episodes: The Articulation of Passion in Eighteenth-Century Prose*. Athens: University of Georgia Press, 1990.
McKenzie, Gordon. *Critical Responsiveness: A Study of the Psychological Current in Later Eighteenth-Century Criticism*. Berkeley: University of California Press, 1949.
MacLean, Norman. "From Action to Image: Theories of the Lyric in the Eighteenth Century." In R. S. Crane, ed., *Critics and Criticism: Ancient and Modern*. Chicago: University of Chicago Press, 1952.
Macpherson, C. B. *The Political Theory of Possessive Individualism*. Oxford: Oxford University Press, 1962.
Manning, Peter J. "Childe Harold in the Marketplace: From Romaunt to Handbook." *Modern Language Quarterly* 52 (1991): 170-90.
———. *Reading Romantics: Texts and Contexts*. New York: Oxford University Press, 1990.
Marshall, David. *The Figure of Theater: Shaftesbury, Defoe, Adam Smith, and George Eliot*. New York: Columbia University Press, 1986.
———. *The Surprising Effects of Sympathy: Marivaux, Diderot, Rousseau, and Mary Shelley*. Chicago: University of Chicago Press, 1988.
———. "True Acting and the Language of True Feeling: Mansfield Park." *Yale Journal of Criticism* 3 (1989): 87-106.
Masse, Michelle. *In the Name of Love: Women, Masochism, and the Gothic*. Ithaca, N.Y.: Cornell University Press, 1992.
Maus, Katherine Eisaman. "Proof and Consequences: Inwardness and Its Exposure in the English Renaissance." *Representations* 34 (1991): 29-52.
Mayo, Robert. "The Contemporaneity of the Lyrical Ballads." *PMLA* 69 (1954): 486-522.
Mellor, Anne K. *Romanticism and Gender*. New York and London: Routledge, 1993.
Mermin, Dorothy. "The Female Poet and the Embarrassed Reader: Elizabeth Barrett Browning's Sonnets from the Portuguese." *ELH* 48 (1981): 351-67.
Miall, David S. "Wordsworth and the Prelude: the Problematic of Feeling." *Studies in Romanticism* 31 (1992): 233-53.
Miller, D. A. "The Late Jane Austen." *Raritan* 10 (1990): 55-79.
Miller, David. *Philosophy and Ideology in Hume's Political Thought*. Oxford: Oxford University Press, 1981.
Miller, J. Hillis. *The Disappearance of God: Five Nineteenth-Century Writers*. Cambridge, Mass.: Harvard University Press, 1963.
Miller, Naomi J. "Rewriting Lyric Fictions." In Anne M. Haselkorn and Betty S. Travitsky, eds., *The Renaissance Englishwoman in Print: Coun-*

terbalancing the Canon. Amherst: University of Massachusetts Press, 1990.

Moler, Kenneth. *Jane Austen's Art of Allusion.* Lincoln: University of Nebraska Press, 1968.

Monthly Review, 1784.

Moorman, Mary. *William Wordsworth: The Early Years 1770–1805.* Oxford: Oxford University Press, 1957.

More, Hannah. "Essay on the Danger of Sentimental or Romantic Connexions." In *Essays on Various Subjects Principally Designed for Young Ladies.* London, 1777.

———. "Prospectus" for the Cheap Repository of Publications on Religious and Moral Subjects. *Monthly Magazine* 4 (Jan, 1797): 14 [1795].

Morgan, Susan. *In the Meantime: Character and Perception in Jane Austen's Fiction.* Chicago: University of Chicago Press, 1980.

Morris, David B. "Gothic Sublimity." *New Literary History* 16 (1985): 299–319.

Mossner, Ernest Campbell. *The Life of David Hume.* Austin: University of Texas Press, 1954.

Mullan, John. *Sentiment and Sociability: The Language of Feeling in the Eighteenth Century.* Oxford: Oxford University Press, 1988.

Nell, Victor. *Lost in a Book: The Psychology of Reading For Pleasure.* New Haven: Yale University Press, 1988.

The New Monthly Magazine, 1818.

Nussbaum, Felicity. *The Autobiographical Subject: Gender and Ideology in Eighteenth-Century England.* Baltimore: Johns Hopkins University Press, 1989.

Nussbaum, Martha C. *Love's Knowledge: Essays on Philosophy and Literature.* New York: Oxford University Press, 1990.

Oxenhandler, Neal. "The Changing Concept of Literary Emotion: A Selective History." *New Literary History* 20 (1988): 105–21.

Page, Judith. *Wordsworth and the Cultivation of Women.* Berkeley and Los Angeles: University of California Press, 1994.

Page, Norman. *The Language of Jane Austen.* Oxford: Basil Blackwell, 1972.

Parker, Reeve. "'Oh Could You Hear His Voice!': Wordsworth, Coleridge, and Ventriloquism." In Arden Reed, ed., *Romanticism and Language.* Ithaca, N.Y.: Cornell University Press, 1984.

Paulson, Ronald. *Representations of Revolution, 1789–1820.* New Haven: Yale University Press, 1983.

Pilkington, Laetitia. *The Memoirs of Mrs. Laetitia Pilkington, 1712–50.* Ed. Iris Barry. London: George Routledge and Sons, 1928.

Pinch, Adela. "Emotion and History: A Review Article." *Comparative Studies in Society and History* 37 (1995): 100–109.
Pinchbeck, Ivy. *Women Workers and the Industrial Revolution, 1750–1850*. London: George Routledge and Sons, 1930.
Piozzi, Hester Lynch Thrale. *Thraliana: The Diary of Mrs. Hester Lynch Thrale, 1776–1809*. Ed. Katharine C. Balderston. 2 vols. Oxford: Oxford University Press, 1942.
Plowden, Alison. *Caroline and Charlotte*. London: Sidgwick and Jackson, 1989.
Pocock, J. G. A. "The Mobility of Property and the Rise of Eighteenth-Century Sociology." In *Virtue, Commerce, and History*. Cambridge: Cambridge University Press, 1985.
Polwhele, Richard. *The Unsex'd Females: A Poem, Addressed to the Author of the Pursuits of Literature*. London, 1798.
Poovey, Mary. "Ideology and The Mysteries of Udolpho." *Criticism* 21 (1979): 307–30.
———. *The Proper Lady and the Woman Writer: Ideology as Style in the Works of Mary Wollstonecraft, Mary Shelley, and Jane Austen*. Chicago: University of Chicago Press, 1984.
Priestley, Joseph. *A Course of Lectures on Oratory and Criticism*. London, 1777.
Punter, David. *The Literature of Terror: A History of Gothic Fictions from 1765 to the Present Day*. London: Longman, 1980.
Radcliffe, Ann. *Gaston de Blondeville; or the Court of Henry III Keeping Festival in Ardenne and St. Albans Abbey: A Metrical Tale*. 4 vols. London, 1826.
———. *A Journey Made in the Summer of 1794, through Holland and The Western Frontier of Germany, with a Return down the Rhine; to which are added Observations during a Tour to the Lakes of Lancashire, Westmoreland, and Cumberland*. London, 1795.
———. *The Mysteries of Udolpho*. Ed. Bonamy Dobrée. Oxford: Oxford University Press, 1966.
Railo, Eino. *The Haunted Castle: A Study of the Elements of British Romanticism*. London: Routledge, 1927.
Rashkin, Esther. *Family Secrets and the Psychoanalysis of Narrative*. Princeton: Princeton University Press, 1992.
Reed, Mark L. *Wordsworth: The Chronology of the Early Years, 1770–1799*. Cambridge, Mass.: Harvard University Press, 1967.
Reid, Thomas. *An Inquiry into the Human Mind, On the Principles of Common Sense*. 3d ed. London and Edinburgh, 1779.

Reiman, Donald, ed. *The Romantics Reviewed: Contemporary Reviews of British Romantic Writers*. 9 vols. New York: Garland, 1972.
Richardson, Alan. "Romanticism and the Colonization of the Feminine." In Anne K. Mellor, ed., *Romanticism and Feminism*. Bloomington: Indiana University Press, 1988.
Richardson, Joanna. *George the Magnificent: A Portrait of George IV*. New York: Harcourt, Brace and World, 1966.
Richetti, John. *Philosophical Writing: Locke, Berkely, Hume*. Cambridge, Mass: Harvard University Press, 1983.
Rogers, Katharine. *Feminism in Eighteenth-Century England*. Urbana: University of Illinois Press, 1982.
Rorty, Amélie O. "From Passions to Emotions and Sentiments." *Philosophy* 57 (1982): 159–72.
Ross, Marlon. *The Contours of Masculine Desire: Romanticism and the Rise of Women's Poetry*. New York: Oxford University Press, 1989.
Ruoff, Gene W. "Anne Elliot's Dowry: Reflections on the Ending of *Persuasion*." In Harold Bloom, ed., *Jane Austen*. New York: Chelsea House, 1986.
Rzepka, Charles. *The Self as Mind: Vision and Identity in Wordsworth, Coleridge, and Keats*. Cambridge, Mass: Harvard University Press, 1986.
Samuels, Shirley, ed. *The Culture of Sentiment: Race, Gender, and Sentimentality in Nineteenth-Century America*. New York: Oxford University Press, 1992.
Sanchez-Eppler, Karen. *Touching Liberty: Abolition, Feminism, and the Politics of the Body*. Berkeley: University of California Press, 1993.
Sapiro, Virginia. *A Vindication of Political Virtue: The Political Theory of Mary Wollstonecraft*. Chicago: University of Chicago Press, 1992.
Scheman, Naomi. *Engenderings: Constructions of Knowledge, Authority, and Privilege*. New York: Routledge, 1993.
Schiesari, Juliana. *The Gendering of Melancholia: Feminism, Psychoanalysis and the Symbolics of Loss in Renaissance Literature*. Ithaca, N.Y.: Cornell University Press, 1992.
Schor, Esther. *Bearing the Dead: The British Culture of Mourning from the Enlightenment to Victoria*. Princeton: Princeton University Press, 1994.
Scott, Joan. "The Evidence of Experience." *Critical Inquiry* 17 (1991): 773–97.
Sedgwick, Eve Kosofsky. "The Character in the Veil: Imagery of the Surface in the Gothic Novel." *PMLA* 96 (1981): 255–70.
———. *Epistemology of the Closet*. Berkeley: University of California Press, 1990.

———. "A Poem Is Being Written." *Representations* 17 (1987): 110–43.
Sennett, Richard. *The Fall of Public Man.* New York: Knopf, 1977.
Seward, Anna. *The Letters of Anna Seward.* 6 vols. Edinburgh, 1811.
Shakespeare, William. *Shakespeare's Sonnets.* Ed. Stephen Booth. New Haven: Yale University Press, 1977.
Shaver, Chester, and Alice C. Shaver. *Wordsworth's Library.* New York: Garland, 1979.
Simpson, David. "What Bothered Charles Lamb About Poor Susan?" *Studies in English Literature* 26 (1986): 589–612.
———. *Wordsworth's Historical Imagination: The Poetry of Displacement.* London: Methuen, 1987.
Siskin, Clifford. *The Historicity of Romantic Discourse.* New York: Oxford University Press, 1988.
Smith, Adam. *The Theory of Moral Sentiments.* Ed. D. D. Raphael and A. L. Macfie. Oxford: Oxford University Press, 1976.
Smith, Charlotte. *The Poems of Charlotte Smith.* Ed. Stuart Curran. New York: Oxford University Press, 1993.
Smith, Norman Kemp. *The Philosophy of David Hume.* London: Macmillan, 1941.
Southam, B. C. *Jane Austen: The Critical Heritage.* London: Routledge and Kegan Paul, 1968.
Sperry, Willard. *Wordsworth's Anti-Climax.* Cambridge, Mass: Harvard University Press, 1935.
Spring, David. "Interpreters of Jane Austen's Social World." In Janet Todd, ed., *Jane Austen: New Perspectives. Women and Literature,* new ser. 3 (1983): 53–72.
Starr, G. A. *Defoe and Spiritual Autobiography.* Princeton: Princeton University Press, 1965.
Staves, Susan. "Eighteenth-Century Feminism." *The Eighteenth Century: Theory and Interpretation* 26 (1985): 170–75.
Steele, Richard. *Selections from the Tatler and the Spectator.* Ed. Angus Ross. Harmondsworth: Penguin, 1982.
Stewart, Kathleen. "Nostalgia—A Polemic." *Cultural Anthropology* 3 (1988): 227–41.
Stewart, Maaja. *Domestic Realities and Imperial Fictions: Jane Austen's Novels in Eighteenth-Century Contexts.* Athens: University of Georgia Press, 1993.
Stewart, Susan. "Notes on Distressed Genres." In *Crimes of Writing: Problems in the Containment of Representation.* Oxford: Oxford University Press, 1991.

---. *On Longing: Narratives of the Miniature, the Gigantic, the Souvenir, the Collection*. Durham, N.C.: Duke University Press, 1993 [1984].

Stone, Lawrence. *The Family, Sex, and Marriage in England, 1500–1800*. New York: Harper and Row, 1977.

Swann, Karen. "'Christabel': The Wandering Mother and the Enigma of Form." *Studies in Romanticism* 23 (1984): 533–53.

---. "Literary Gentlemen and Lovely Ladies: The Debate on the Character of Christabel." *ELH* 52 (1985): 394–418.

---. "Public Transport: Adventuring on Wordsworth's Salisbury Plain." *ELH* 55 (1988): 811–34.

---. "Suffering and Sensation in *The Ruined Cottage*." *PMLA* 106 (1991): 83–94.

Tanner, Michael. "Sentimentality." *Proceedings of the Aristotelian Society*, new ser. 77 (1976–77): 127–47.

Tanner, Tony. *Jane Austen*. Cambridge, Mass.: Harvard University Press, 1986.

Tave, Stuart M. "Jane Austen and One of Her Contemporaries." In John Halperin, ed., *Jane Austen: Bicentenary Essays*. Cambridge: Cambridge University Press, 1975.

Thomas, Keith G. "Jane Austen and the Romantic Lyric: Persuasion and Coleridge's Conversation Poems." *ELH* (1987): 893–924.

Tickell, Richard. *The Wreath of Fashion, or, The Art of Sentimental Poetry*. London, 1778.

Todd, Janet. *Sensibility: An Introduction*. London: Methuen, 1986.

Tompkins, Jane P. *Sensational Designs: The Cultural Work of American Fiction, 1790–1860*. New York: Oxford University Press, 1985.

Tucker, Susie I. *Enthusiasm: A Study in Semantic Change*. Cambridge: Cambridge University Press, 1972.

Turner, Rufus Paul. "Charlotte Smith (1749–1806): New Light on Her Life and Literary Career." Ph. D. diss., University of Southern California, 1966.

Tuveson, Ernest. *The Imagination as a Means of Grace: Locke and the Aesthetics of Romanticism*. Berkeley: University of California Press, 1960.

Vrettos, Athena. *Somatic Fictions: Imagining Illness in Victorian Culture*. Stanford: Stanford University Press, 1995.

Wasserman, Earl. "The Inherent Values of Eighteenth-Century Personification." *PMLA* 65 (1950): 435–63.

Webb, R. K. *The British Working-Class Reader, 1790–1848: Literacy and Social Tension*. London: Allen and Unwin, 1955.

Whelan, Frederick. G. *Order and Artifice in Hume's Political Philosophy*. Princeton: Princeton University Press, 1985.
Williams, Raymond. *The Country and the City*. Oxford: Oxford University Press, 1973.
———. "David Hume: Reasoning and Experience." In Hugh Sykes Davies and George Watson, eds., *The English Mind*. Cambridge: Cambridge University Press, 1964.
Wolfson, Susan J. "*Lyrical Ballads* and the Language of (Men) Feeling: Wordsworth Writing Women's Voices." In Thais Morgan, ed., *Men Writing the Feminine: Literature, Theory, and the Question of Genders*. New York: SUNY Press, 1994.
———. "Romanticism and the Measures of Meter." *Eighteenth-Century Life* 16 (1992): 221–46.
Wollstonecraft, Mary. *A Vindication of the Rights of Men*. London, 1790.
———. *A Vindication of the Rights of Woman*. Ed. Carol H. Poston. New York: W. W. Norton, 1975.
Wordsworth, William. *Poems and Extracts Chosen by William Wordsworth for An album Presented to Lady Mary Lowther*. Ed. H. Littledale. London, 1905.
———. *Poetical Works of William Wordsworth*. Ed. E. de Selincourt and Helen Darbishire. 5 vols. Oxford: Oxford University Press, 1940–49.
———. *The Prelude, 1799, 1805, 1850*. Ed. Jonathan Wordsworth, M. H. Abrams, and Stephen Gill. New York: W. W. Norton, 1979.
———. *Prose Works*. Ed. W. J. B. Owen and Jane Worthington Smyser. 3 vols. Oxford: Oxford University Press, 1974.
Wordsworth, William, and S. T. Coleridge. *Lyrical Ballads*. Ed. R. L. Brett and A. R. Jones. London: Methuen, 1963.
Wordsworth, William, and Dorothy Wordsworth. *The Letters of William and Dorothy Wordsworth: The Later Years, 1821–1850*. Ed. E. de Selincourt, revised by Alan G. Hill. Oxford, Oxford University Press, 1979.
Wright, Walter Francis. *Sensibility in English Prose Fiction 1760–1814: A Reinterpretation*. Urbana: University of Illinois Press, 1937.
Zaretsky, Eli. *Capitalism, the Family, and Personal Life*. New York: Harper and Row, 1976.

Index

In this index "f" after a number indicates a separate reference on the next page, and "ff" indicates separate references on the next two pages. A continuous discussion over two or more pages is indicated by a span of numbers.

Aarsleff, Hans, 197n1
Abraham, Nicolas, and Maria Torok, 132–33
Abrams, M. H., 197n1
Armstrong, Nancy, 197n21
Austen, Jane: reading in, 137–39, 156–63; and epistemology of emotion, 142–45; memory in, 150–52. Works: *Emma*, 142–44, 167; *Mansfield Park*, 146, 170; *Northanger Abbey*, 112, 139; *Persuasion*, 138–40, 142, 144–63; *Sanditon*, 166–67
Averill, James H., 78, 99, 204n8

Baier, Annette C., 23f, 41
Baillie, Joanna, 2–3
Barbauld, Anna Laetitia, 186–87
Barker-Benfield, G. J., 55, 195nn5, 11
Bate, Jonathan, 167
Bate, Walter Jackson, 198n3

Beattie, James, 46, 199n25
Beer, Gillian, 210n25
Benjamin, Walter, 150–51, 153–54
Berlant, Lauren, 70–71
Bewell, Alan J., 204n8, 205n19
Bogel, Fredric V., 197n21
Booth, Stephen, 171
Borch-Jacobsen, Mikkel, 197n24
Boyd, Julian, and Zelda Boyd, 207n42
Box, M. A., 43, 198n9
Brennan, Teresa, 197n24
Brissenden, R. F., 18
Bronson, Bertrand H., 46
Brown, Gillian, 196n15
Brown, Marshall, 197n21
Burke, Edmund, 111–12, 113ff
Butler, Marilyn, 195n5
Byron, George Gordon, Lord, 184–85

Campbell, Colin, 195n11

Caroline, Princess (later Queen), 187, 189–92
Caruth, Cathy, 197n1, 205n17
Castle, Terry, 209n11, 210n26
Chapone, Hester, 2
Charlotte, Princess, 177–92; funeral of, 177; political importance of, 177–78, 184–85; spread of mourning of, 182; and epistemology of emotion, 182–83, 186–92
Christensen, Jerome, 27, 31f, 197nn1,23, 198n17, 199n21, 205n21
Clark, Anna, 190
Code, Lorraine, 12
Coleridge, Samuel Taylor, 72, 93
Compagnon, Antoine, 215n13
Conger, Syndy McMillen, 195n5
Cottom, Daniel, 213n29
Coward, Rosalind, 135
Cowper, William, 101
Croft, Sir Richard (doctor to Princess Charlotte), 187–89
Curran, Stuart, 202n20
Cvetkovich, Ann, 196n15, 214n7

Davenport, Allen, 185
Davidoff, Leonore, and Catherine Hall, 190, 209n13
Davies, Hugh Sykes, 197n1
de Bolla, Peter, 197n21, 211n2
de Grazia, Margreta, 170
Deleuze, Gilles, 198n11
De Quincey, Thomas, 171–78
Donaldson, John, 47
Douglas, Ann, 196n15

Eagleton, Terry, 195n11
Edgeworth, Maria, 153

Ellison, Julie, 195n11, 196n14
Emotion: and feminism, 12–13, 53–55, 70–71; and language, 16, 45–50, 63, 75, 82, 87, 117, 126–27. *See also* Personification
Empiricism and emotion, 6, 17–24, 32–37, 69–71, 73, 113–16, 124, 150, 164
"Era of sensibility," 11

Favret, Mary A., 213n24
Feminism, 12–13, 53–55, 70–71, 135–36
Ferguson, Frances, 48, 196n13, 210n23
Freud, Sigmund, 75, 91, 131, 150–51; "A Child Is Being Beaten," 83–86, 94–97. *See also* Psychoanalysis
Fried, Debra, 199n19

Gass, William, 159
Gilbert, Sandra M., and Susan Gubar, 213n20
Glen, Heather, 99
Goldsmith, Oliver, 56
Green, André, 197n24

Hartley, David, 90
Hartman, Geoffrey, 73
Hemans, Felicia, 183
Henderson, Andrea, 197n21, 210n22
Hertz, Neil, 215n13
Hirschman, Albert O., 195n11
Homans, Margaret, 201n3
Huish, Robert, 179–84
Hume, David, 1, 3–4, 114f; on sympathy, 19, 24–32, 34–40,

Index

43f; on miracles, 20; on skepticism, 20ff; on pride, 21–26; on plagiarism, 26–27; on exile, 26–32; on relation between impressions and ideas, 32–36; on force or vivacity, 33–39, 199n24; and autobiography, 200n30. Works: *An Enquiry Concerning Human Understanding*, 17, 19–20, 36; "On the Delicacy of Taste and Passion," 51–53, 140–42; *A Treatise of Human Nature*, 17ff, 20–44
Hunt, Leigh, 162

Inchbald, Elizabeth, 144
Individualism, 13–15, 17–18, 27–28, 73
Izenberg, Gerald N., 196n18

Jacobus, Mary, 196n14, 207n47
Johnson, Barbara, 200n40
Johnson, Claudia L., 195nn5,11, 201n8

Kahane, Claire, 210n27
Kames, Henry Home, Lord, 4–6, 49–50, 115, 165f
Kelly, Gary, 211n36
Kiely, Robert, 124
Knapp, Steven, 197n1, 200n39

Lamb, Charles, 69, 102–4
Laplanche, Jean, 91–92
Laqueur, Thomas, 190
Law, Jules David, 197n1
Levinson, Marjorie, 202n23
Lewis, Judith Schneid, 188
Locke, John, 23, 33, 35, 83–84
Luhmann, Niklas, 196n18

McCalman, Iain, 190
McKenzie, Alan T., 196n19, 197n2
McKenzie, Gordon, 200n32
Macpherson, C. B., 196n18
Marshall, David, 196n12, 199n17
Maus, Katherine Eisaman, 14
Mellor, Anne K., 196n14
Miall, David S., 205n15
Miller, David, 197n23
More, Hannah, 97, 206n25
Morgan, Susan, 143
Mullan, John, 195n11, 196n12

Novel of manners, 140–45
Nussbaum, Felicity, 197n21
Nussbaum, Martha, 143

Personification, 18, 21, 23–24, 38; and epistemology of emotion, 44–50
Pilkington, Laetitia, 74–75
Pocock, J. G. A., 195n11, 196n18
Priestley, Joseph, 46–47
Psychoanalysis, 15–16, 75, 83–86, 91–97, 131–36, 150–51, 210n27

Quotation: and Charlotte Smith, 60–65; and ventriloquism, 94, 96–97, 158, 161–63, 165–76, 179

Radcliffe, Ann: and Edmund Burke, 111–15; and nostalgia, 118–25, 134; emotional occupation in, 125–27; and psychoanalysis, 130–34, 210n27. Works: *A Journey Made in the Summer of 1794*, 119–22; *The*

Mysteries of Udolpho, 112–19, 121–36, 137
Reading, 75–76, 80, 83–89, 138, 156–63; women's, 56–57, 137–139, 161–63
Richetti, John, 40–41
Romanticism, 11–12, 17, 165, 167
Rorty, Amélie O., 22
Ross, Marlon, 196n14, 197n21, 202n14
Rzepka, Charles, 197n21

Samuels, Shirley, 196n15
Sanchez-Eppler, Karen, 196n15
Scheman, Naomi, 195n10, 211n38
Schor, Esther, 178, 186, 195n11, 202n16
Scott, Joan, 53
Scott, Sir Walter, 140–42
Sedgwick, Eve, 95, 123, 196n16, 208n5
Sennett, Richard, 197n21
Sentimentality, 55, 57, 68–71, 75–82
Shakespeare, William: quotation of, 165, 169–72
Simpson, David, 103–4
Smith, Charlotte: Elegiac Sonnets, 55, 58–71; epistemology of emotion in, 55, 66–70; contemporary views of, 58, 61, 66; quotation in, 60–65; poems addressed to, 79–80
Sonnet: and personal emotion, 58, 69, 170–71. See also Smith, Charlotte; Wordsworth, William, "Sonnet on Seeing Miss Helen Maria Williams Weep at a Tale of Distress"
Stack, Richard, 46
Starr, G. A., 200n28

Steele, Richard, 81
Stewart, Susan, 119, 134, 209n13
Stone, Lawrence, 197n21
Swann, Karen, 204n8, 214n7
Swift, Jonathan, 103
Sympathy, 19, 24–32, 34–40, 43f, 81, 86, 99, 145, 188

Tickell, Richard, 1–2
Todd, Janet, 195n5
Tompkins, Jane P., 196n15
Tuveson, Ernest, 197n1

Vrettos, Athena, 214n7

Webb, R. K., 206n25
Whelan, Frederick G., 197n23
Williams, Raymond, 41
Wolfson, Susan J., 108–9, 204n9, 205n24
Wollstonecraft, Mary, 2, 54–55, 112, 135
Wordsworth, William, 49; contemporary views of, 72–73, 106; emotional extravagance in, 72–76, 106–10; and masochism, 84–86, 91–97; meter in, 87–91; and ventriloquism, 94, 96–97. Works: "Goody Blake and Harry Gill," 88–94, 109; "Poor Susan," 98–106, 107; Preface to Lyrical Ballads, 73, 75, 85–89, 94, 105–6, 109; The Prelude, 74, 82, 104–5, 168–70; "Sonnet on Seeing Miss Helen Maria Williams Weep at a Tale of Distress," 76–82; "Strange Fits of Passion I Have Known," 73, 106–10; The Vale of Esthwaite, 93

Zaretsky, Eli, 197n21

Library of Congress Cataloging-in-Publication Data

Pinch, Adela
  Strange fits of passion : epistomologies of emotion, Hume to Austen / Adela Pinch.
       p.   cm.
  Includes bibliographical references and index.
  ISBN 0-8047-2548-9 (cloth) : ISBN 0-8047-3656-1 (pbk.)
(pbk. : alk. paper)
  1. English literature—18th century—History and criticism.
2. Emotions in literature. 3. Hume, David, 1711–1776—Contributions in philosophy of passions. 4. English literature—19th century—History and criticism. 5. Radcliffe, Ann Ward, 1764–1823. Mysteries of Udolpho. 6. Wordsworth, William, 1770–1850—Knowledge—Psychology. 7. Smith, Charlotte Turner, 1749–1806. Sonnets.
8. Austen, Jane, 1775–1817. Persuasion. 9. Emotions (Philosophy)—History—18th century. I. Title.
PR448.E46P56   1996
820.9'353—dc20   95-52593
                                                                        CIP

Original printing 1996
Last figure below indicates year of this printing:
05 04 03 02 01 00 99

The authorized representative in the EU for product safety and compliance is:
Mare Nostrum Group
B.V Doelen 72
4831 GR Breda
The Netherlands

www.ingramcontent.com/pod-product-compliance
Lightning Source LLC
Chambersburg PA
CBHW020646230426
43665CB00008B/337